INVITATION

It is often difficult for art-lovers seeking an introduction to a subject to find the right approach amid the bewildering array of literature available. Read on; you'll not be bored!

The aim of this book is to provide an entertaining but well-founded introduction to the world of the artists' group the Blue Rider, which flourished in German in the early years of the twentieth century.

The first seven chapters lead readers through the exciting period from 1908 until the First World War and let them witness the birth of the group. The views of the artists are described as well as their often complicated personal relationships with each other. The most important works are introduced and their significance examined.

In the last chapter there is, literally, much to discover, including the places in Bavaria where the members of the Blue Rider left their traces. The museums where you can admire the works of Kandinsky & Co. will be described, as will, as far as is possible today, the locations where it all happened. Where did the artists live; where were their studios; and where was the famous salon of Marianne von Werefkin, in which the artists drank, smoked and spent long nights in animated discussion?

My sincere thanks go to the great authority on the Blue Rider, Dr. Annegret Hoberg of the Lenbachhaus in Munich, who encouraged me to embark on this project and to whom I am grateful for important advice. I dedicate this book to my grandchildren Jonathan, Gabriel, and Rebecca.

Eckhard Hollmann

THE BLUE RIDER

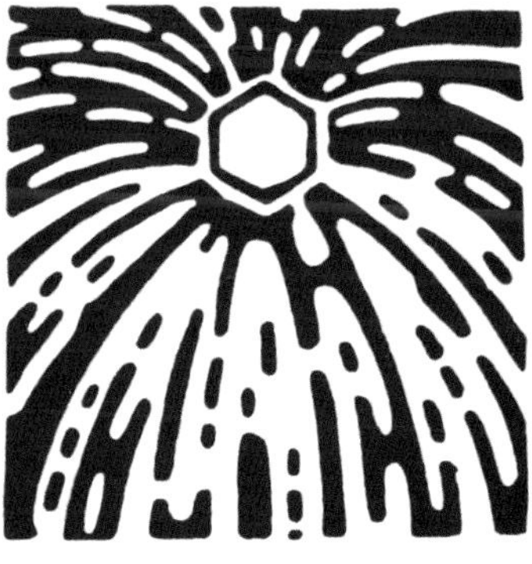

PRESTEL

MUNICH · LONDON · NEW YORK

1. MUNICH, CITY OF ART

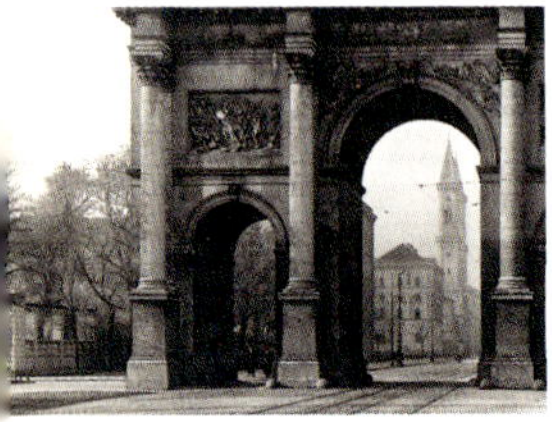

PAGE 8

During the last decade of the nineteenth century, Munich's art scene was a veritable hive of activity. In the city's artists' district, Schwabing, the bohemian crowd met at the Café am Siegestor, and the cabaret *Die Elf Scharfrichter (The Eleven Executioners)* met in Café Stefanie. This scene became the breeding ground from which in 1901 there emerged an artists' group with the programmatic name of the Phalanx. Inspired mainly by Wassily Kandinsky, this would give rise to the Neue Künstlervereinigung München (NKVM; New Artists' Association of Munich), from which in turn the Blue Rider would be formed.

2. FOUNDATION

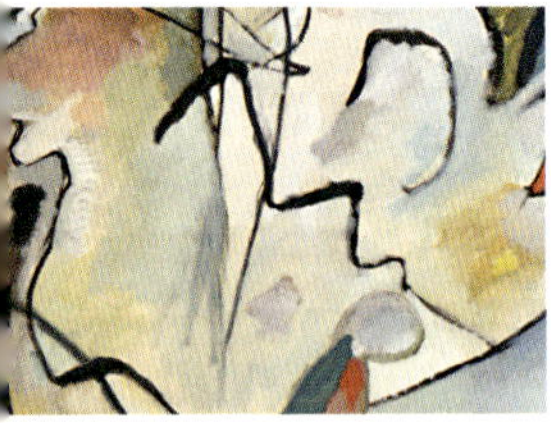

PAGE 42

Ultimately it was a friendship between artists that gave the world a completely new attitude to art and made an important contribution to the modern age: Wassily Kandinsky and Franz Marc founded the artists' association the Blue Rider (Der Blaue Reiter) in 1911 with an exhibition in Munich and expressed their hope for a new, modern, and challenging conception of art: "We, on the other hand, believe – or at least we hope we may be allowed to believe – that far away from all these groups of 'Wild Ones' standing in the foreground here in Germany there may be some silent powers which are struggling to achieve the same distant, lofty goals … We stretch out our hand to them in the dark without knowing who they are."
Did Kandinsky and Marc succeed in uniting these "silent powers" and in becoming the leaders of a new conception of art?

3. THE PROTAGONISTS

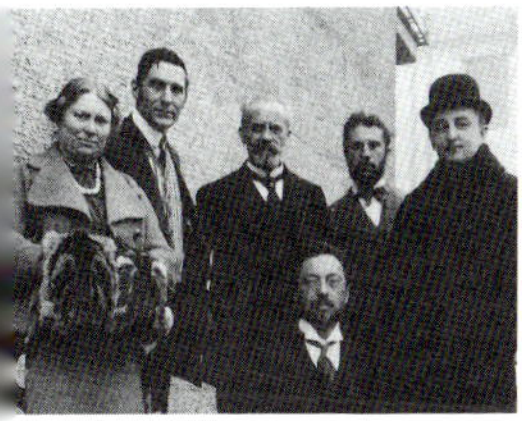

PAGE 88

Wassily Kandinsky, a Russian lawyer, studied painting in Munich and turned the art scene upside-down. Gabriele Münter became his student, mistress, and an important ally. They developed a close friendship with Franz and Maria Marc, who settled in Sindelsdorf, not far from Murnau, where Kandinsky and Münter lived.

Important members of the group included the brooding and solitary Alfred Kubin, August Macke with his painted prisms in bright colors, and Paul Klee, who later became a teacher at the Bauhaus, and whose pictures are often praised as "painted music."

4. SATELLITES

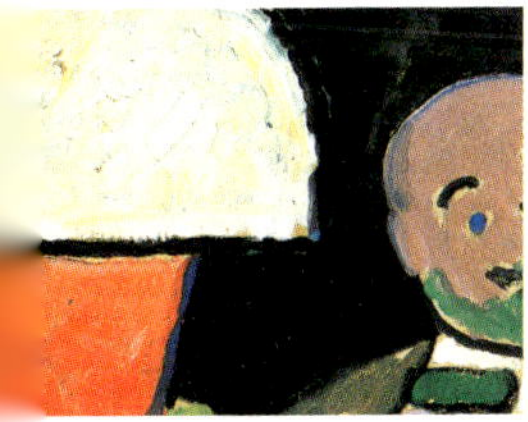

PAGE 120

Marianne von Werefkin, Alexej von Jawlensky, Heinrich von Campendonk, and the composer Arnold Schönberg were not permanent members of the Blue Rider. They nonetheless played a very important role in the development of the artistic theories of the group and the presentation of their exhibitions.

5. ACTIVITIES

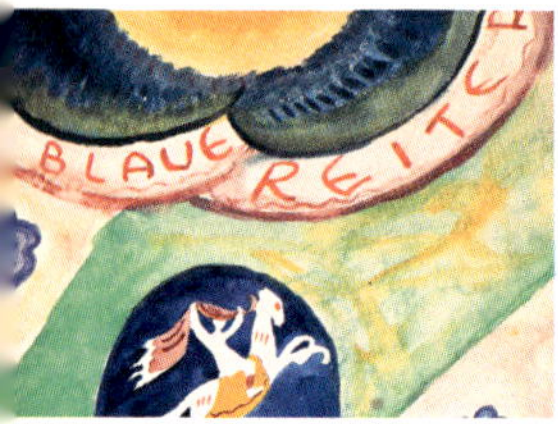

PAGE 128

For the supporters of the Blue Rider, the year 1912 got off to a very successful start.

They had left the New Artists' Association of Munich to form their own artists' group and had produced a theoretical basis in the form of the almanac *Der Blaue Reiter*. Wassily Kandinsky and Franz Marc were the driving forces who encouraged the artists to continue to develop and to realize new ideas.

6. INNOVATIONS

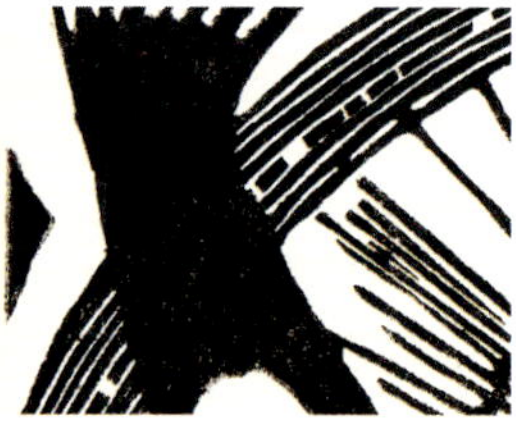

PAGE 142

"What will survive of my work?" Many people, not only artists, ask themselves this question. The painters of the Blue Rider not only enlivened the art scene of the time; they also created works which would stand the test of time.

After all, the first totally abstract painting in the history of art was not produced in one of the world's great art metropolises, but in Murnau, a little market town in Upper Bavaria. Its creator, Wassily Kandinsky, was fond of being photographed in traditional Bavarian dress. That, on the other hand, did not prevent him and his friend Franz Marc from making an intensive study of "world art," "folk art," and "primitive art" and using them for their own work.

7. RECEPTION

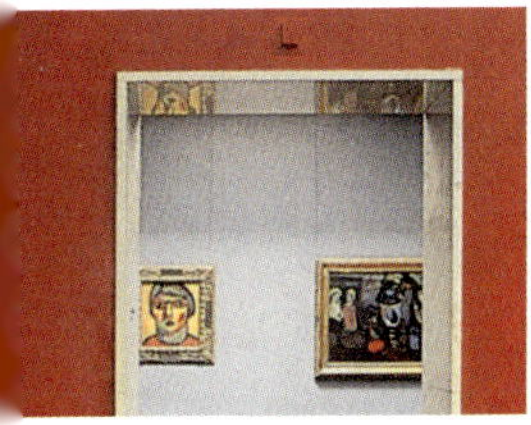

PAGE 152

The outbreak of the First World War brought to an abrupt end the activities of the Blue Rider. Kandinsky had to leave Germany and returned to Russia. August Macke and Franz Marc were killed in France. "I saw Kubin sink into an ever-deepening mood of despair," wrote his brother-in-law after a visit at Christmas 1915. Klee and Kandinsky would later be summoned to work at the Bauhaus in Weimar. Proscribed as "degenerate art," in 1937 the traces of the Blue Rider were in danger of being lost altogether. But this did not happen. In 1949 the major exhibition *Der Blaue Reiter* in the Haus der Kunst in Munich sparked a renaissance of the ideas and works of this extraordinary artists' group.

8. DISCOVERIES

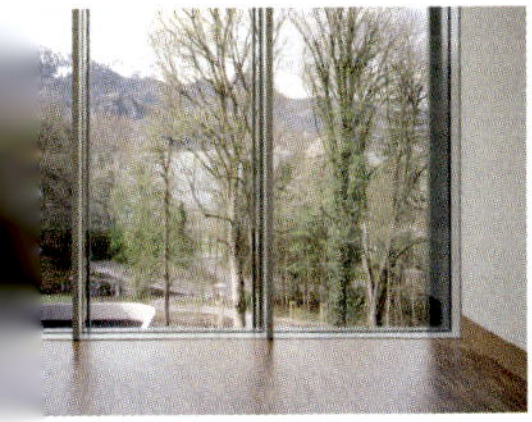

PAGE 156

This chapter will lead you in the footsteps of the Blue Rider to important places and sights in Upper Bavaria. The starting point for this tour is the Lenbachhaus in Munich, which holds by far the most comprehensive collection of works relating to the Blue Rider. Things become more private and intimate in Murnau, where Wassily Kandinsky and Gabriele Münter lived in the "Russian House," which you can visit. The Schloss Museum Murnau shows pictures by Gabriele Münter and a large collection of reverse-glass painting, an art form which Kandinsky and Münter practiced and developed. It is also worthwhile making a detour to visit the Franz Marc Museum in Kochel, perched high above the Kochelsee.

1. MUNICH, CITY OF ART

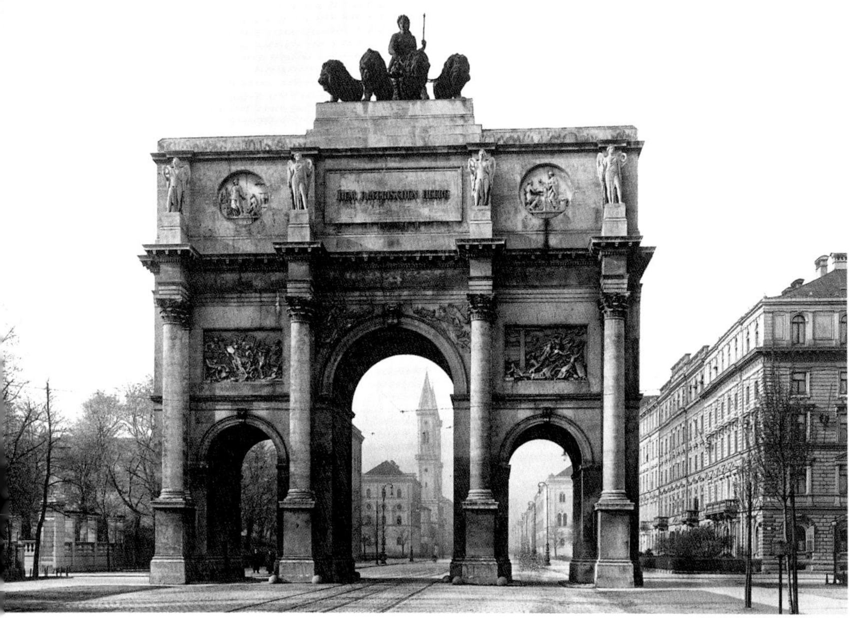

View from the Siegestor of Ludwigstrasse with the Ludwigskirche, Munich, photograph, 1906

FROM KING LUDWIG I TO THE TURN OF THE CENTURY

King Ludwig I of Bavaria established and enhanced Munich's reputation as a "modern" city of art during his reign from 1825 until the revolution of 1848. He brought together important architects, artists, and writers. Over a period of ten years from 1826, Leo von Klenze supervised the building of the Alte Pinakothek museum, an impressive structure made of unfaced bricks which clearly shows its debt to the Italian Renaissance. It forms a worthy framework for one of the most exciting and comprehensive collections of classical art in Germany, which succeeding generations of artists have repeatedly studied and admired, including the protagonists of the Blue Rider. Klenze also built Wittelsbacher Platz, the most beautiful square in Munich. It lies just a stone's throw from Odeonsplatz and Friedrich von Gärtner's Feldherrenhalle (Field Marshals' Hall), which was modeled on the Loggia dei Lanzi in Florence. From here the equestrian statue of Ludwig I surveys Munich's "via triumphalis," which continues as far as the Siegestor (Victory Arch).

The writers who lived in Munich at this time included Heinrich Heine, Ludwig von Brentano, and Gottfried Keller. The fine arts were represented by Peter von Cornelius and Johann Friedrich Overbeck, both members of the Nazarene movement, as well as the sculptor Bertel Thorvaldsen and the landscape painter Carl Rottmann.

Maximilian II (r. 1848–1864) did not want to be outdone by his predecessor when it came to architecture. He had Maximilianstrasse, the Bayerisches Nationalmuseum, and the Maximilianeum (initially an institute of higher learning, now the seat of the Bavarian parliament) built as examples of "grand romantic architecture." From 1869 international art exhibitions were held under the aegis of the Münchner Künstlergenossenschaft (Munich Society of Artists) in the Glaspalast ("Glass Palace"), an ultra-modern glass-and-iron construction which had been inaugurated in 1854. This further enhanced Munich's reputation as an "international city of art." Another important step for the development of fine art was the construction of the new building for the Akademie der bildenden Künste (Academy of Fine Arts) in 1876–1885 under Ludwig II (r. 1864–1886), the much-loved – and much-derided – "Fairy Tale King." As an admirer of Richard Wagner, he was responsible for the construction of

Neuschwanstein, Linderhof, and Herrenchiemsee, the three Bavarian "fairy tale castles" which still attract millions of visitors every year. His tragic death in Lake Starnberg, which has still not been properly explained, further contributed to the Ludwig myth.
Major changes occurred in the art scene during the reign of the Prince Regent, Luitpold (r. 1886–1912). A bourgeois-radical artistic approach which was completely independent of the court was established, starting with the Munich Secession in 1892 and ending in 1911 with the first exhibition of the Blue Rider and the publication of their almanac of the same name.

THE "PAINTER PRINCES" AND BOHEMIAN SOCIETY

For several years from 1896, the "painter prince" Franz von Lenbach (1836–1904) was the undisputed leader of the Munich Society of Artists, at that time the only artists' association. As early as 1892 he had moved into his Tuscan-style town villa, which can only be described as "enchanting" and which is currently being modernized for the third millennium by a rebuilding project under the direction of Sir Norman Foster. Today the former residence of this conservative artist, of all places, is the home of the Städtische Galerie im Lenbachhaus, which includes the world's most extensive collection of works by Blue Rider artists. Just imagine this "revaluation of all values": when Franz von Lenbach died in 1904, twelve years had already passed since the founding of the Secession – the withdrawal of the progressive artists from the Munich Society of Artists – while the periodical *Die Jugend [Youth]* and the related art movement, Jugendstil (the German form of Art Nouveau), were at the height of their power. Wilhelm Leibl, who had been unable to achieve recognition with his "French Realism," had died in May 1900 and Wassily Kandinsky's Phalanx group had just disbanded. The association of the "Wild Ones," the Neue Künstlervereinigung München (NKVM; New Artists' Association of Munich), had formed under the direction of Wassily Kandinsky, Alexej von Jawlensky, and their associates. What a juxtaposition of opinions, styles, and approaches!
Nor should we forget that in all camps it was not only excellent works that were being produced, but also artistically weak ones.

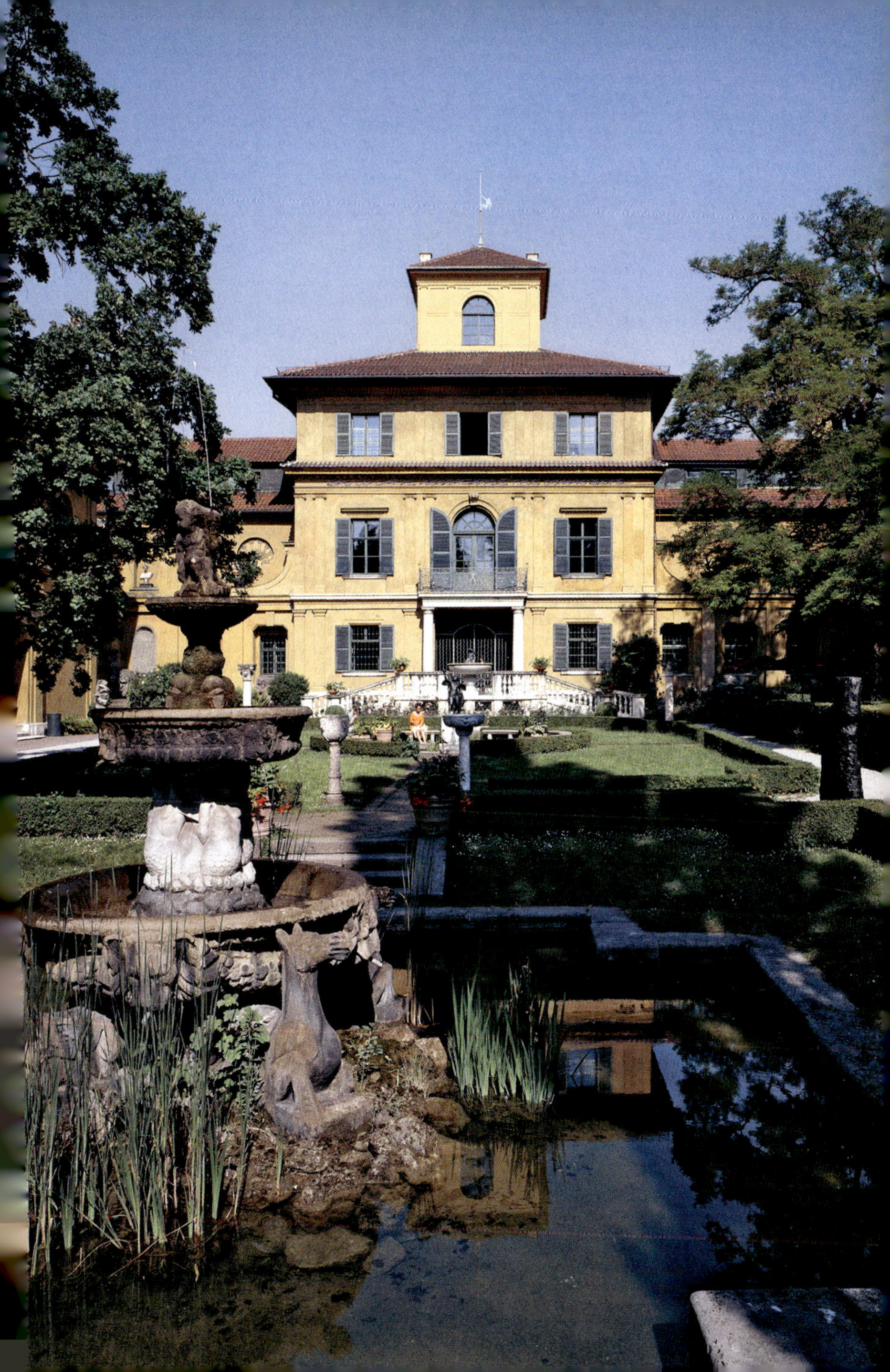

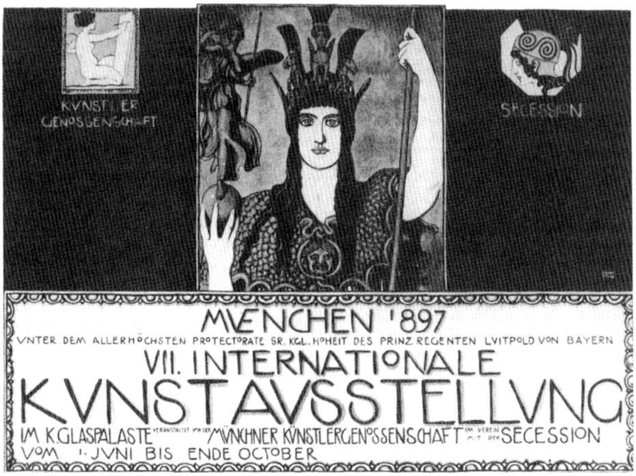

Franz von Stuck,
VII International Art
Exhibition, 1897

Right page:

Simplicissimus,
vol. 10, no. 1

Ludwig von Zumbusch,
Advertisement for the
Munich periodical *Jugend*,
1898

Remembering this makes it possible for us to view them with the objectivity of hindsight. In those days, as now, the camps were based on ideology, and virtually everyone who rebelled against historicism (the revival of historical styles), salon painting, and Impressionism was welcomed by the "Wild Ones." Indeed, many people find it difficult to regard Maria Marc as a serious artist, and Arnold Schönberg was at best a talented amateur as a painter; he was recruited by Kandinsky for the Blue Rider not because of his painting, but because of his music and his progressive approach to art. Kandinsky hoped that they would be able to undertake "synesthetic" experiments together, blending music and the visual arts.

It would be very interesting to know which of the big names among today's artists will still be appreciated in a hundred years' time, and whether there are still some figures unrecognized today who will one day be counted among the greatest artists of the twenty-first century.

Franz von Stuck (1863–1928) from Lower Bavaria, the second of Munich's "painter princes," also has a place in art history. In 1906 he was knighted as Ritter von Stuck and was at the same time a member of the aesthetically oriented Monist League (a scientific, religious, and political association) founded by the naturalist Ernst Haeckel. Today Stuck, one of the protagonists of the Munich Secession, is still sometimes decried as a "salon painter," though he was an excellent artist who was open to new impulses. He supported the Jugendstil

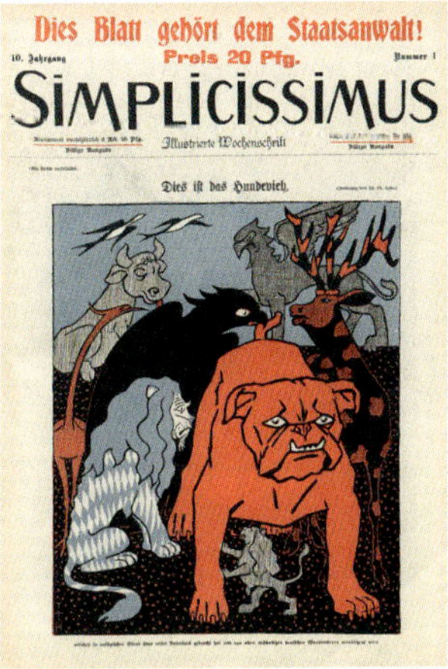

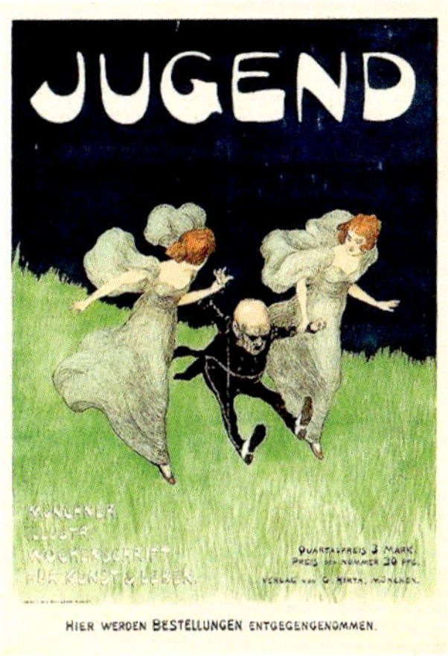

movement in no small measure, and as a professor at the Munich academy was one of the teachers of the avant-garde: both Kandinsky and Paul Klee studied under him. A visit to the Villa Stuck, his Munich residence, today a museum with a very interesting program of exhibitions, is always worthwhile.

The third member of the trio of great painters in Munich is Friedrich August von Kaulbach (1850–1920), who also resided in a magnificent city villa (today the Historical Institute) in what is now Kaulbachstrasse. He made a reputation for himself above all as a portrait painter.

The protagonists of the Blue Rider may have broken with many traditions, but they were also firmly rooted in them: Stuck was at times strongly influenced by Franz von Lenbach, and, as noted, Kandinsky and Klee in their turn studied under Franz von Stuck. Kandinsky could doubtless only develop what he would later insist on as the "inner necessity" of painting, his universal philosophy which embraced world art as well as folk art, in the tensions arising from his simultaneous admiration for and rebellion against his teachers.

Nor should the city's remarkably lively modern cultural scene be forgotten in a survey of the development of modern art in Munich. Literature in Munich experienced a golden age with Thomas Mann, Rainer Maria Rilke, Frank Wedekind, and Ernst von Wolzogen. In 1896 Georg Hirth founded the Munich periodical *Jugend*, which would become the most important voice of German Jugendstil. In the same year Albert Langen published the first issue of the satirical journal *Simplicissimus.*

Schwabing's bohemian crowd met at the Café am Siegestor, and the cabaret *Die Elf Scharfrichter (The Eleven Executioners)* met in Café Stefanie. This scene served as the counter to official art and was the breeding ground from which emerged the artists' group and painting school with the programmatic name Phalanx in 1901. Inspired mainly by Wassily Kandinsky, this would ultimately give rise to the New Artists' Association of Munich, from which in turn the Blue Rider would be formed.

THE PHALANX (1901–1904)

Wassily Kandinsky, the Russian lawyer and economist with a master's degree from the University of Moscow, left Russia in December 1896 to study art in Munich. He started off in the private painting school of the Slovenian artist Anton Ažbé. In 1901 Kandisky founded the Phalanx together with the sculptor Wilhelm Hüsgen, the writer Gustav Freytag, and a number of artists from the circle of the cabaret *Die Elf Scharfrichter.* The group wanted to be seen as the antithesis of conservative art. They were strongly influenced by Jugendstil, and Kandinsky introduced Old Russian and medieval motifs.

The Phalanx school also admitted women, which the Academy at the time had not yet started to do. In 1902 Gabriele Münter enrolled at the Phalanx school, an event which was to have major repercussions for Kandinsky. The group organized a total of twelve exhibitions, which are important primarily because they showed pictures not only by their own members and students, but also by progressive artists from Germany and France, including Lovis Corinth, Alfred Kubin, Claude Monet (whose works were shown for the first time in Munich in 1903 in the Seventh Phalanx Exhibition), Paul Signac, Henri de

Kandinsky with his painting class from the Phalanx art school in Kochel, 1902

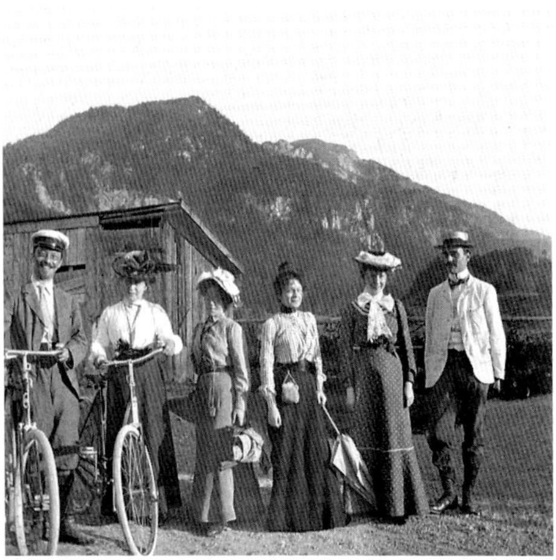

Toulouse-Lautrec, Wilhelm Trübner, Felix Vallotton, and Albrecht Weisgerber.

"The desire first apparent here, that the Phalanx association should also provide the participating artists with opportunities to show their work and gain commissions, reappears eight years later on another level of development in the founding of the New Artists' Association of Munich. It shows that from the start Kandinsky was a skillful and determined strategist when it came to art, who attempted to use in a novel way for himself and his goals the mechanisms of the modern art market, which was just beginning to evolve at that time." [1]

In the summer of 1903, some of the members of the Phalanx went on a painting trip to Kallmünz in the Upper Palatinate. Gabriele Münter was one of the participants. Here she painted small oil landscapes in the style of Kandinsky and using a palette knife. He continued to develop his painting method using patches of bright color against a dark background, and both of them learned the technique of making colored woodcuts.

Münter and Kandinsky developed a close relationship; whether she seduced him or he her on one of their bicycle rides together has remained their secret. In any case, the two became "betrothed," though Kandinsky was already married to his cousin Anya Semjakina, who had accompanied him from Moscow to Munich and who lived with him in an apartment in Munich (see p. 161).

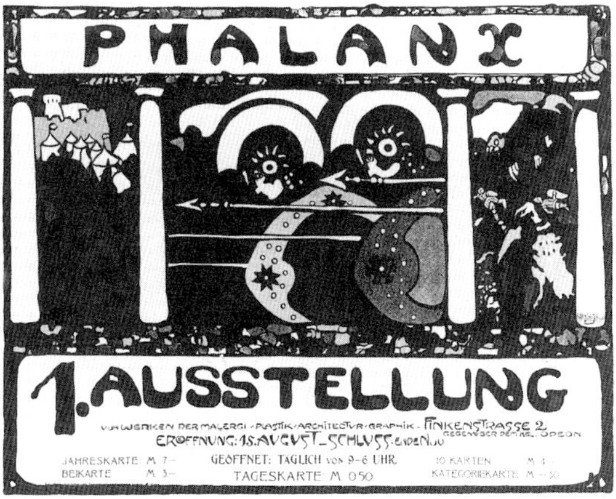

Wassily Kandinsky, Poster for the first Phalanx exhibition, 1901

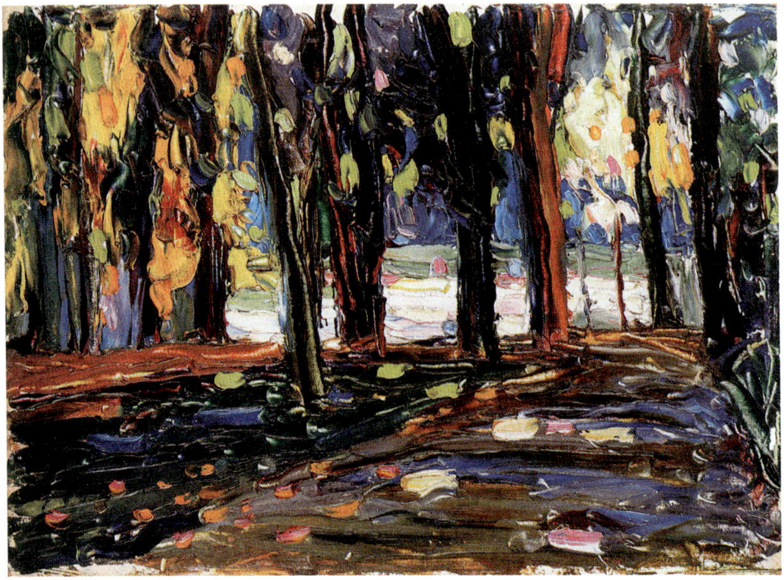

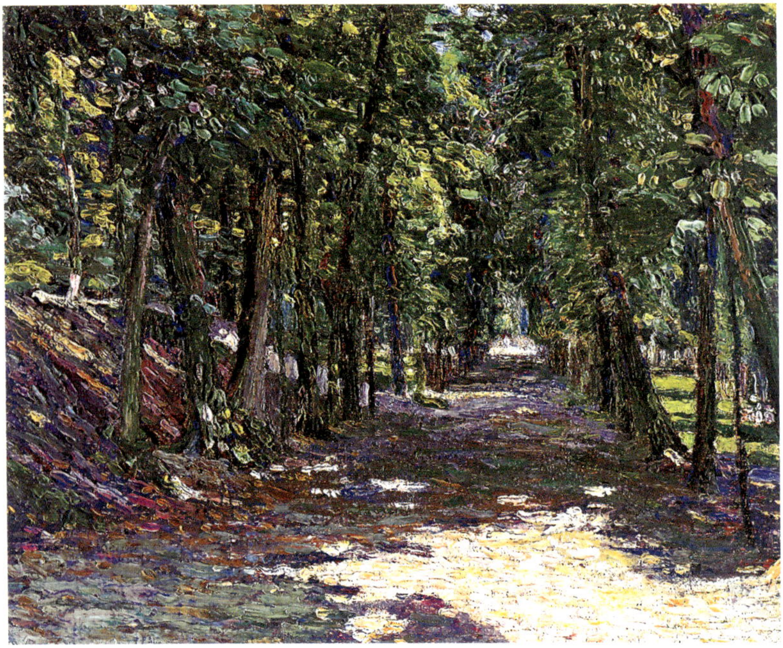

This is no doubt the reason for the restless life that Münter and Kandinsky led during the following four years, marked as it was by travel and lengthy periods abroad: Bonn in 1904, Tunis during the winter of 1904–1905, a joint flat in Dresden in 1905, Rapallo during the winter of 1905–1906, and Paris from June 1906 until June 1907, where they absorbed ideas from the contemporary woodcuts being produced by the French artists of the "Nabis" group and saw pictures by Vincent van Gogh and Paul Gauguin. In June 1908 the couple decided to return to Munich following stays in Berlin and South Tyrol.
During their excursions they discovered the little market town of Murnau am Staffelsee, 80 kilometers (50 miles) south of Munich, where they spent long holidays painting. Murnau was to become for both of them the most important location during the years they spent together.

Left Page:

Wassily Kandinsky
IN THE PARK AT SAINT CLOUD, 1906

Gabriele Münter
AVENUE IN THE PARK AT SAINT CLOUD, 1906

MURNAU 1908: THE ARTISTIC BREAKTHROUGH

Full of enthusiasm, Kandinsky and Münter told their Munich artist friends of their discovery and persuaded Marianne von Werefkin and Alexej von Jawlensky to take rooms in Murnau for the months of August and September, in order to spend the summer painting together outdoors in the countryside.
They also wanted to evaluate together the artistic impulses which the two couples had experienced during their journeys to France. Above all they studied the two-dimensional painting and bright colors of the Nabis [2] and the paintings of Paul Gauguin. A heated debate raged in the art world at the time regarding Gauguin's guidelines for "Synthetism" (according to which a picture should express its content in universally comprehensible forms and signs) and "cloisonnism" (in which strongly colored figures and objects are separated from each other by black contours; from the French *cloisonner*, "to separate"). [3] The cult picture of the Nabis was *Talisman*, a small oil painting by Paul Sérusier, which he had painted in 1888 according to Gauguin's instructions: "How do you see this tree? Is it yellow? Then take the most beautiful yellow in your palette. And this shadow? It's actually blue, isn't it? Don't be afraid, paint it as blue as you possibly can." [4]

Paul Sérusier
TALISMAN, 1888

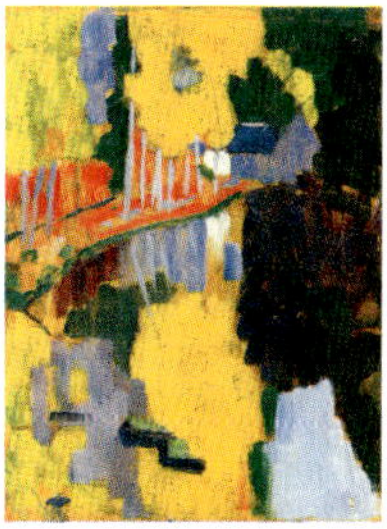

Following the ideas of Wassily Kandinsky, folk art was also used to serve the artists' own means of expression. Münter learned the technique of reverse-glass painting from the last glass painter in Murnau, Heinrich Rambold. The application of the paint to the reverse of the sheet of glass encouraged the ability to think in abstract terms. When painting a human face, glass artists don't first paint the nose and then add a spot of light; they first paint the spot of light and then the nose, and next the mouth and eyes (if required, spots of light are always put down first of all). Only then will they paint the hair, and the outline of the face last. So the picture is built up in layers; the painter has to think of it like a negative. Simplified forms and a clear, brilliant range of colors are the result. After initially copying reverse-glass folk paintings, Münter soon started to create her own designs. Kandinsky too embarked on works using this technique.

Religious subjects also provided the motifs for Kandinsky's "semi-abstract" paintings. In this context, memories of a journey he had undertaken as a young man in the Vologda region in 1889 were important: "I shall never forget the large wooden houses, covered with wood carvings. In these wonderful houses I experienced something which I have never seen again since that time. They taught me to move within the picture, to live in the picture. The table, the benches [...] the cupboards and every item were all painted with brightly colored, generously proportioned ornaments. There were folk pictures on the walls [...] When I finally entered the room I felt I was surrounded on all sides by the painting into which I had stepped."[5]

In 1908 Kandinsky came a step nearer his goal: to walk through the space of a picture which is not the image of a real space but an invention created by oneself and distinct from reality.

Wassily Kandinsky
ALL SAINTS I, 1911

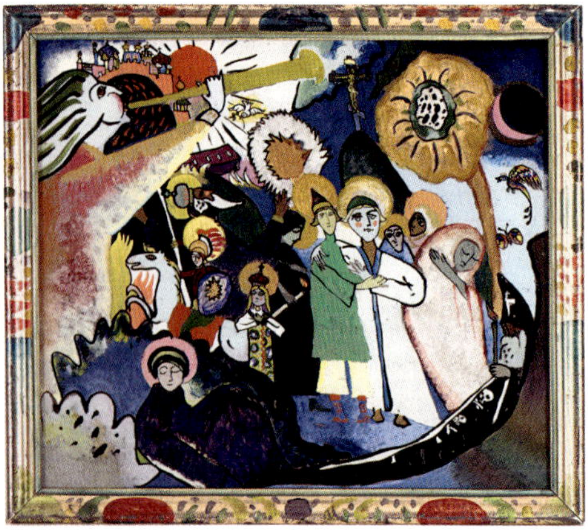

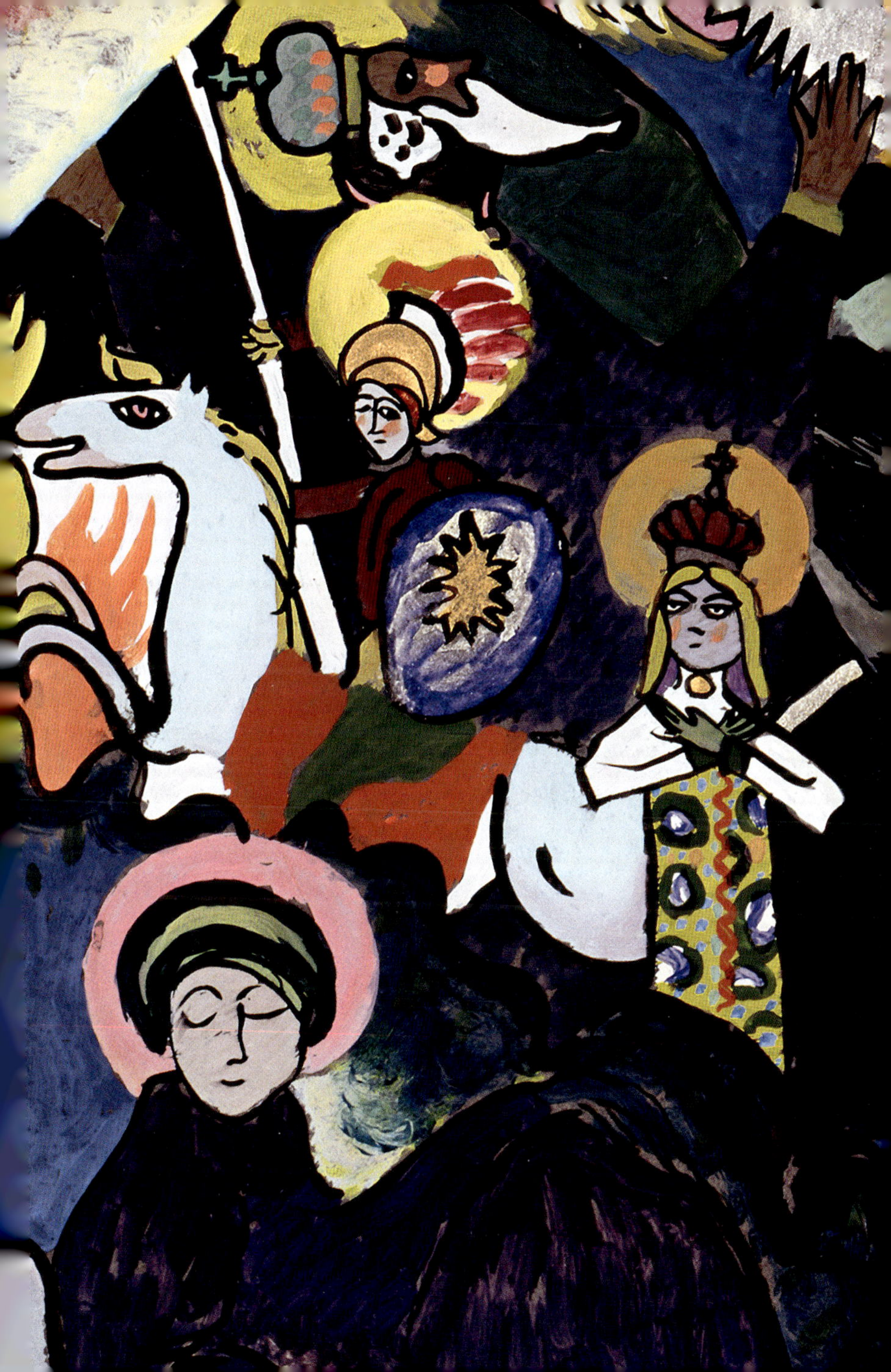

THE NEW ARTISTS' ASSOCIATION OF MUNICH 1909–1912

There is a manuscript by Gabriele Münter dated January 22, 1909, which is regarded as the founding document of the New Artists' Association of Munich (Neue Künstlervereinigung München; NKVM), though the actual name of the association is not mentioned. Though future members had not yet agreed as to the name of the association, they were in agreement as to the form the organization would take, as well as their future steps and common goals:

> "The goal of the association is to stage art exhibitions in Germany and abroad. It has been decided that:
>
> 1. The association must be registered.
> 2. There is no limit on the number of members.
> 3. All persons can be elected as members who receive the votes of the majority of members. The annual subscription shall be 10 M[arks].
> 4. All those persons who pay a single amount of 100 M[arks] at least once may be elected as patrons of the arts.
> 5. All those persons who receive a two-thirds majority vote can be elected as honorary members.
> 6. Regular members are entitled to submit two pictures for showing in the exhibitions without the approval of the jury. The remaining works submitted for exhibition are subject to selection by the jury, which shall consist of all ordinary members present at the time at the place of exhibition in Munich.
> 7. The hanging panel shall be elected annually by a normal majority vote.
> 8. The committee shall consist of the First, Second and Deputy Chairman, the First and Second Secretary, and the Treasurer. The following were elected as members of the committee: First Chairman: Wassily Kandinsky, artist; Second Chairman: Alexej Jawlensky, artist. Deputy Chairman: Miss Johanna Kanoldt
>
> First Secretary: Dr. Oscar Wittenstein
> Second Secretary and Treasurer: Miss Johanna Kanoldt."[6]

The members of the New Artists' Association of Munich were Wassily Kandinsky, Alexej von Jawlensky, Gabriele Münter, Marianne von Werefkin, Alexander Kanoldt, Karl Hofer, Alfred Kubin, Adolf Erbslöh, and ten other artists and supporters. Kanoldt had already moved to Munich from Karlsruhe, where he had attended the Academy, in 1908.

Kubin had already exhibited works with the Phalanx in 1904. Kandinsky had an extremely high opinion of his dark drawings and at the same time worried, in a touching manner, about Kubin's state of mind. With regard to the latter's novel *Die andere Seite [The Other Side]* he wrote to him in 1911: "These last few days I have thought that we have heard nothing from you, where you might be and what you are doing. And then a message came from you that did not please me in the least. Please try to banish your dark thoughts with all your energy, to overcome them. You are a person with fine feelings, with great sensitivity. How is it, then, that you can only feel *one* side of 'life'? What keeps the other side hidden from your view? Or better: Why do you only *see the other side?* In this remarkable book you are right a thousand times. It is almost a vision of evil. But now you must knock the head off your wax doll and stamp it to dust under your feet. Just as you have seen evil so vividly, so you are sure to see things very differently too. I am suddenly quite certain of that."[7]

Kandinsky, who was elected Chairman of the New Artists' Association of Munich "because no one else could take it on," as Gabriele Münter tartly remarked, soon developed a clear programmatic goal. He referred above all to Gauguin's motto "Vive la sintaize!" The meaning of the term "synthesis" was discussed animatedly in the "salon" of Marianne von Werefkin and Alexej von Jawlensky; the latter lived in Giselastrasse and the main participants referred to themselves as "Giselisten" (Giselists). According to these discussions, what new ideas in painting had to emerge?

Gauguin demanded the simplification of forms and the use of only clear, brilliant colors. From the synthesis of these two elements he aimed to arrive at a new pictorial language. In 1910 Kandinsky described how the artist friends approached this goal of "synthesis" in different ways: "Some place themselves facing nature and change it in line with their innermost needs. Others treat nature in the same way but do not have it in front of them while they are actually working. And yet others create things that they have in most cases never seen in nature."[8] Along with himself, he included Alfred Kubin in this third category.

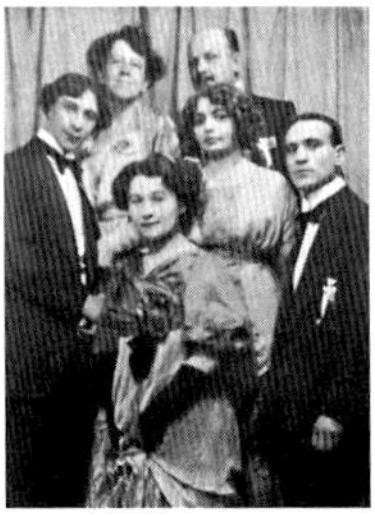

Marianne von Werefkin and Alexej von Jawlensky (top) with Alexander Sakharoff, his sister and a friend; in front, Helene Neznakomova, 1909

Kandinsky also saw it as his task to enlighten important museum people, publicists and collectors in particular, not to mention the general public, about the goals of the New Artists' Association of Munich, and to campaign on behalf of the new painting style. In the spring of 1909, shortly after his election as chairman of the group, he approached Hugo von Tschudi, the newly appointed general manager of the Bavarian museums, who had been forced to leave Berlin because of his progressive approach. Tschudi reacted immediately and attended a small, improvised exhibition by the group in Jawlensky and Werefkin's studio in Giselastrasse. This powerful museum director was very open to their work. "His remarks were splendid," noted Kandinsky in delight.

THE FIRST EXHIBITION OF THE NEW ARTISTS' ASSOCIATION OF MUNICH

It was not least as a result of Hugo von Tschudi's support this the new artists' association was able to open its first comprehensive exhibition with about 130 exhibits in the Galerie Thannhauser in Munich, in Theatinerstrasse, on December 1, 1909. The public "complained, threatened, spat"; the critics reacted with horror: "A number of what we hope must be very young people offer in the lovely toplit room at the Moderne Galerie a premature Fasching [carnival] amusement, an artists' prank with nothing missing except, unfortunately, humor. The exhibition of the Neue Künstlervereinigung, about which I am writing, is in fact governed by the dark sign of a tortured involuntary comedy of that sort of distressing ridiculousness which will arouse no pleasure in anyone who is sensitive in any way, but will rather give rise to feelings of consternation and embarrassment. [...]

If it is not a simple outbreak of excited childishness, then the diagnosis can only be one of scornful arrogance. We should not forget that the bizarre, the pathological aspects of the French artists under discussion here were highly attractive to the perverse taste of certain fragile classes of Central European society."[9]

Right page:

Marianne von Werefkin
CRUCIFIX IN LANDSCAPE, 1909

Gabriele Münter
JAWLENSKY AND WEREFKIN, 1909

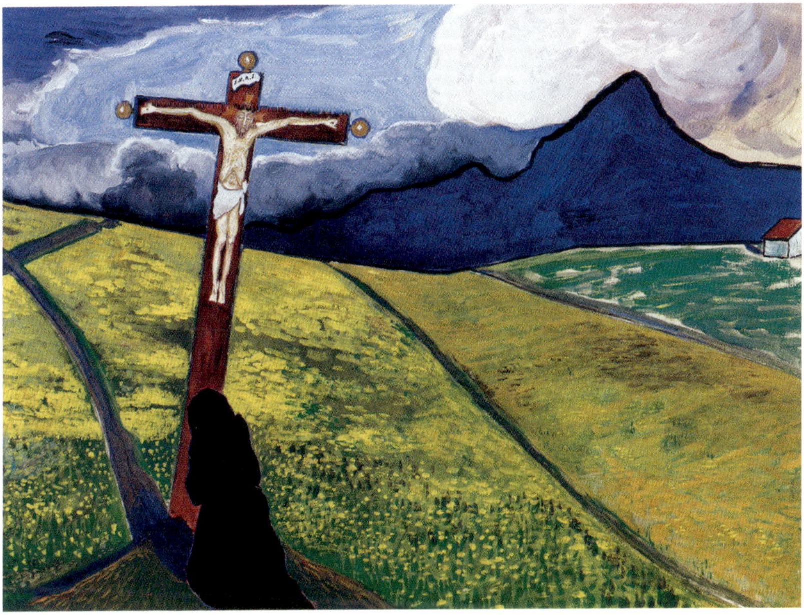

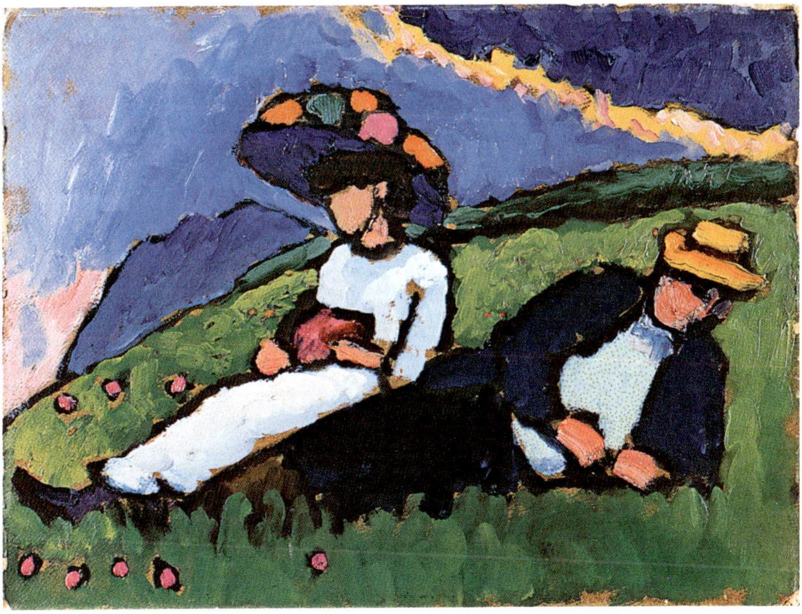

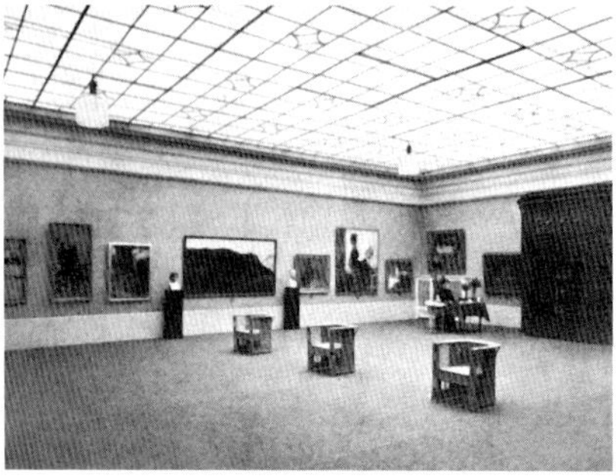

Moderne Galerie Heinrich Thannhauser, Munich, skylit gallery, 1909

Hugo von Tschudi apparently felt an affinity with these "fragile classes" of the bourgeoisie, since he took it upon himself to defend the artists. Kandinsky observed in a letter to Franz Marc that "not a single voice was raised in defense of the exhibition. Not a single Bavarian voice, but a Prussian one. This voice was that of Hugo von Tschudi, the general manager of all Bavarian art museums. [...] It was thanks to him that we [were able to] put on our exhibition, and it was thanks to him that the immediate closure demanded by the press did not take place. And it was he, too, who visited the exhibition to encourage the gallery owner, who sometimes completely lost his head."[10]

Pages 25–36

Wassily Kandinsky, Poster for the first exhibition of the New Artists' Association of Munich, 1909

Franz Marc **DOG LYING IN THE SNOW**, 1910-1911

Alexej von Jawlensky **PORTRAIT OF THE DANCER ALEXANDER SAKHAROFF**, 1909

Adolf Erbslöh **NUDE WITH GARTER**, 1909

Paul Baum **FLAT LANDSCAPE IN AUTUMN WITH MEADOWS AND POND**, *c.* 1907

Vladimir von Bechteiev **PORTE DE FRANCE, TUNIS**, *c.* 1906

Gabriele Münter **STILL LIFE WITH ARMCHAIR**, 1909

Wassily Kandinsky **MURNAU – LANDSCAPE WITH TOWER**, 1908-1909

Alfred Kubin **WOMEN WITH GROUNDED SHIP**, *c.* 1907-1908

Karl Hofer **ON A SOUTHERN SHORE**, *c.* 1909

Pierre Girieud **JUDAS**, 1908

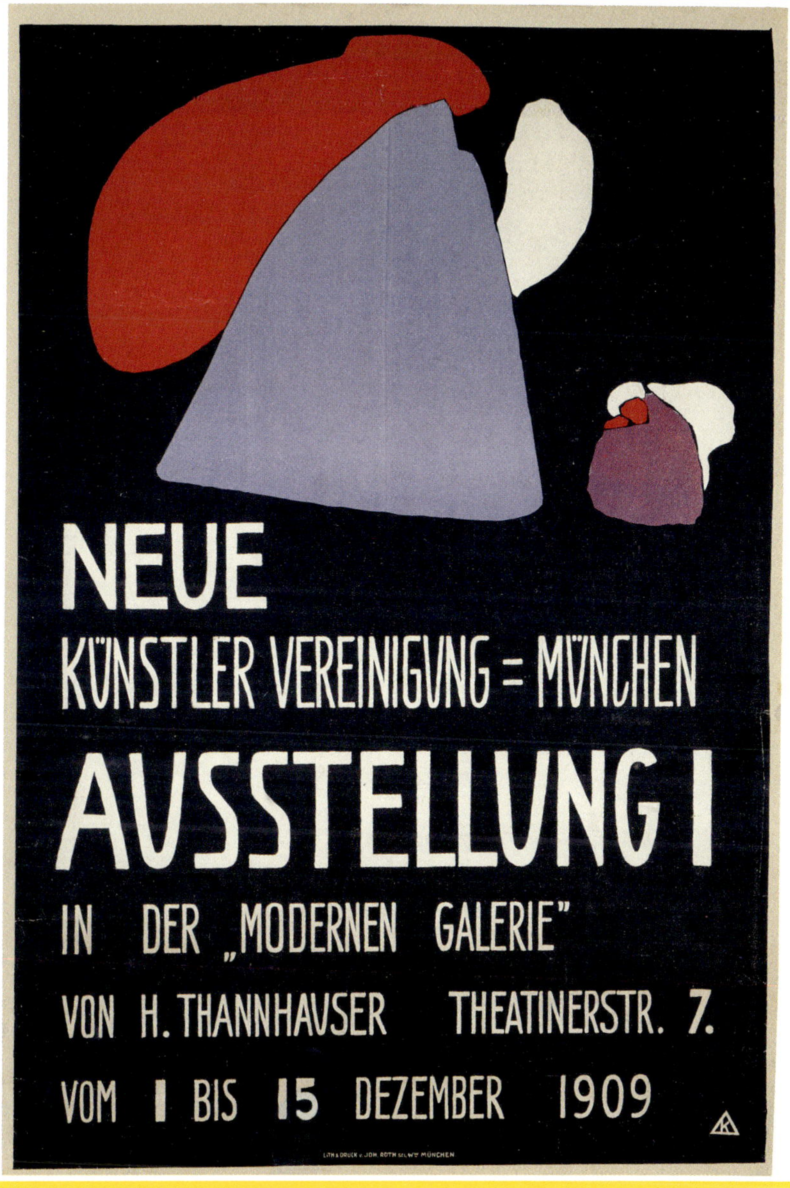
NEUE
KÜNSTLER VEREINIGUNG = MÜNCHEN
AUSSTELLUNG I
IN DER „MODERNEN GALERIE"
VON H. THANNHAUSER THEATINERSTR. 7.
VOM 1 BIS 15 DEZEMBER 1909
LITH & DRUCK v. JOH. ROTH SEL. Wwe MÜNCHEN

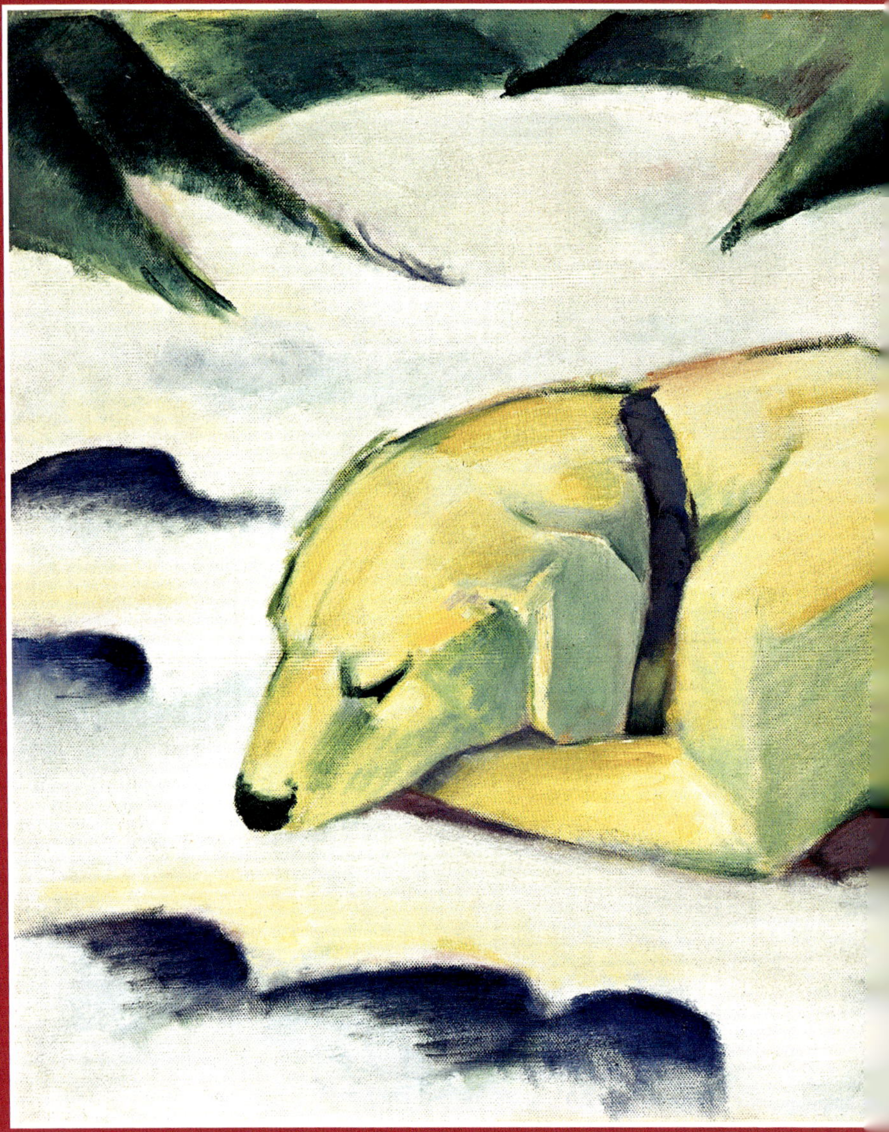

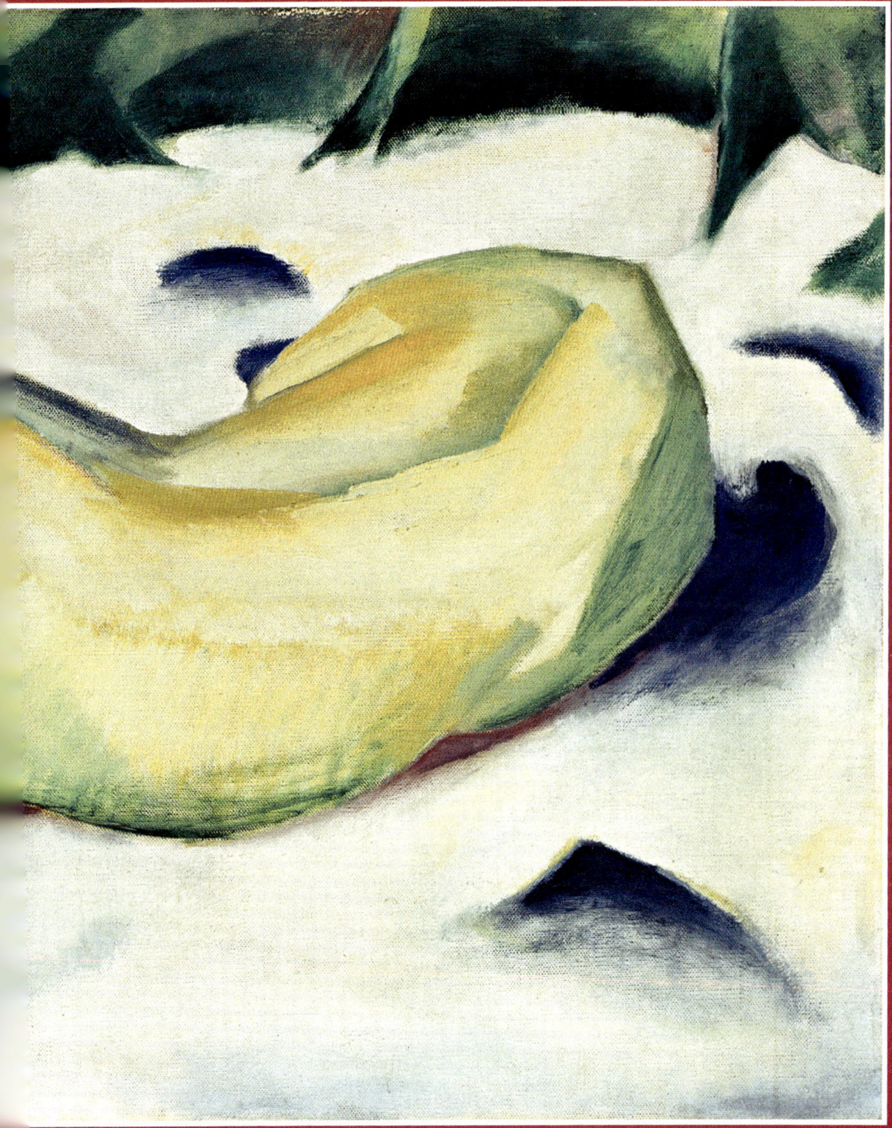

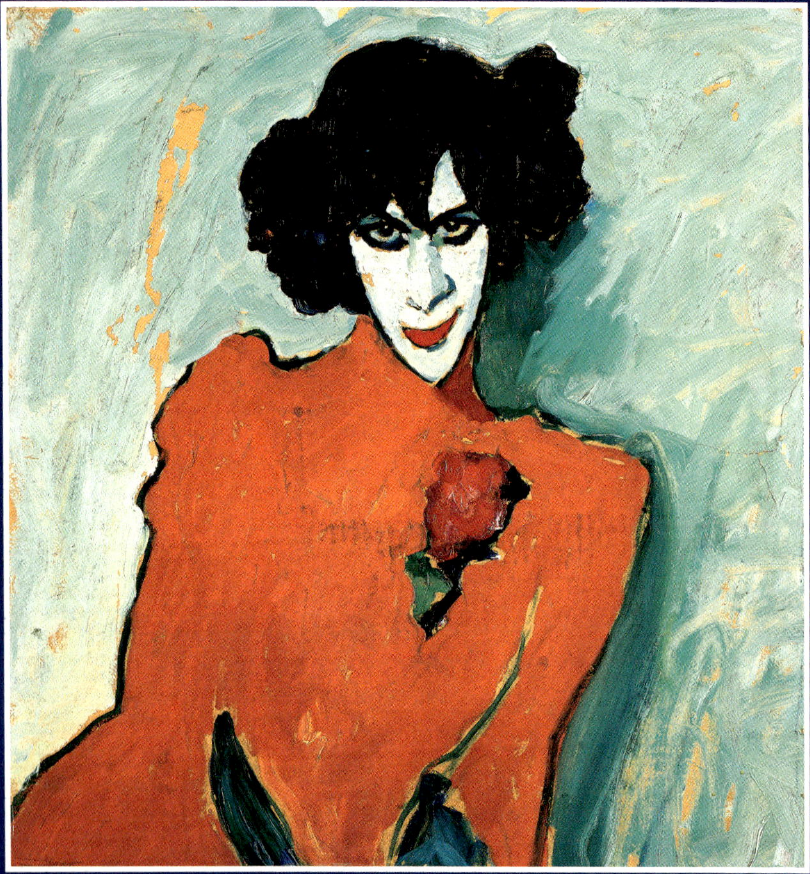

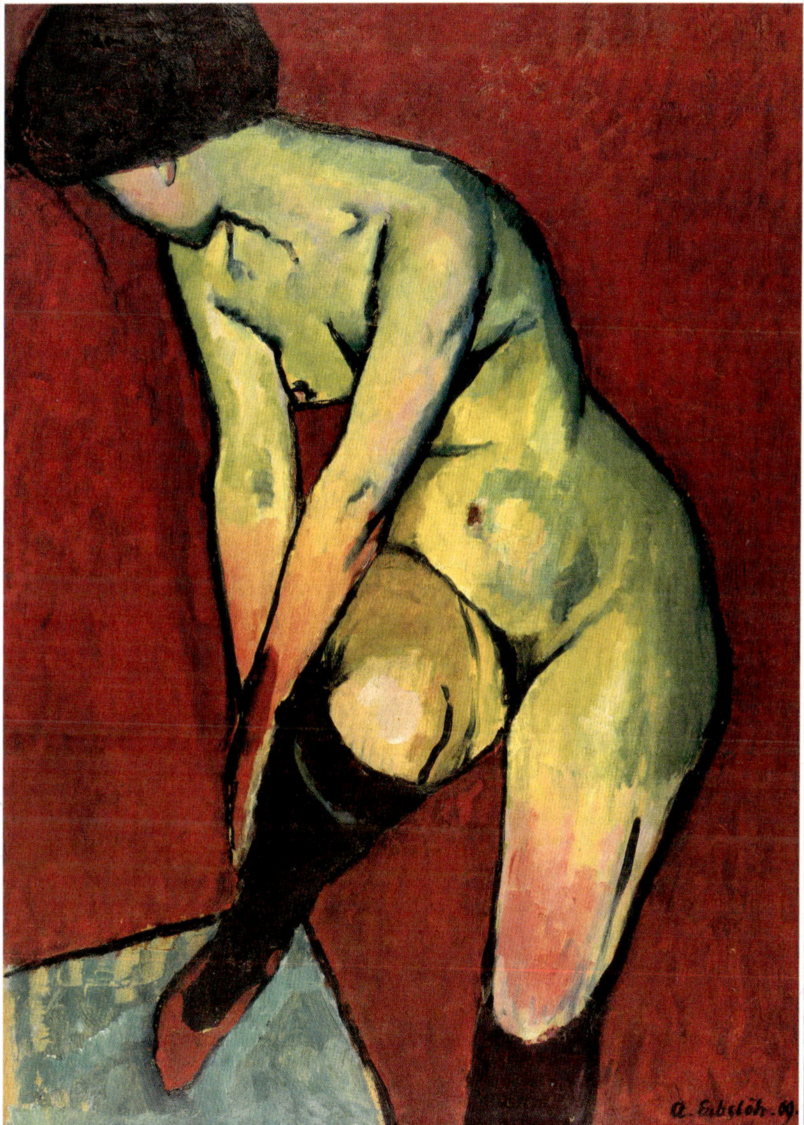
A. Erbslöh. 09.

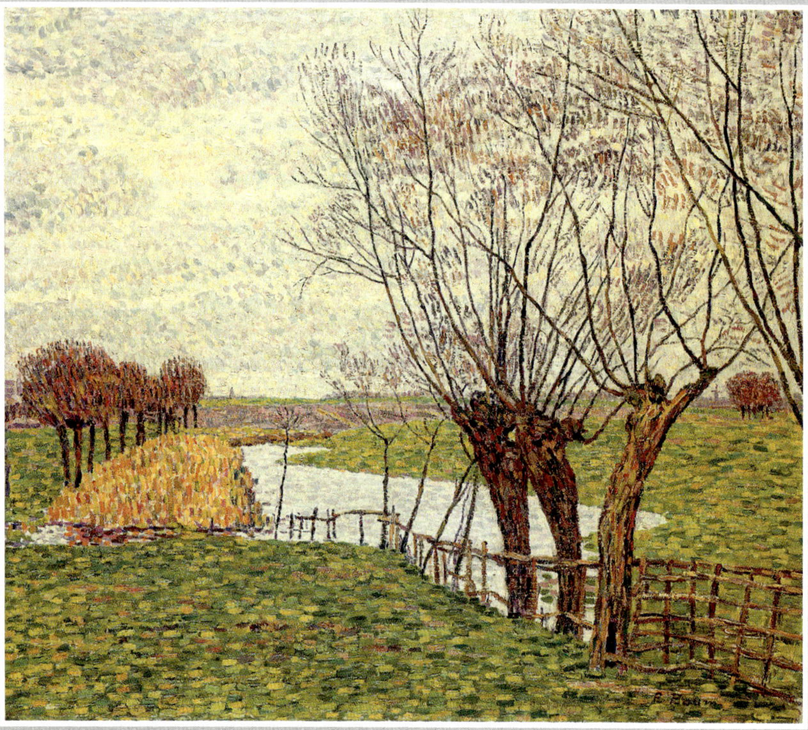

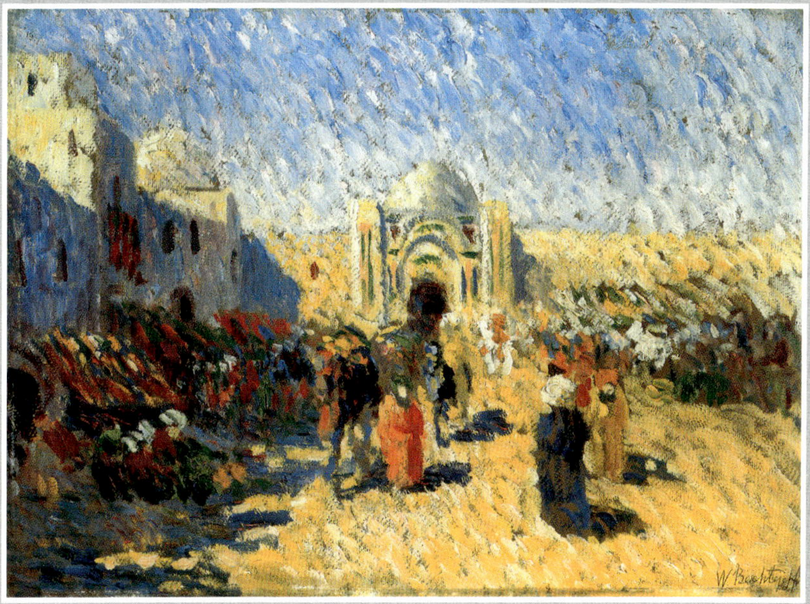

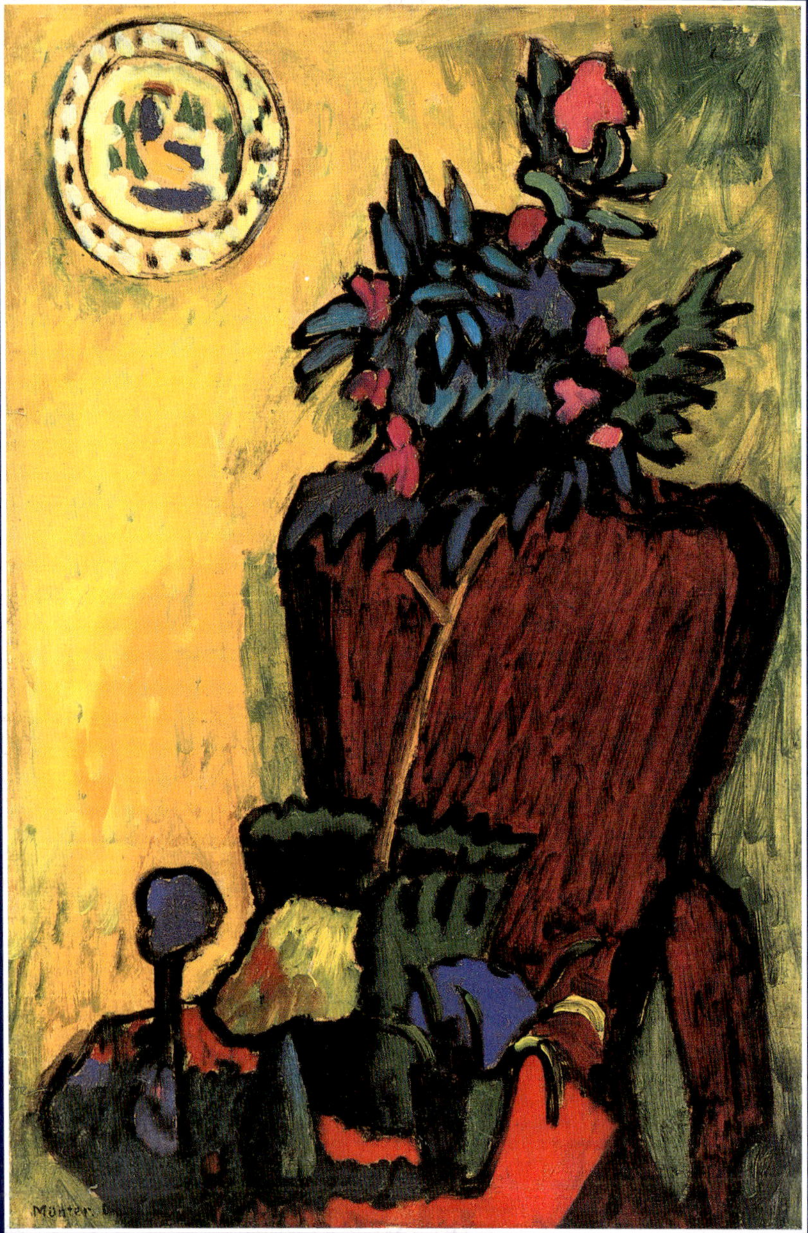
Münter

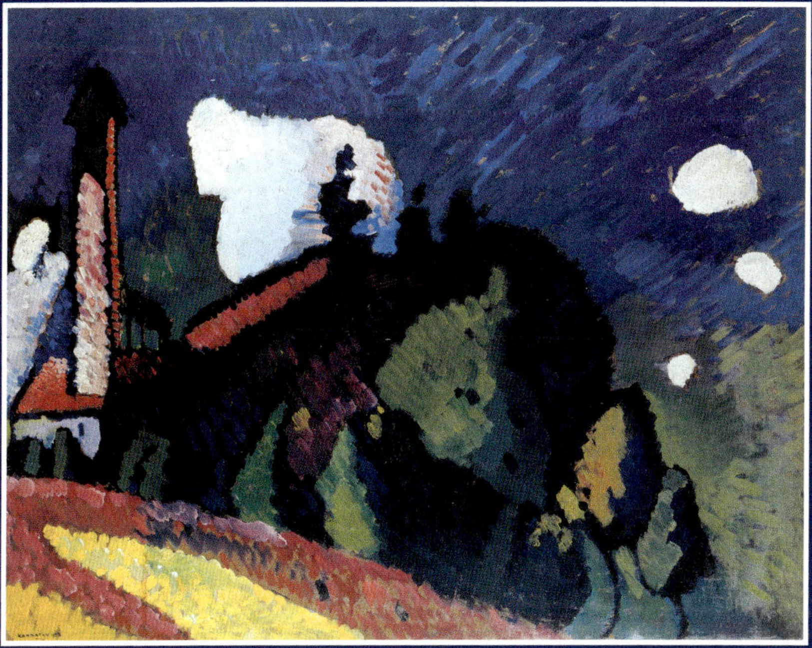

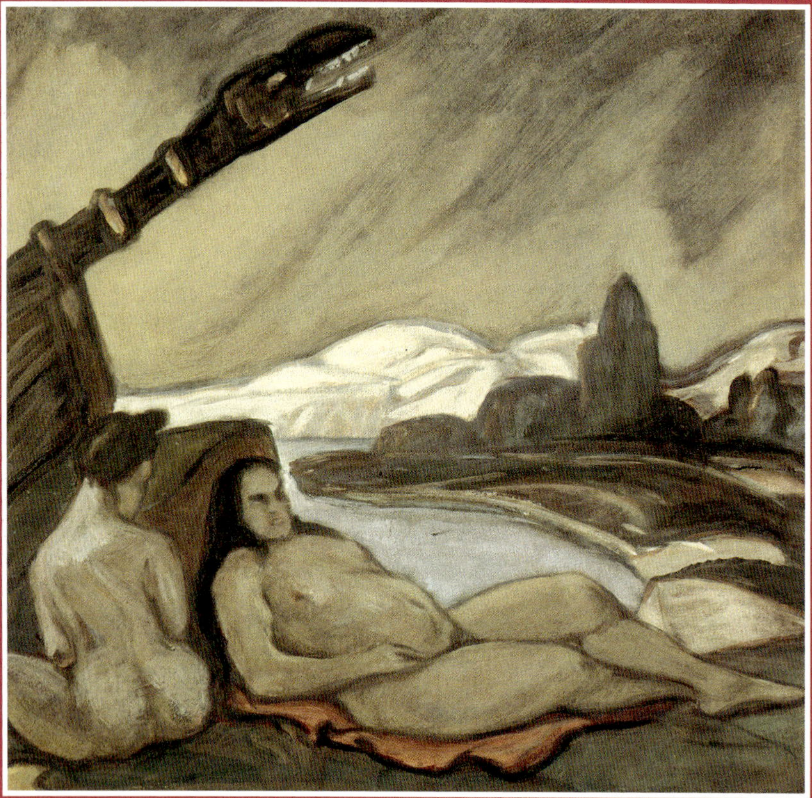

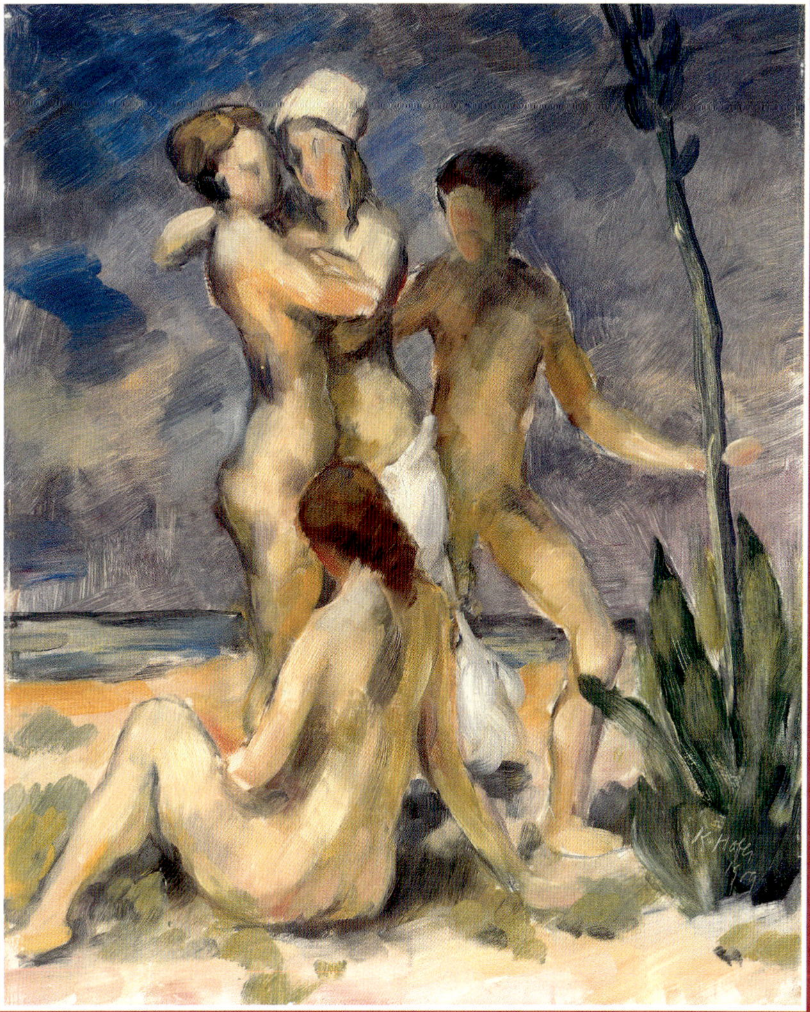

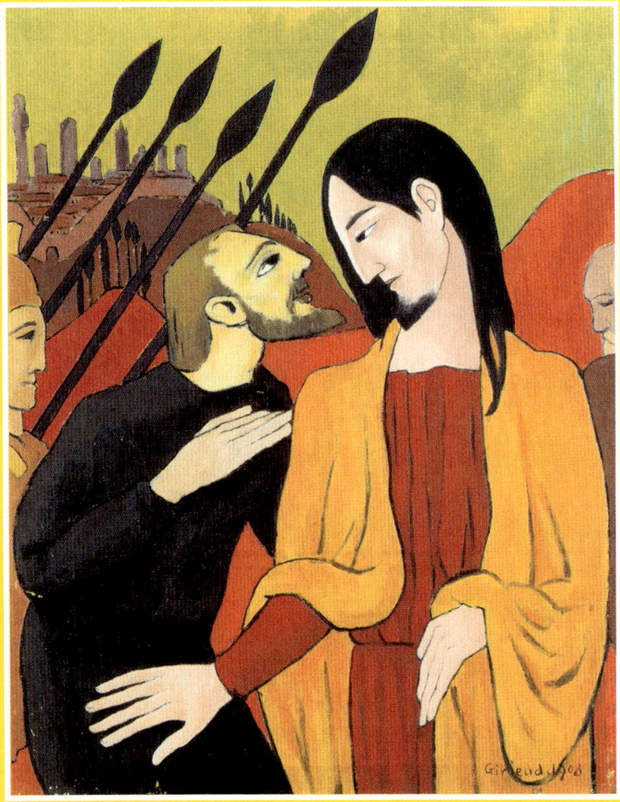
Girieud 1908

THE SECOND EXHIBITION OF THE NEW ARTISTS' ASSOCIATION OF MUNICH

It was certainly mainly thanks to Hugo von Tschudi's influence that the second major exhibition of the New Artists' Association of Munich was held one year later. This in no way lessens the vast achievement of the gallery owner Heinrich Thannhauser (1859–1934). It took a great deal of enthusiasm and courage to dare to put on another exhibition after the commercial failure of the first one. After all, Thannhauser was not only an enthusiastic admirer and supporter of modern art – he had already shown in his gallery works by the French Impressionists as well as Georges Braque and Pablo Picasso – but also a successful businessman.

This time he placed his hopes entirely on the French avant-garde. The exhibition opened on September 1, 1910, in the Arco-Palais at Theatinerstrasse 7, the main location of his gallery. It included works by Picasso, Braque, André Derain, Kees van Dongen, Georges Rouault, and Maurice de Vlaminck. Members of the New Artists' Association of Munich and Russian artists also participated. Once again violent disapproval was voiced by the press; the criticisms were similar to those heard during the previous year's exhibition. An article signed "G. J. W." summarized the overall mood: "The charming name of Munich, so full of promise in all matters relating to art, is obliged to serve as an advertisement for an artists' society which blends together Romanic and Slavic elements that are furthermore alien and hostile to the Munich art tradition. [...] One finds oneself tearing one's hair in despair, so to speak, when one stands in front of these strange pictures. For a long time it is impossible not to believe that we are dealing here with a practical joke. And when one finally decides, for better or worse, to take the matter seriously, then well-justified doubts of a pathological nature begin to surface. An insane mass suggestion must have been at work here. These thirty-odd people [...] have suddenly been taken over by a mad genius. [...] Not only do they paint the most incomprehensible mysteries, but they also write arcane things about their art. In both flickers the mysterious fire of profundity. They are really serious about it and in their overheated imagination even convince themselves that their art is honest. And so they rave with paintbrush and pencil like feverish invalids, like morphine and hashish addicts."[11]

Erma Bossi
AT THE OPERA,
c. 1909/1910

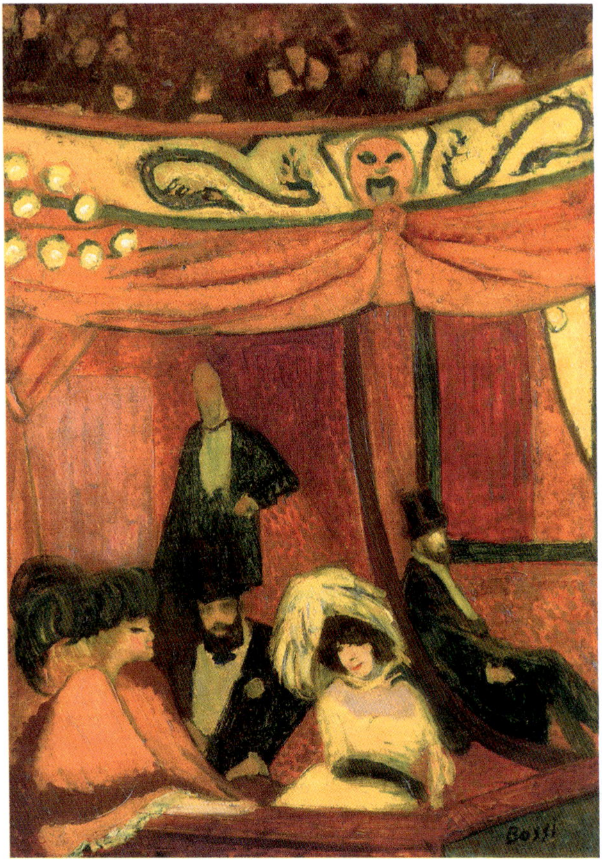

The comments of the critic M. K. Rohe in the *Münchner Neueste Nachrichten* were similar: "There are only two possible explanations for this absurd exhibition: either we assume that the majority of the members and guests of the association are incurably mad, or else we are dealing with pranksters whose desire to create a sensation is not unknown nowadays, and who are attempting to take advantage of the economic situation."[12]

In order to understand this total rejection, we must remember two things. It is linked both with the wide range of styles prevailing on the eve of the First World War, and also with the nervous and agitated atmosphere in the cultural sphere. Academic painting was still regarded as the standard by which all works were judged; perfection of representation was the ultimate criterion of quality in art. People had only just started to discover beauty and harmony in the shimmering world of colors of the Impressionists, and to understand Jugendstil as a legitimate form of art, and then along came the German Expressionists, especially the artists of the Dresden-based group *Die Brücke [The Bridge]* and the Munich New Artists' Association, and confronted them with "deformed" faces, figures, objects and landscapes in brilliant, ungraduated colors. This brutality contradicted the sense of aesthetics of the time so fundamentally that even the overwhelming majority of the elite middle classes rejected the new language of colors and forms. This makes the courage and determination of the young artists, not to mention the gallery owners who supported them, look all the more remarkable.

Of particular importance for art in Munich was the visit to the gallery of one young artist who was also searching for truth and authenticity in art, for an unsentimental opportunity to express great feelings: Franz Marc. He visited both exhibitions of the New Artists' Association of Munich and was enchanted. Full of enthusiasm, he wrote a letter to the gallery, in which he observed: "The completely spiritualized and dematerialized subjectivity of the feeling which our fathers, the artists of the nineteenth century, never even tried to achieve in their pictures, this bold attempt to spiritualize the 'matter' which Impressionism got bogged down in, is a necessary reaction that started in Pont-Aven under Gauguin and that is already manifest in countless attempts. What seems to us to be so promising in this new approach that the New Artists' Association has adopted is that the pictures, in addition to their highly spiritualized purpose, also contain very valuable examples of space arrangement, rhythm and color theory."[13] Kandinsky and his supporters were so delighted with Marc's text that they added it to the catalogue for the subsequent venues of the exhibition, alongside the damning comments by M. K. Rohe in the *Münchner Neueste Nachrichten* ("incurably

August Macke
AT THE CIRCUS, 1911

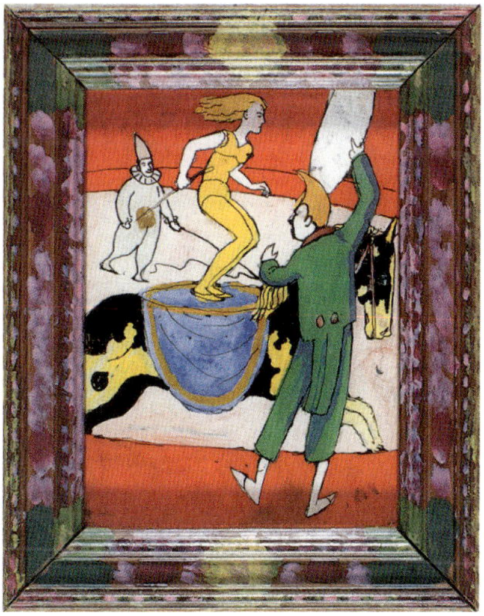

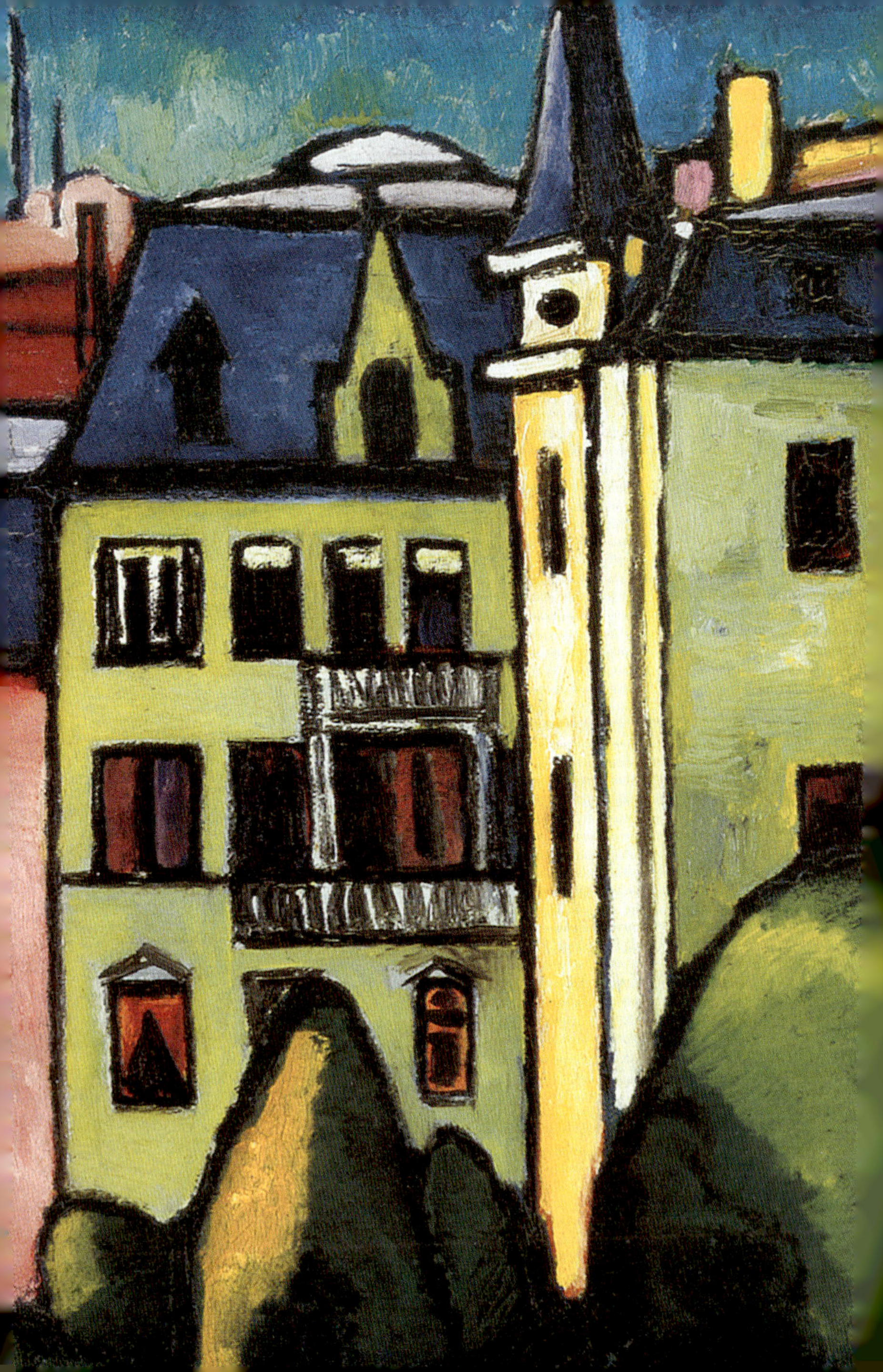

mad"). During the following weeks, Franz Marc made the acquaintance of most of the artists in the group, the only exception being Kandinsky, who was away in Russia. On New Year's Eve 1911 the day came at last. Franz Marc was invited to Giselastrasse in Schwabing, to the salon of the "Giselisten" surrounding Werefkin and Jawlensky. There he met Gabriele Münter and Wassily Kandinsky and noted later: "Spent the entire evening talking to Kandinsky and Münter – fantastic people."[14] Maria Marc, that diligent chronicler of the events relating to the Blue Rider, observed: "Kandinsky surpasses them all; I can understand exactly why little Münter, whom I greatly like, should love him 'passionately'."[15] And so what would later become the quartet of Kandinsky and Münter, Franz and Maria Marc, was now complete and an artistic friendship formed which like no other would advance the development of modern painting in Germany, both in theory and practice.

Alexander Kanoldt
A RAY OF SUNSHINE, 1910

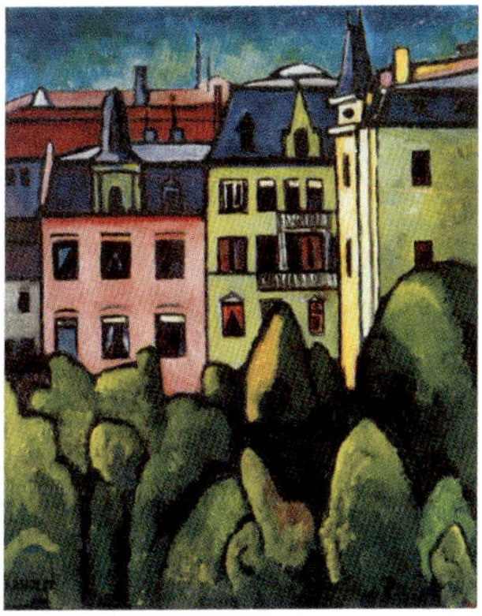

2. THE FOUNDING

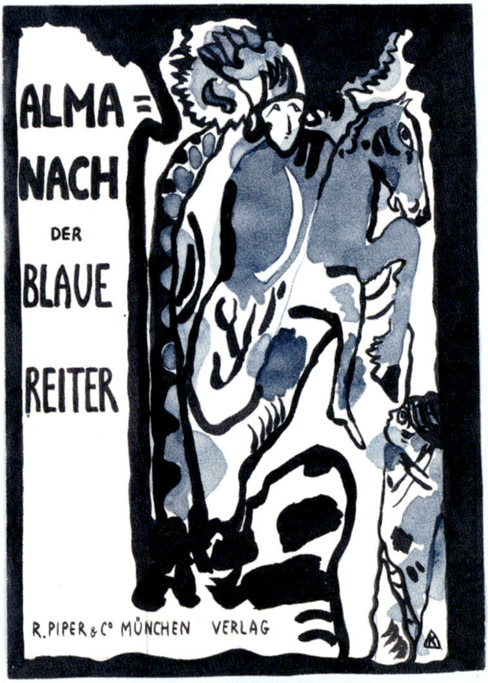

Wassily Kandinsky
Title woodcut for the almanac *Der Blaue Reiter*, 1911

THE YEAR 1911

Things moved quickly after that. On January 2 the program included a concert; the music was by Arnold Schönberg. Kandinsky was enchanted by the new, unaccustomed sounds, which were exactly what he wanted to paint. Not a portrait of the composer, nor a realistic landscape into which he might be transported while listening to the music, and most definitely not a still life with musical instruments. No, he wanted to paint the music as he had heard it, to transpose onto the canvas what he had experienced while listening to it. This sparked a lively discussion within the group, especially between Kandinsky, Marc, and Schönberg (who not only composed music but also liked to paint), on the subject of "synesthesia," the crossing of the border between fine art and music. They soon came to the conclusion that this subject was tremendously important for modern art.

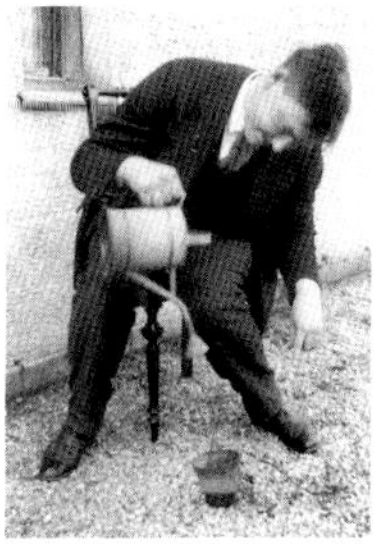

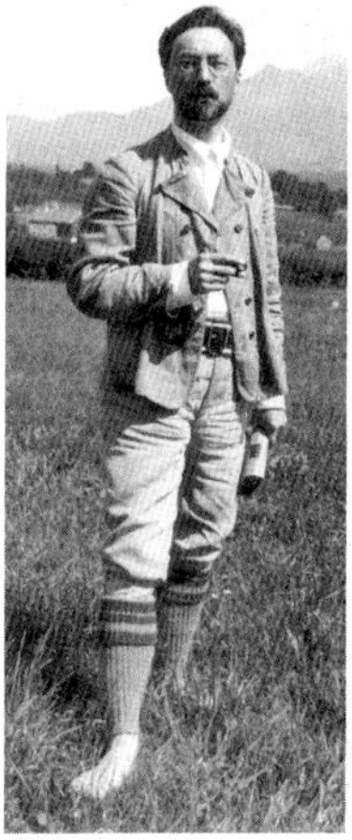

In February, Jawlensky, Werefkin, and Erbslöh visited Franz and Maria Marc in Sindelsdorf on the Kochelsee, where the couple had rented a house. They were greatly impressed. The artist became a member and third chairman of the New Artists' Association of Munich. His contact with Kandinsky was particularly close, even though the latter had just resigned from his position as first chairman. The reason for this step was that his views "regarding the activities of our association and the way it is run" were no longer shared by the other committee members.[16] The contact between Kandinsky and Marc became closer; they visited each other in Munich, Sindelsdorf, and Murnau.

In the dispute which now followed between the "moderates" (Erbslöh, Wittenstein) and the "progressives" (Kandinsky, Münter), Marc unequivocally and energetically took Kandinsky's side. Primarily, the dispute was about whether external artists and especially foreigners should be invited to participate in the planned third exhibition.

As a result of the disagreement, which was now no longer merely a matter of memberships and organizational affairs, but rather a question of real differences of artistic approach, Kandinsky decided to make clear his opinion in a publication. In June 1911 he developed the basic principles for an almanac which was to explain his basic

August Macke watering the "Tender Plant of Modern Art," 1912

Kandinsky with cigarette and book in a meadow near Murnau, c. 1910

Right page:

Poster for a concert of Arnold Schönberg's compositions in Munich on January 2, 1911

Wassily Kandinsky, Sketch for **IMPRESSION III (CONCERT)**, 1911

artistic beliefs through the example of art from different countries and epochs. For him it was a matter of including not just important and recognized artists, but also folk art from all over the world. In doing so he created something truly revolutionary. We must remember that at that time there flourished the cult of genius, which celebrated not only "painter princes" like Lenbach and Makart, but also the *artiste maudit*, the "accursed artist" who, despite his lack of success, and in spite of the enormous deprivation and impoverishment of his lifestyle, clung determinedly to his artistic convictions, often to the bitter end (Van Gogh, Gauguin).

In any case, art was always seen as being linked to a particular type of artistic personality. Folk art was regarded at best as "providing the subject" for fine art, as was the "anonymous" art of primitive peoples, which was viewed in ethnological museums as exotic, but not really considered to be art. Opinions differed sharply on these and other questions.

Finally, on December 2, 1911, the dispute took a decisive turn. The jury rejected Kandinsky's picture *Composition V. The Last Judgment* for the planned Munich New Artists' Association. They said that it exceeded the agreed dimensions of 4 square meters (43 square feet) and could therefore not be shown. Since Kandinsky himself had been the one to propose the "4-square-meter rule" two years previously, the jury members had every reason to consider themselves in the right. In any case, a majority of the jury members voted against the inclusion of Kandinsky's painting.

This was preceded by heated arguments between the "radicals" Kandinsky, Münter, and Marc on the one hand and the "moderates" around Erbslöh and Kanoldt on the other, who could not or would not accept Kandinsky's increasing abandonment of the realistic subject of the picture and his orientation toward complete abstraction and "pure form." That in turn was what Kandinsky could not accept, and for Münter and Marc, too, this went too far. And so on the evening of December 2 the three of them announced that they were leaving the New Artists' Association of Munich, which they had helped to found a few years previously. As so often, the fronts in this controversy did not always advance in a straightforward manner. Werefkin and Jawlensky remained members of the association, but took the side of Kandinsky & Co. as far as the disputed artistic questions were concerned. Maria Marc wrote that same evening to

Wassily Kandinsky **IMPRESSION III (CONCERT)**, 1911

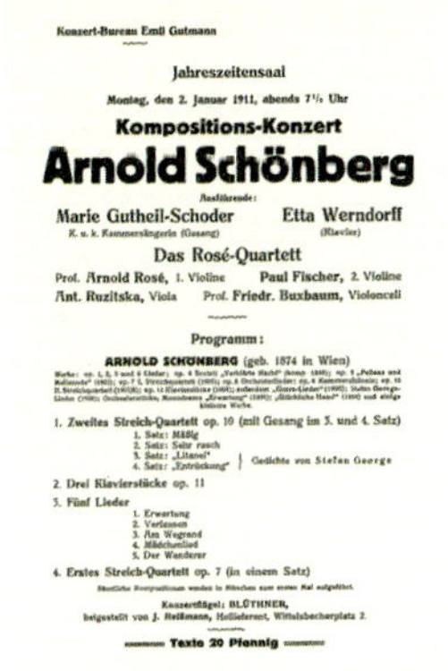

Konzert-Bureau Emil Gutmann

Jahreszeitensaal

Montag, den 2. Januar 1911, abends 7½ Uhr

Kompositions-Konzert

Arnold Schönberg

Ausführende:

Marie Gutheil-Schoder K. u. k. Kammersängerin (Gesang)

Etta Werndorff (Klavier)

Das Rosé-Quartett

Prof. **Arnold Rosé,** 1. Violine — **Paul Fischer,** 2. Violine

Ant. Ruzitska, Viola — Prof. **Friedr. Buxbaum,** Violoncell

Programm:

ARNOLD SCHÖNBERG (geb. 1874 in Wien)

1. **Zweites Streich-Quartett** op. 10 (mit Gesang im 3. und 4. Satz)
   1. Satz: Mäßig
   2. Satz: Sehr rasch
   3. Satz: „Litanei"
   4. Satz: „Entrückung" } Gedichte von Stefan George
2. **Drei Klavierstücke** op. 11
3. **Fünf Lieder**
   1. Erwartung
   2. Verlassen
   3. Am Wegrand
   4. Mädchenlied
   5. Der Wanderer
4. **Erstes Streich-Quartett** op. 7 (in einem Satz)

Konzertflügel: BLÜTHNER,
beigestellt von J. Reißmann, Hoflieferant, Wittelsbacherplatz 2.

Texte 20 Pfennig

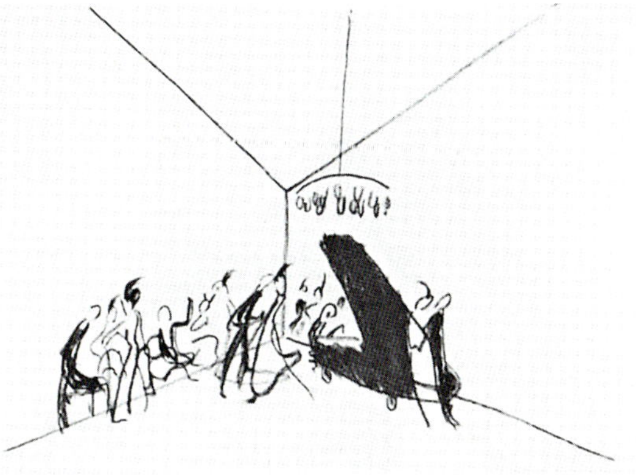

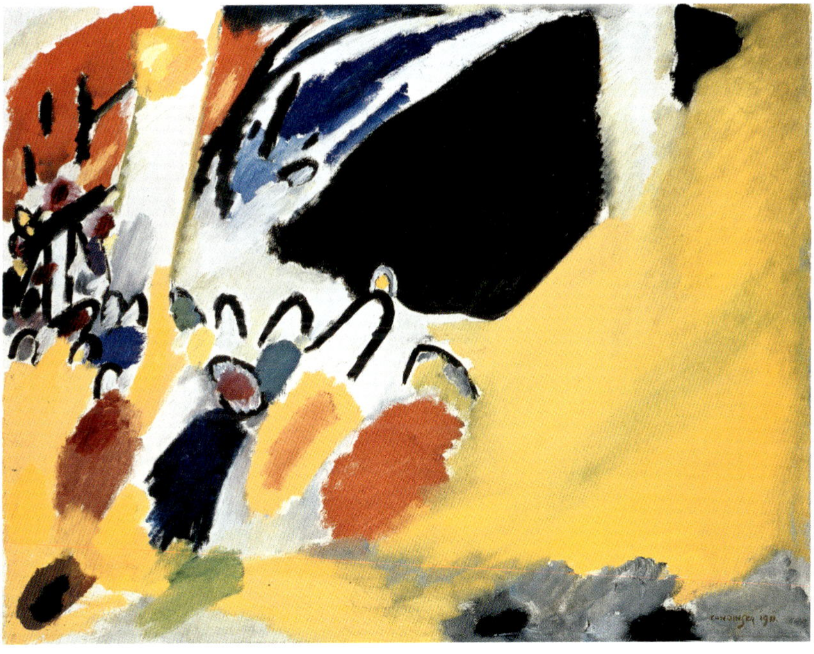

August Macke in Bonn and circulated a comment by Werefkin: "So, gentlemen, now we are losing the two most admirable members and a wonderful picture as well, and we will soon find ourselves wearing nightcaps." [17]

This led to a split: Kandinsky, Marc, and Münter left the association and put together their own exhibition within just sixteen days: *The First Exhibition of the Editorial Board the Blue Rider.* It was held parallel to the third exhibition of the New Artists' Association of Munich in the Galerie Thannhauser. The preparation time was extremely short and so it seems possible that the long-term dispute in the Munich New Artists' Association had prompted at least Kandinsky and Marc to prepare an alternative plan some weeks previously. Kandinsky put it like this a couple of decades later: "Since we both saw the 'quarrel' coming well in advance, we had prepared another exhibition." However it may have been, and although the announced programmatic paper was not yet available, the day the exhibition opened, December 18, 1911, can be described as the official date of the founding of the Blue Rider.

HOW THE BLUE RIDER GOT ITS NAME

What was the origin of this memorable, fine sounding and evocative name?

From the outset, Kandinsky wanted a mounted figure on a galloping or leaping horse. Two of Kandinsky's eleven sketches for the cover he produced in the autumn of 1911 include the name the Blue Rider, but only the last one clearly refers to the mounted knight, St. George. The image was inspired by Russian folk prints (so-called *lubki*) and Bavarian glass painting.

The mounted savior, therefore, accompanied by the use of the "heavenly" color blue, leads us to think that Kandinsky was searching for a symbol for the spiritual renewal of art. He could hardly have found a better one!

However, if we are to believe Kandinsky himself, this inspired choice of name was the result of an utterly prosaic event: "We thought up the name the Blue Rider around the coffee table in the gazebo in Sindelsdorf; we both loved blue, Marc horses, I riders. So the name more or less invented itself. And the fantastic coffee of Marc's wife Maria tasted even better."[18]

THE ALMANAC OF THE BLUE RIDER

Kandinsky had continued to cling to the idea of the almanac despite all the disputes which arose from the difficult "final phase" of the New Artists' Association of Munich, and despite the effort involved. He succeeded in arousing the enthusiasm of his fellow campaigners, especially Franz Marc, for his project. The latter wrote to August Macke on September 8, 1911: "We want to establish an almanac which will become the mouthpiece of all truly new ideas of our time. Painting, drama, music etc. [...] We especially want to explain many things using material to serve as a comparison. Your old plans of developing comparative art history will have their place here. We shall show old glass paintings, French and Russian folk pictures, alongside new works by outsiders and by us, and in between from time to time 'Munich modern painting' by way of comparison. We hope for so many beneficial and inspiring impulses, also directly for our own works, to clarify our ideas, so that this almanac has become all we ever dreamed of."[19]

The young August Macke, who was only twenty-two at the time, had moved with his wife from Bonn to Tegernsee for a year. It was here that Elisabeth planned to give birth to her child, who had been conceived before their marriage. Elisabeth's uncle, the Berlin factory owner and art collector Bernhard Koehler, was to become an important patron of the Blue Rider. One day, Macke appeared in Marc's studio in Schwabing together with his cousin, the painter Helmuth Macke, as well as the son of this rich uncle, who like his father was also called Bernhard. Marc and Macke took to each other immediately, and their friendship was to endure until the latter's premature death in 1914. For Marc the subsequent encounter with Bernhard Koehler senior was also a stroke of luck: from June 1910 the latter paid him a monthly allowance which was offset against the purchase of pictures. So Marc always had enough money to live on, an almost indescribable stroke of good fortune for the uncompromising young painter, who was able henceforth to devote himself entirely to the theoretical and practical development of his artistic aims. This also profited the intensive editorial work with Kandinsky and Münter on the almanac, which began with great enthusiasm in September 1911.

They continually revised the concept, wrote letters and sent offers for contributions to artists all over the world. They searched through mountains of pictorial material searching for items that supported their theories in a meaningful way. Their considerations were also devoted in detail to the graphic design and presentation of the almanac. In present-day terms, Kandinsky and Marc were simultaneously publishers, authors, editors, and book designers. Gabriele Münter helped them with copy-editing. During the most intensive phase of the editorial work in October, the group was also joined by August and Elisabeth Macke. "Everything was examined, discussed and accepted or rejected, and not without disputes and disagreement," noted Elisabeth Macke.[20]

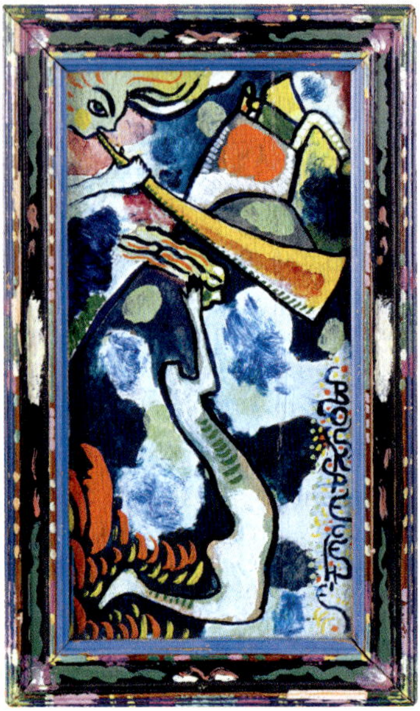

Wassily Kandinsky
THE LAST JUDGEMENT, 1911

During the many discussions within the New Artists' Association of Munich in the preparatory phase for the first Blue Rider exhibition, Kandinsky's and Marc's views and expectations on the subject of art theory had crystallized to such an extent that they wanted to present them to the art world and the general public in order to stimulate debate. The main protagonists were concerned with nothing less than the fundamental renewal and re-assessment of fine art. The first volume was to provide the basis for this.

Today the choice of the term "almanac" for a document with such revolutionary ideals seems old-fashioned. Just imagine if Karl Marx had chosen to call his world-shattering manifesto *The Communist Almanac* – we might have been spared a great deal!

On the other hand we must also remember that in the early years of the twentieth century the world was simply full of manifestos, protests, and calls to action, especially in the fields of social theory and art. Kandinsky wanted to produce an "almanac" in the original sense of the word: a publication which would appear at regular intervals. In fact the word "almanac" can possibly be traced back to the Arabic *al manăch*, a sort of calendar containing stories. It was from this that the European form of the almanac had developed:

Right page:

Wassily Kandinsky
COMPOSITION V, 1911 (detail)

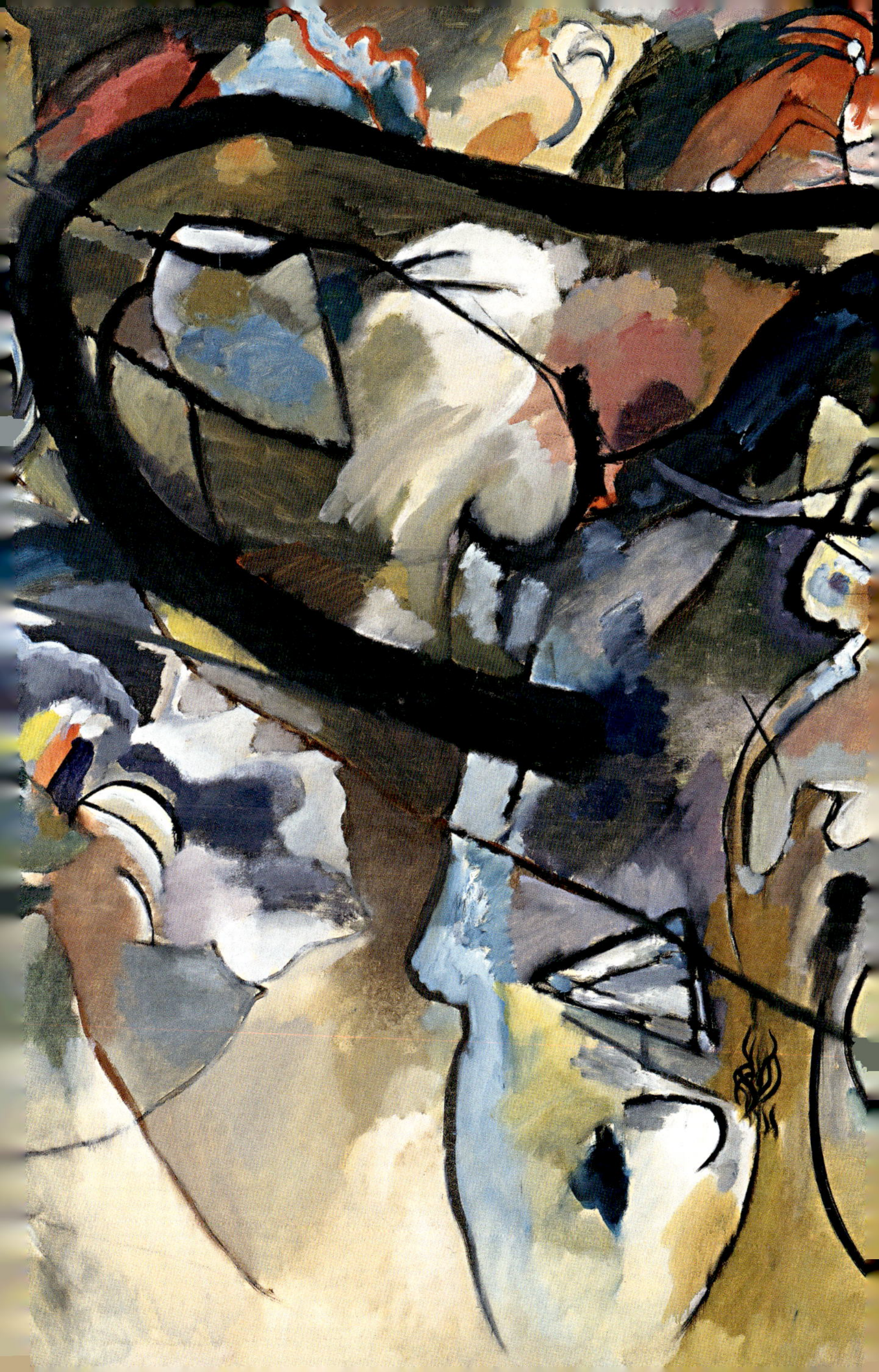

a calendar for the year, decorated and complemented by stories, poems, and other texts suitable for the season in question. Ultimately, the term "almanac" started to be used for a periodical in the broadest sense.

And so it is not surprising that the publisher Reinhard Piper spoke out energetically against the use of the term in the title of the book, since that would have obliged him to continue the project. The term, therefore, no longer appeared on the title when the publication was finally published by the Piper Verlag in Munich in March 1912, nor when it was reprinted in 1914 in a second edition. Nonetheless the term "almanac" has remained, which can only be explained by the genesis of the book. In the history of art the titles *Almanach der Blaue Reiter* or *Almanach des Blauen Reiters* have prevailed.

Armed with the obligatory white gloves, I had the indescribable pleasure of spending many days examining this wonderful testimony to classical Modernism. I was able to study the copy in the possession of the Lenbachhaus in Munich at my leisure.

The first impression is overwhelming: a fine binding of dark-blue morocco leather, embossed in gold with the motif of the horse rider in a mountain landscape. Inside are the original graphic sheets, which had been glued in. First of all an energetic colored woodcut by Kandinsky met my gaze. The typography was understated and classic and there was a wealth of interesting illustrations of different works of art, and at the back of the book the musical scores, which were also glued in. Any lover of art and books will experience true happiness when holding the original edition![21]

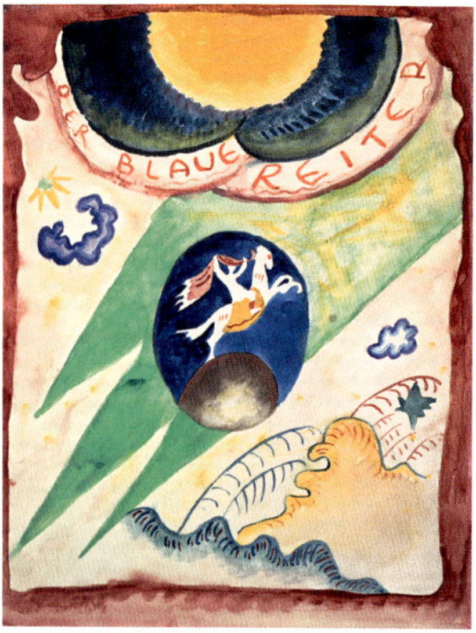

Wassily Kandinsky, Sketch for the cover of the almanac *Der Blaue Reiter*, 1911

What is there to discover? You will search in vain for a table of contents by way of assistance; the book begins programmatically with the essay "Geistige Güter" (Intellectual Property) by Franz Marc. The text is introduced by a lovely vignette and comes straight to the point: "It is remarkable how spiritual property is valued by people so completely differently from material property. For example, if someone conquers a

new colony for his fatherland, the entire country will sing his praises. They will not hesitate for even a single day to take possession of the colony, and technical achievements are greeted with the same jubilation.
However, if someone has the idea of giving his fatherland some new purely intellectual property, this will almost always be rejected with anger and irritation; the gift will be treated with suspicion and they will attempt to get rid of it; if it were allowed today, they would burn the donor for his gift."[22] It is tragic to think that just four years later the writer of these words would suffer this very death: Franz Marc would be killed near Verdun "for the fatherland."
The second contribution in the book, entitled "Die 'Wilden' Deutschlands" (Germany's 'Wild Ones') is also by Franz Marc. He draws a line between the Blue Rider and his colleagues from other modern trends, mentioning the Brücke group in Dresden and the New Secession in Berlin, whom he accuses of concentrating too intensively on formal aspects, asserting that "the renewal [of art] must not be formal, but a renaissance of thought." The essay ends with a sort of auto-suggestion: "We, on the other hand, believe – or at least we hope we may be allowed to believe – that far away from all these groups of 'Wild Ones' standing in the foreground here in Germany there may be some silent power which is struggling to achieve the same distant, lofty goals, and that ideas are maturing somewhere in silence, unbeknown to those who are shouting so loudly in the dispute. We stretch out our hand to them in the dark without knowing who they are."[23]
The third contribution, "Zwei Bilder" (Two Pictures) by Marc, compares an illustration for *Grimm's Fairy Tales* of 1832 with a woodcut produced by Kandinsky in 1910: "The first one is authentic and inwardly completely, like a folk song; it was understood by its time with total naturalness and love. However, we believe that everyone who feels the inwardness and artistic qualities of the old fairy-tale picture will feel, when standing before Kandinsky's picture, which we present for comparison, that it contains the same depth of inwardness and artistic expression."[24]
A contribution by David Burliuk examines the "Wild Ones" (progressive artists) of Russia, and August Macke writes in his contribution "Die Masken" (The Masks) with great respect about what was known at the time as "Negro art." "The disparaging gesture with

Almanac *Der Blaue Reiter*, first page of Franz Marc's essay "Intellectual Property," 1912

which up to that date art experts and artists dismissed all forms of art by primitive peoples to the field of ethnology or crafts is surprising, to say the least." And just a few pages further on he adds: "The bronze statues by the Negro peoples of Benin in West Africa [...] the idols from Easter Island in the farthest Pacific Ocean, the chieftain's necklace from Alaska and the wooden mask from New Caledonia speak the same powerful language as the chimeras of Notre-Dame [the cathedral in Paris] and the tombstone in Frankfurt Cathedral."[25]

Mention should also be made of the contributions by Arnold Schönberg ("Das Verhältnis zum Text"/The Relationship to Text), Theodor von Hartmann ("Die Anarchie in der Musik"/ Anarchy in Music), Leonid Sabaneyev ("Prometheus von Skrjabin"/ The *Prometheus* of Scriabin), and Nikolai Kulbin ("Die freie Musik"/ Free Music), which all examine different aspects of contemporary music and its wide-ranging links with painting. As "proof" of the theories expounded in the essays, scores by Arnold Schönberg, Alban Berg, and Anton Webern were included.

Kandinsky submitted two extensive written contributions, the essay "Über die Formfrage" (On the Question of Form) and the stage composition *Der Gelbe Klang [The Yellow Sound]*. The first of these – a complicated work of art theory – summarizes the ideas to date of the painter-philosopher Kandinsky. He describes the "creative" and "good" as the "white fertilizing stream." This is contrasted with the way man is blinded by the "black, death-bringing hand": "That is the negative, the destructive. That is evil."[26] He formulates his basic theory very vividly and memorably, and would like to see it applied to every form of artistic creativity. "In practical life you will find hardly anyone who will get out of the train in Regensburg if he wants to travel to Berlin. In intellectual life it is quite a common thing to get out in Regensburg. Sometimes even the engine driver does not want to carry on and all the passengers get out in Regensburg. How many people who were looking for God will find themselves standing in front of a carved statue! How many people who were searching for art got caught up in a form which an artist used for *his* purposes, be he Giotto, Raphael, Dürer, or Van Gogh!

And so our final conclusion must be to discover that it is not the most important thing whether the form is personal, national, stylish, whether it corresponds to the main movement of its contempo-

Next page:

Almanac *Der Blaue Reiter*, pages 8–9, with the illustration "Lyrical" from the essay "Two Pictures" by Franz Marc, 1912

GEISTIGE GÜTER

VON FRANZ MARC

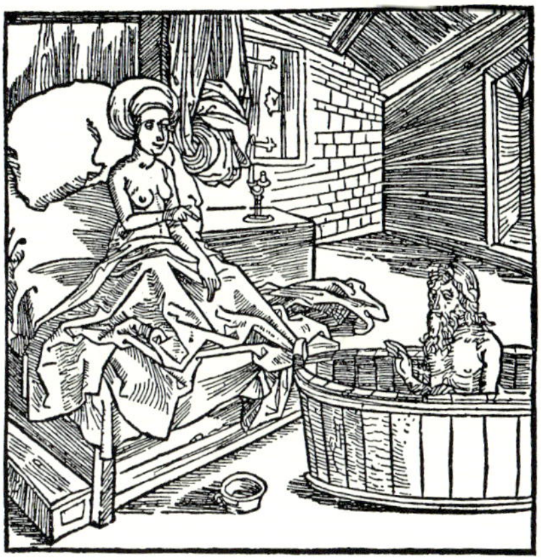

DEUTSCH (15. Jahrh.)

Es ist merkwürdig, wie geistige Güter von den Menschen so vollkommen anders gewertet werden als materielle.

Erobert z. B. jemand seinem Vaterlande eine neue Kolonie, so jubelt ihm das ganze Land entgegen. Man besinnt sich keinen Tag, die Kolonie in Besitz zu nehmen. Mit gleichem Jubel werden technische Errungenschaften begrüsst.

Kommt aber jemand auf den Gedanken, seinem Vaterlande ein neues reingeistiges Gut zu schenken, so weist man dieses fast jederzeit mit Zorn und Aufregung zurück, verdächtigt sein Geschenk und sucht es auf jede Weise aus der Welt zu schaffen; wäre es erlaubt, würde man den Geber noch heute für seine Gabe verbrennen.

Ist diese Tatsache nicht schauerlich?

Ein kleines, heute aktuelles Beispiel verleitet uns zu dieser Einleitung.

Meier-Graefe kam auf den Gedanken, seinen Landsleuten die wunderbare Ideenwelt eines ihnen ganz unbekannten, grossen Meisters zu schenken — es handelt sich hier um Greco; die grosse Allgemeinheit, selbst der Künstler, blieb nicht nur gleichgültig, sondern griff ihn mit wahrer Wut und Entrüstung an. Er hat sich mit dieser einfachen und edlen Handlung in Deutschland fast unmöglich gemacht.

Es ist wahnsinnig schwer, seinen Zeitgenossen geistige Geschenke zu machen.

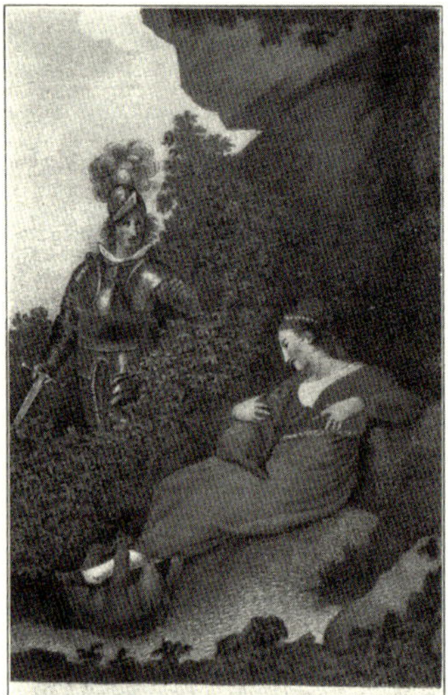

Reinhald das Wunderkind

ZWEI BILDER

VON FRANZ MARC

Die Weisheit muss sich rechtfertigen lassen von ihren Kindern.

Wenn wir so weise sein wollen, unsere Zeitgenossen zu belehren, müssen wir unsere Weisheit rechtfertigen durch unsere Werke und müssen sie zeigen wie eine selbstverständliche Sache.

Wir werden es uns hierbei so schwer wie möglich machen, indem wir die Feuerprobe nicht scheuen, unsere Werke, die in die Zukunft zeigen und noch unerwiesen sind, neben Werke alter, längst erwiesener Kulturen zu stellen. Wir tun es mit dem Gedanken, durch nichts unsere Ideen deutlicher zu illustrieren als durch solche Vergleiche; Echtes bleibt stets neben Echtem bestehen, so verschieden auch sein Ausdruck sein mag. Auch ist die Stunde zu solchen Betrachtungen günstig, da wir glauben, dass wir heute an der Wende zweier langer Epochen stehen; die Ahnung davon ist nicht neu; man hat den Ruf vor hundert Jahren schon lauter gehört. Damals wähnte man sich dem neuen Zeitalter schon sehr nahe, viel näher als wir es heute glauben. Ein ganzes Jahrhundert lag noch dazwischen, in welchem sich eine lange Entwicklung in rasendem Tempo abspielte. Die Menschheit durchjagte förmlich das letzte Stadium einer tausendjährigen Zeit, die ihren Anfang nahm

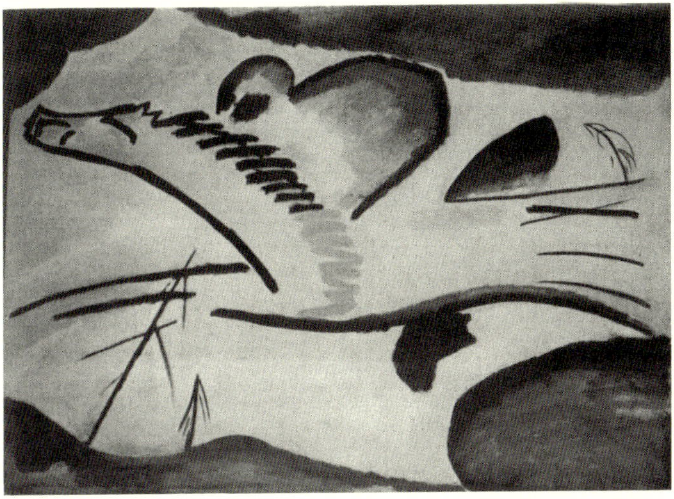

KANDINSKY

nach dem Zusammenbruch der grossen, antiken Welt. Damals legten die „Primitiven“ den ersten Grund für eine lange, neue Kunstentwicklung, und die ersten Märtyrer starben für das neue christliche Ideal.

Heute ist in Kunst und Religion diese lange Entwicklung durchlaufen. Aber noch liegt das weite Land voll Trümmer, voll alter Vorstellungen und Formen, die nicht weichen wollen, obwohl sie schon der Vergangenheit gehören. Die alten Ideen und Schöpfungen leben ein Scheinleben fort, und man steht ratlos vor der Herkulesarbeit, wie man sie vertreiben und freie Bahn schaffen soll für das Neue, das schon wartet.

Die Wissenschaft arbeitet negativ, au détriment de la religion — welches schlimme Eingeständnis für die Geistesarbeit unserer Zeit.

Wohl fühlt man, dass eine neue Religion im Lande umgeht, die noch keinen Rufer hat, von niemand erkannt.

Religionen sterben langsam.

Der Kunststil aber, der unveräusserliche Besitz der alten Zeit, brach in der Mitte des 19. Jahrhunderts katastrophal zusammen. Es gibt seitdem keinen Stil mehr; er geht, wie von einer Epidemie erfasst, auf der ganzen Welt ein. Was es an ernster Kunst seitdem

raries or not, whether it is related to many or few other forms or not, whether it stands completely alone or not etc., etc., but the most important thing in the question of form is whether it has grown from *inner necessity* or not."[27]

With this comment Kandinsky does indeed describe in a very convincing manner one of the main criteria of all art. You cannot just copy art from anywhere, nor can you invent it in a purely theoretical way; you cannot put it together from a variety of different sources, although such processes of course always play a role in the creation of art. What is decisive is always whether the artist can produce from all these influences and models, from his thoughts and experiences, something which is his own, something deeply felt, and create a unity from it.

Kandinsky describes the two poles which mark the way to a valid work of art as the "great realism" and the "great abstraction."

These ideas enlarged the field of vision of the artist friends Marc and Kandinsky in a completely new way. 'Western' art, the art of foreign countries and cultures, folk art, so-called "primitive" art, and the numerous trends, facets and schools of contemporary art, all of which claimed that progress was their prerogative, were put to the

Franz Marc
TWO HORSES, 1911

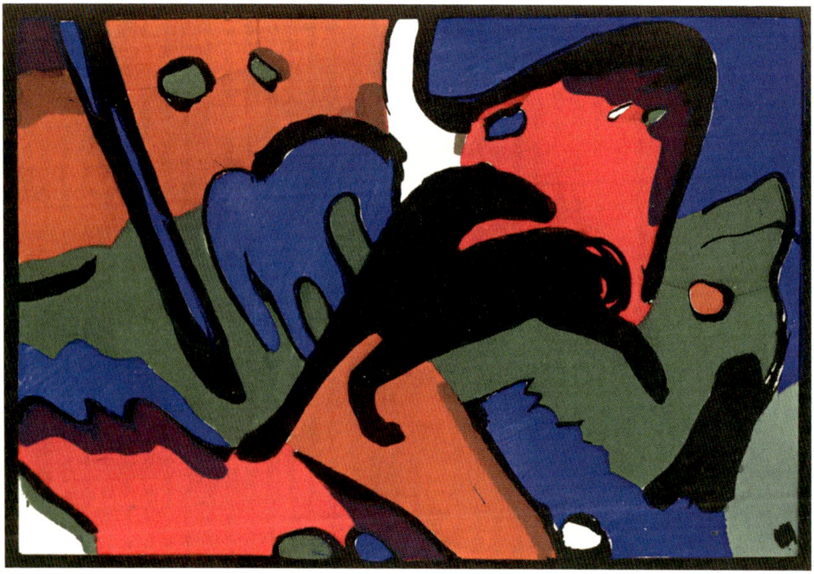

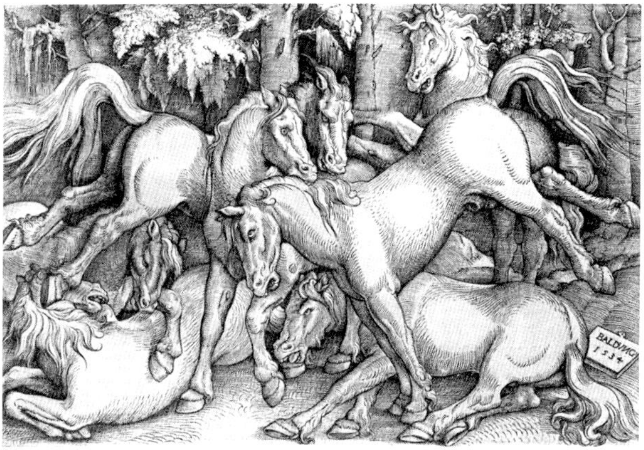

Woodcut by Hans Baldung Grien, from the almanac *Der Blaue Reiter,* 1912

test and examined for their "inner necessity." Only those which satisfied this criterion were admitted to the world of the Blue Rider.

Kandinsky's second contribution to the almanac, the stage composition *The Yellow Sound*, is an example of his synesthetic approach: painting in the form of colored light, the actors' costumes, the masks and dance-like movements of the figures were to be blended together to form a total work of art.

The almanac is paginated, so that pages 1 to 140 have page numbers. The volume owned by the Lenbachhaus in Munich is, however, considerably more voluminous than that. How can we explain this fact? The page numbers were printed only on the pages of text, regardless of whether they included illustrations or not. This text section was then considerably expanded by the inclusion of color plates. The luxury editions also included original prints, lovingly glued in by hand and protected by parchment paper. Furthermore, the pagination takes no account of the full-page black-and-white illustrations. Through this individual treatment, the luxury editions contain varying total volumes. "Copy no. 08 of the museum edition," in the possession of the Lenbachhaus in Munich, contains – if we count all the inserts and supplements – 222 pages.

Wassily Kandinsky,
Vignette for the almanac
Der Blaue Reiter, 1911

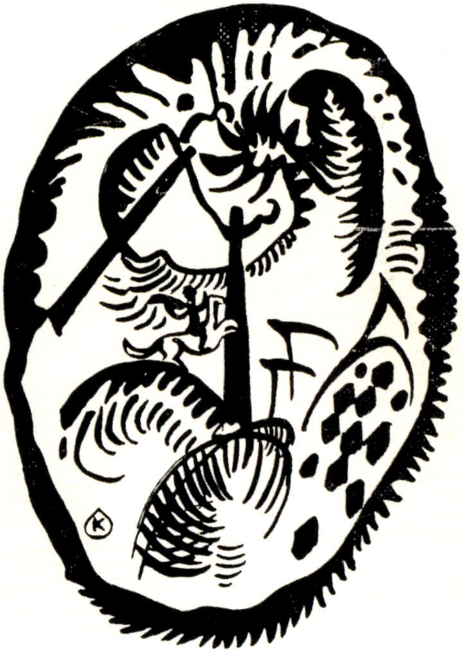

Right page:

Wassily Kandinsky
ARCHER, 1908-1909

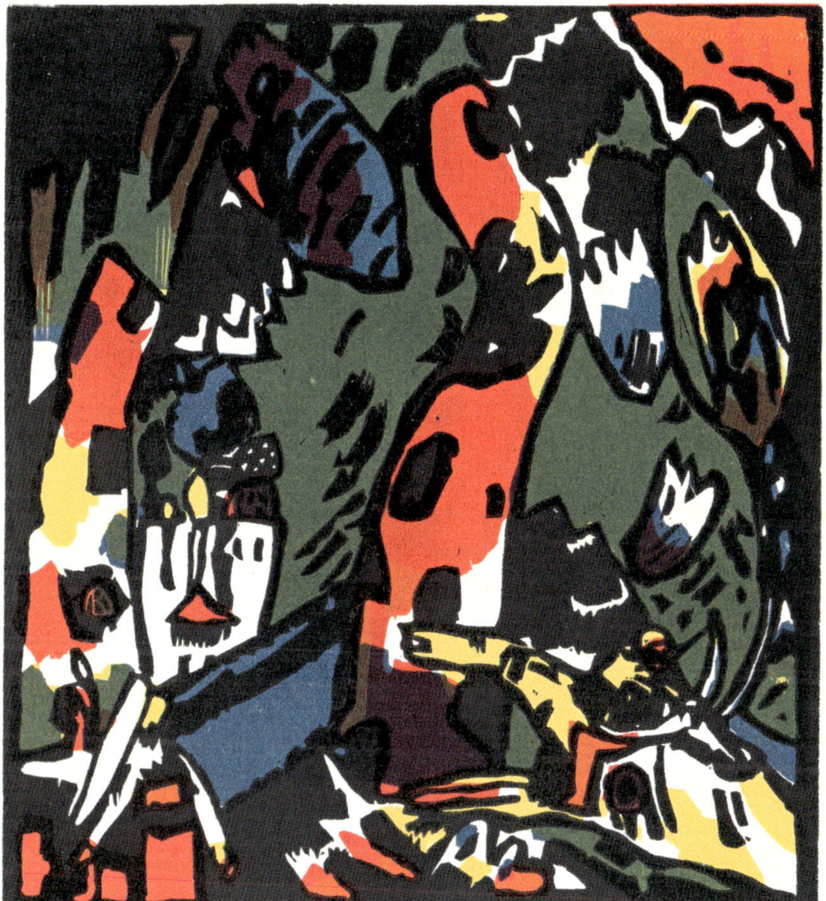

KANDINSKY

First exhibition of the Blue Rider, Galerie Thannhauser, Munich, 1911/12

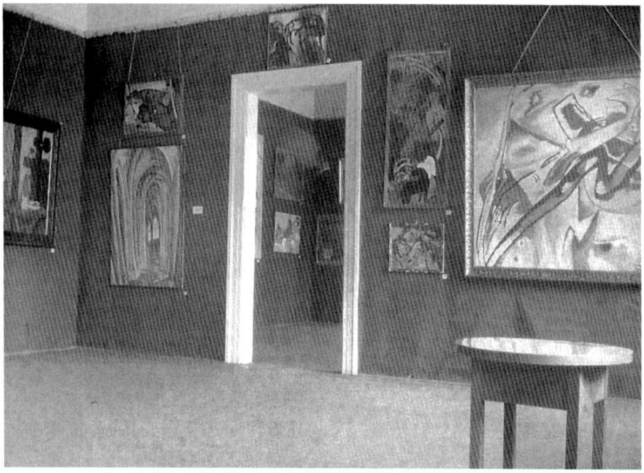

pages 61–74

Wassily Kandinsky, Title woodcut for the almanac *Der Blaue Reiter*, 1911

Vladimir Burliuk **LANDSCAPE**, 1909

Heinrich Campendonk **SEMI-NUDE WITH CAT**, 1912

Eugen von Kahler **THE BATHERS**, 1910-1911

Albert Bloch **THE THREE PIERROTS NO. 2**, 1911

David Burliuk **DNIESTER RAPIDS**, c. 1910

Wassily Kandinsky **IMPROVISATION 26 (ROWER)**, 1912

Franz Marc **THE TIGER**, 1912

Arnold Schönberg **NOCTURNAL LANDSCAPE**, 1910

Robert Delaunay **SAINT SÉVERIN**, 1909-1910

August Macke **LARGE ZOOLOGICAL GARDEN (TRIPTYCH)**, 1913

Gabriele Münter **STILL LIFE WITH ST. GEORGE**, 1911

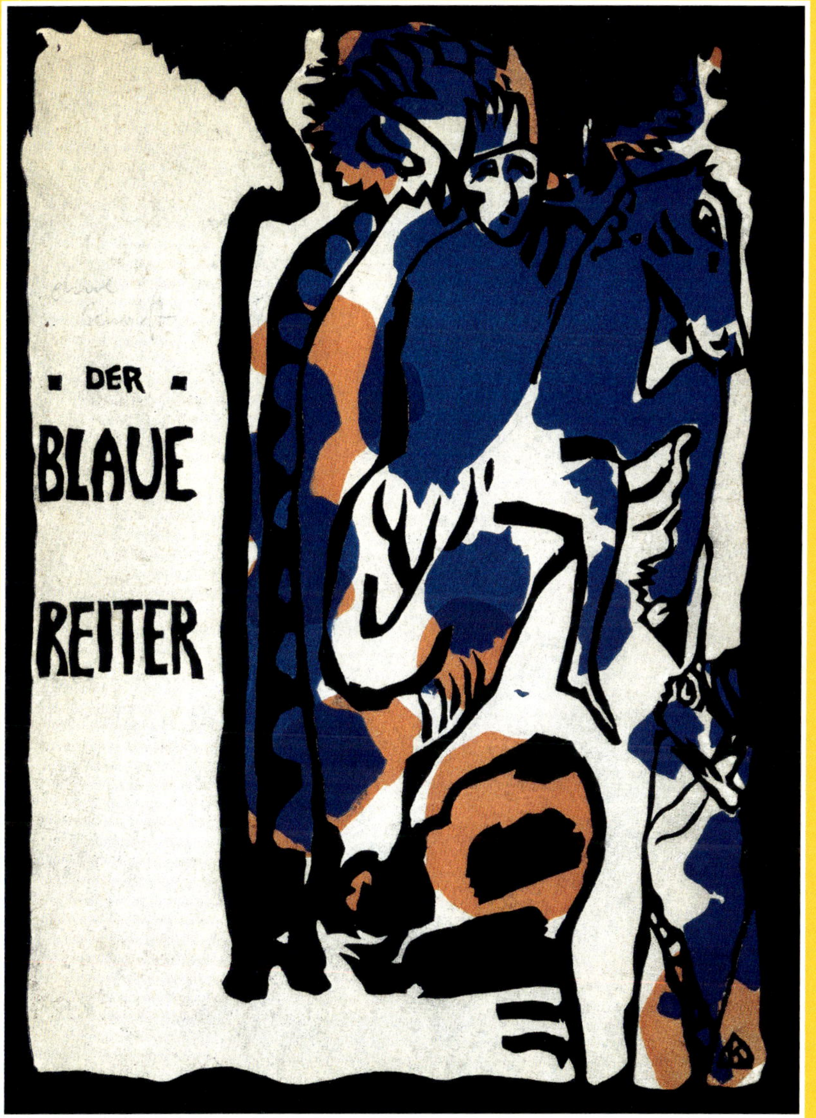
DER
BLAUE
REITER

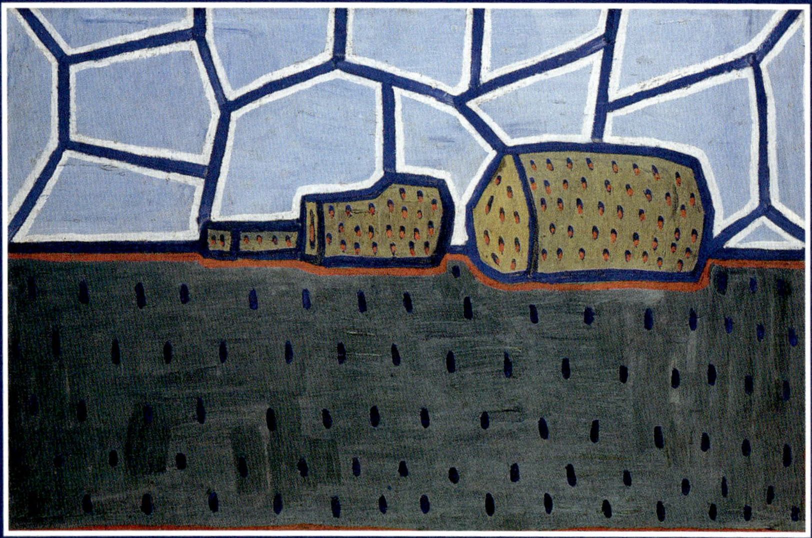

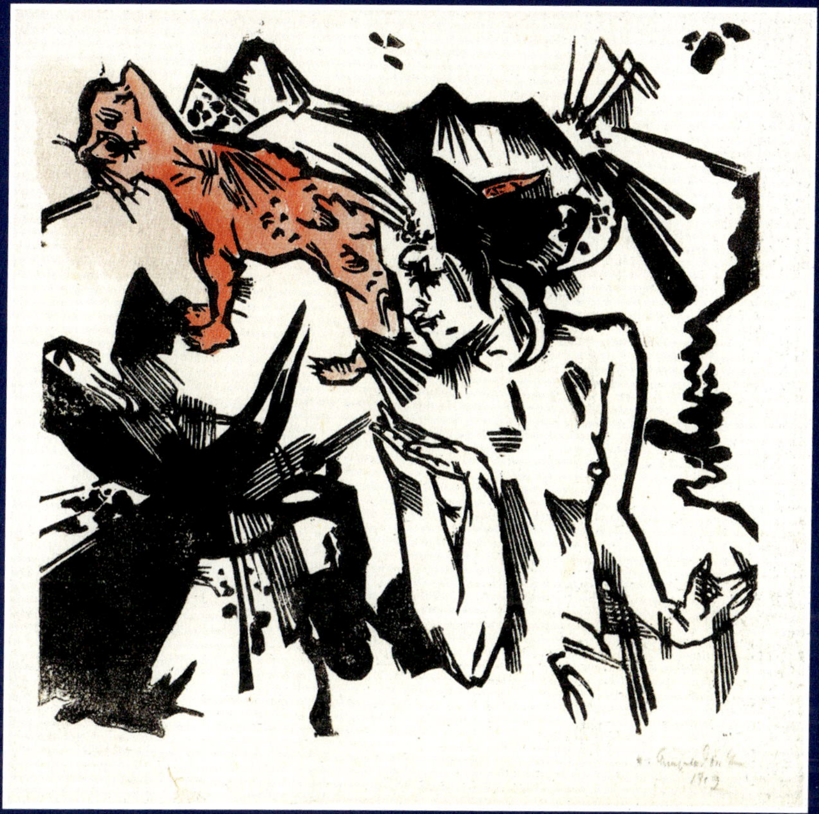

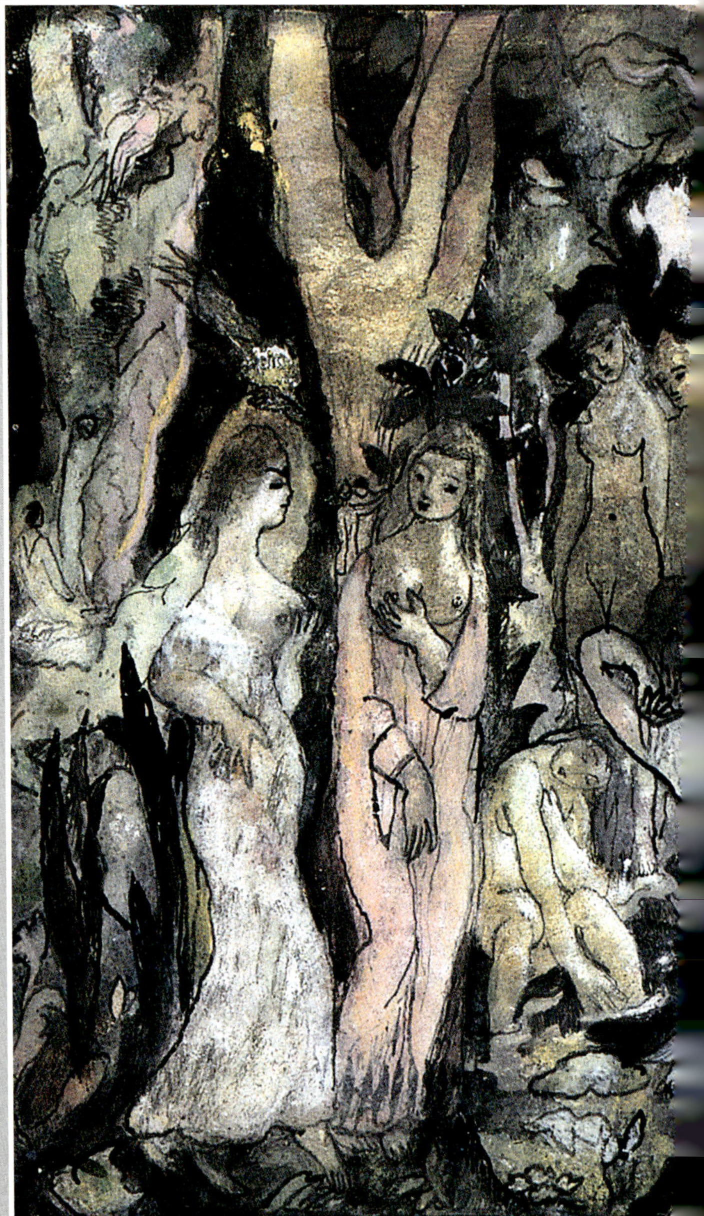

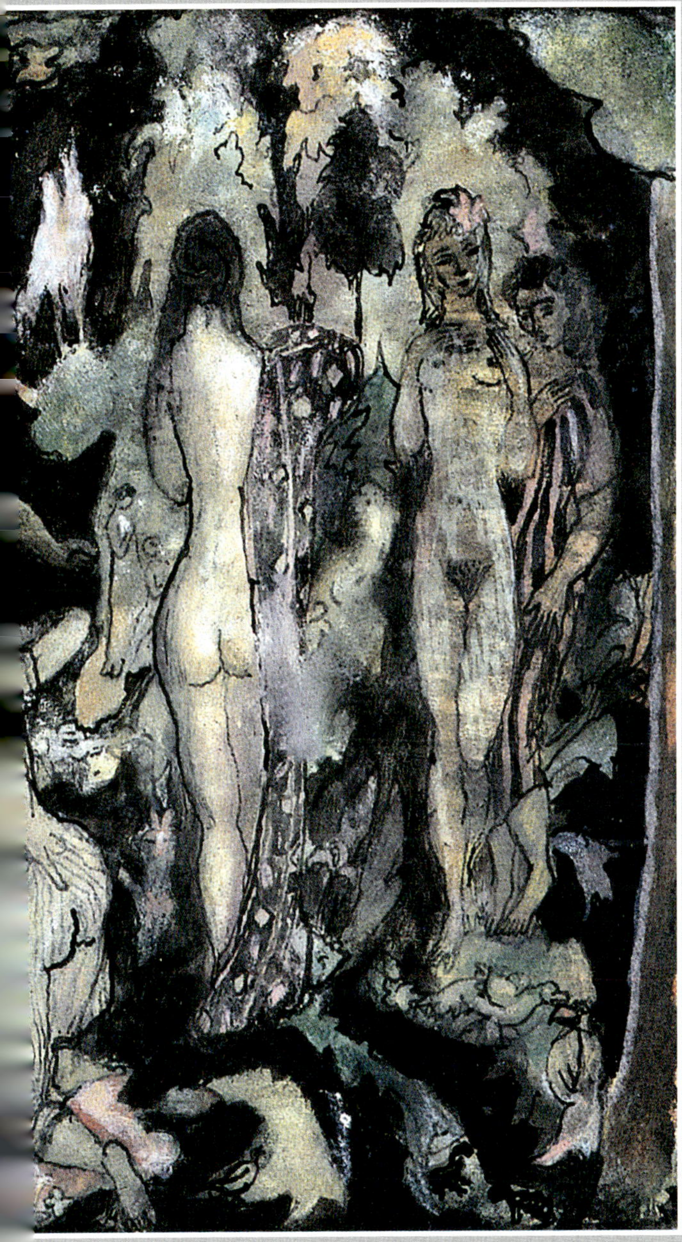

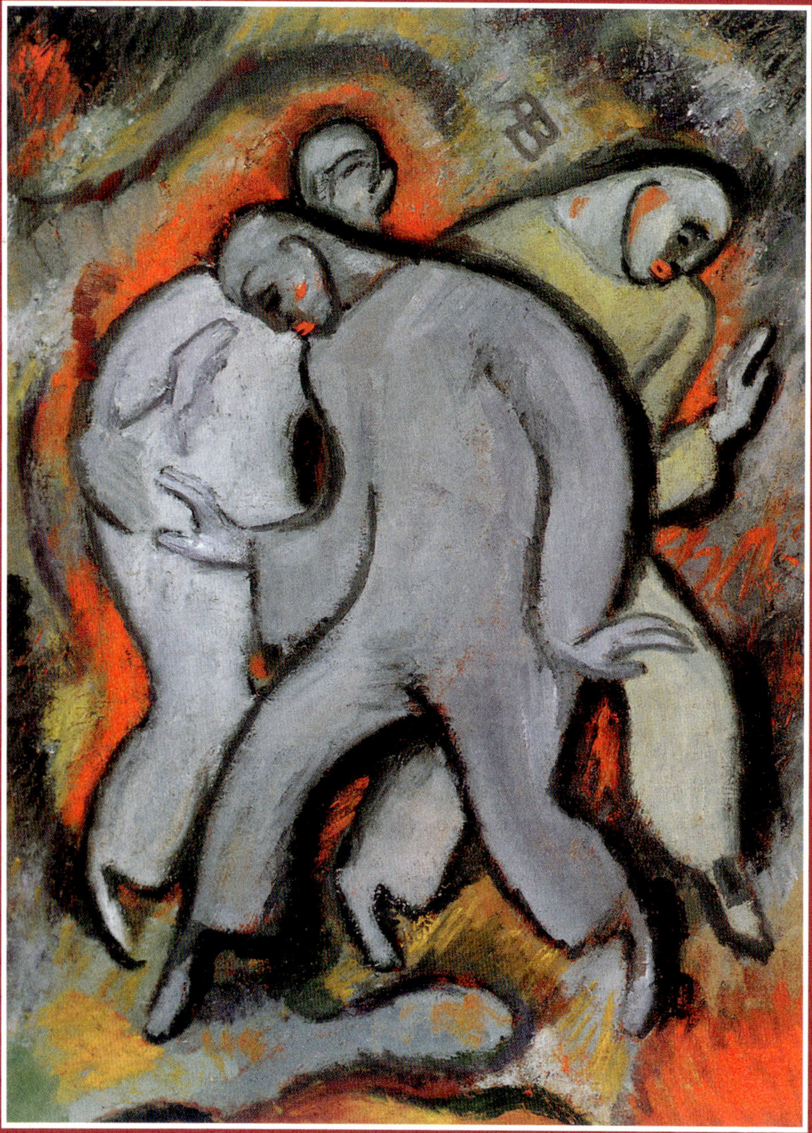

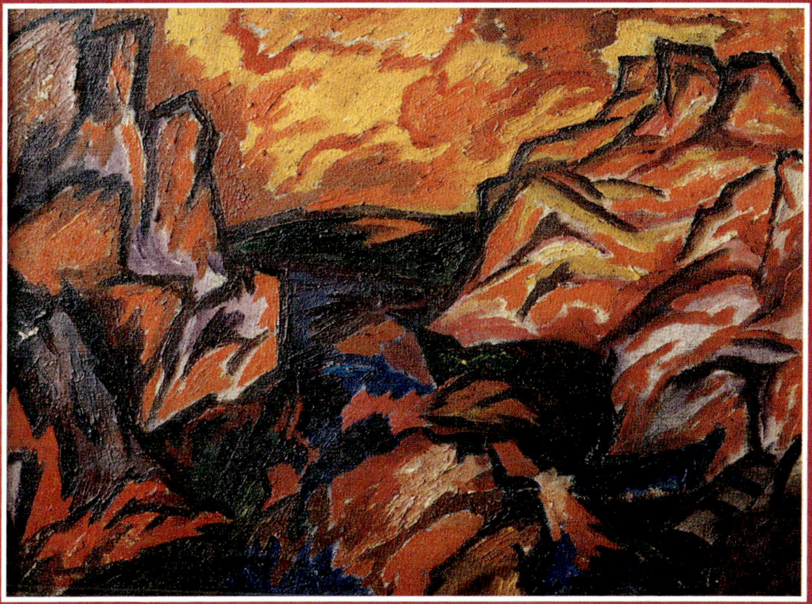

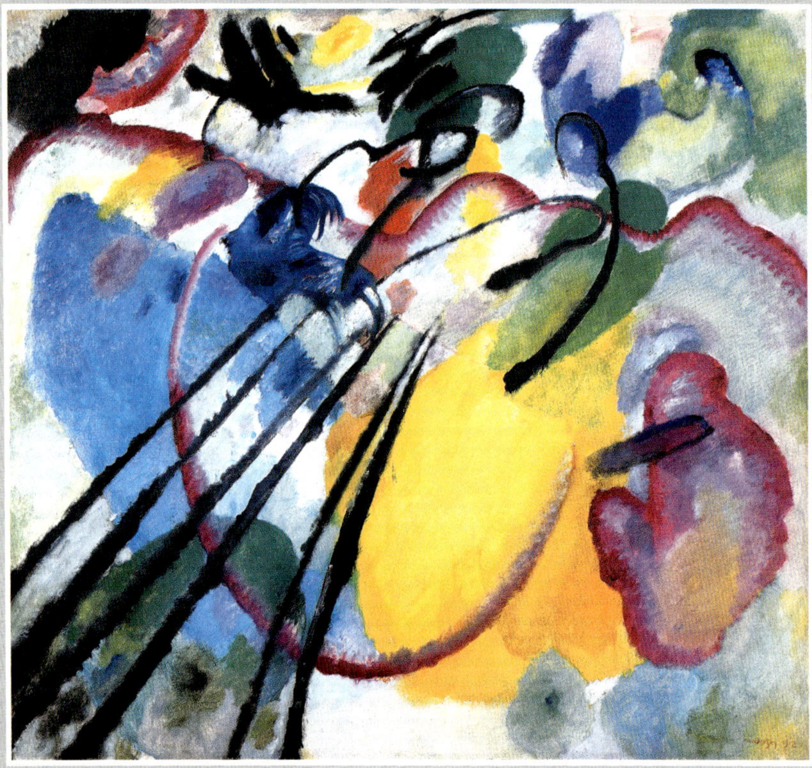

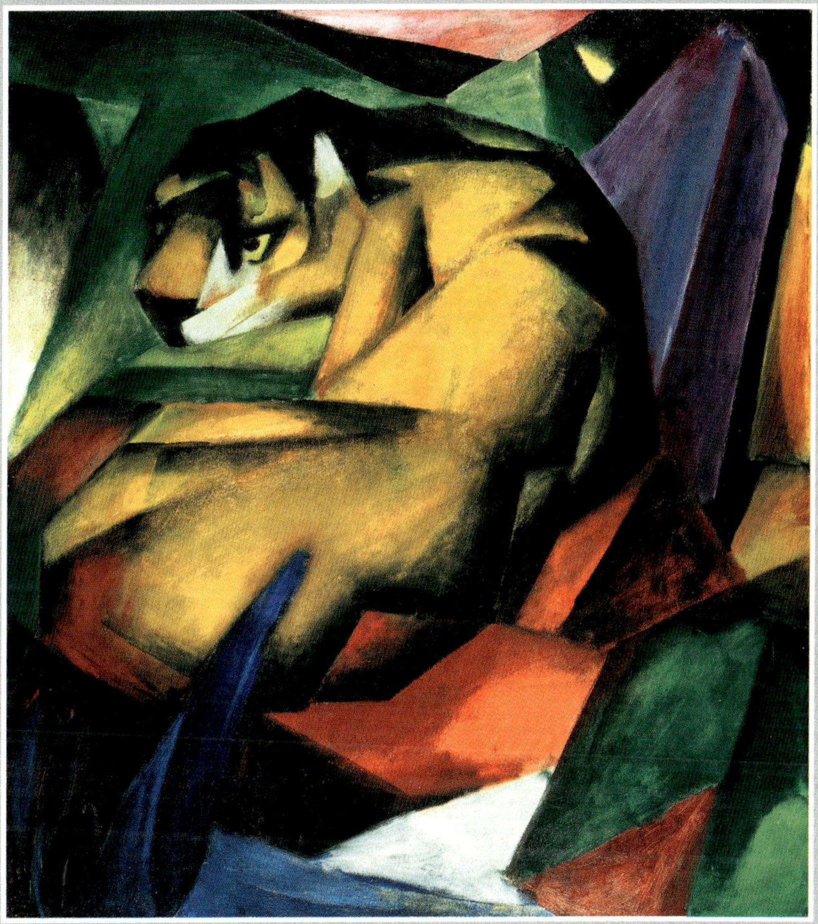

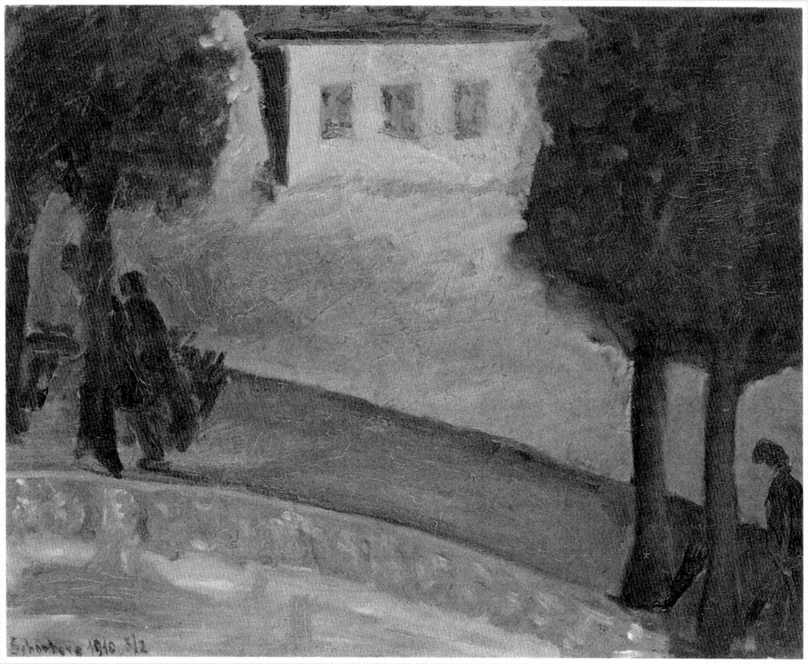

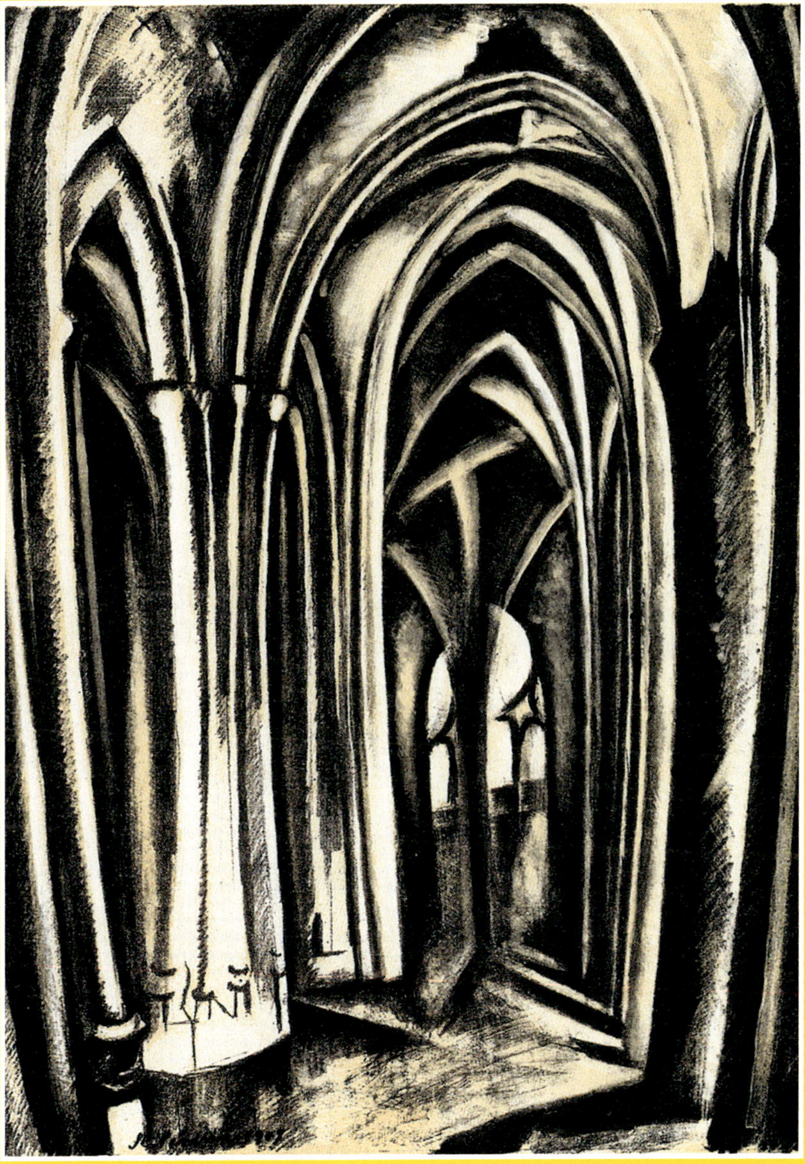

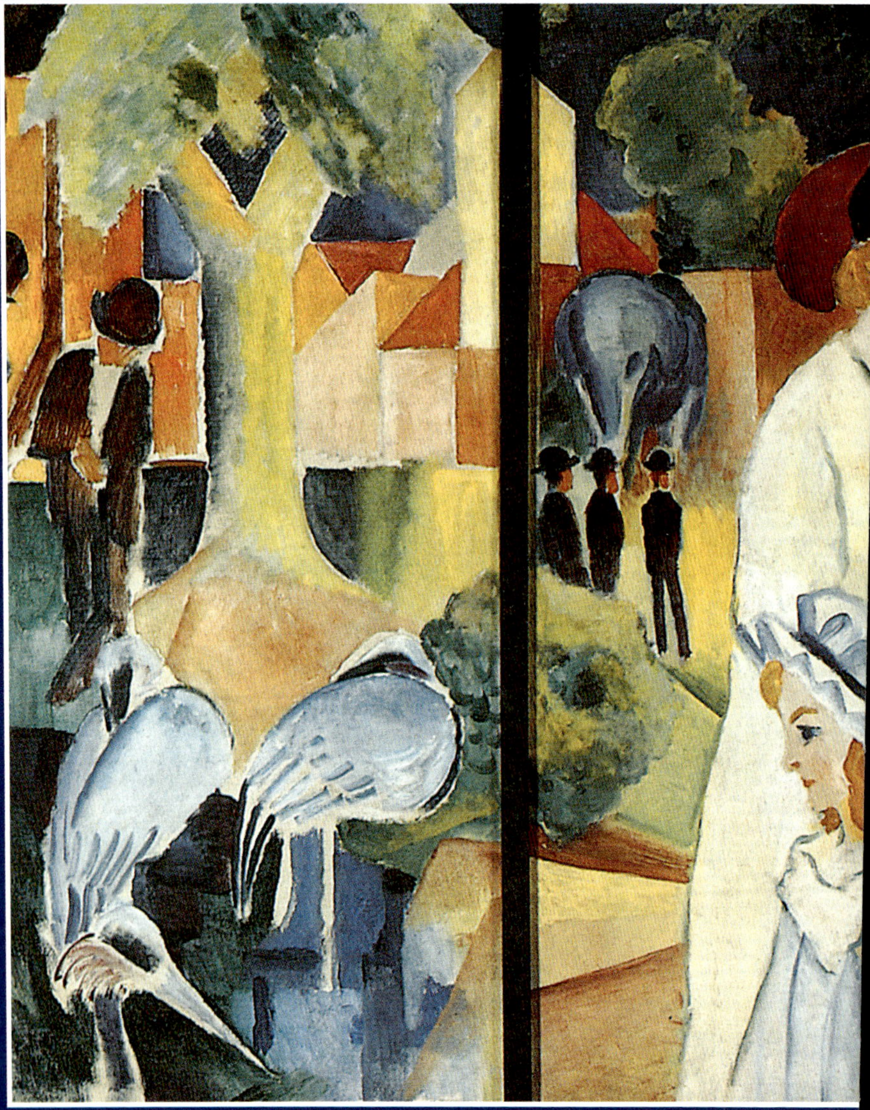

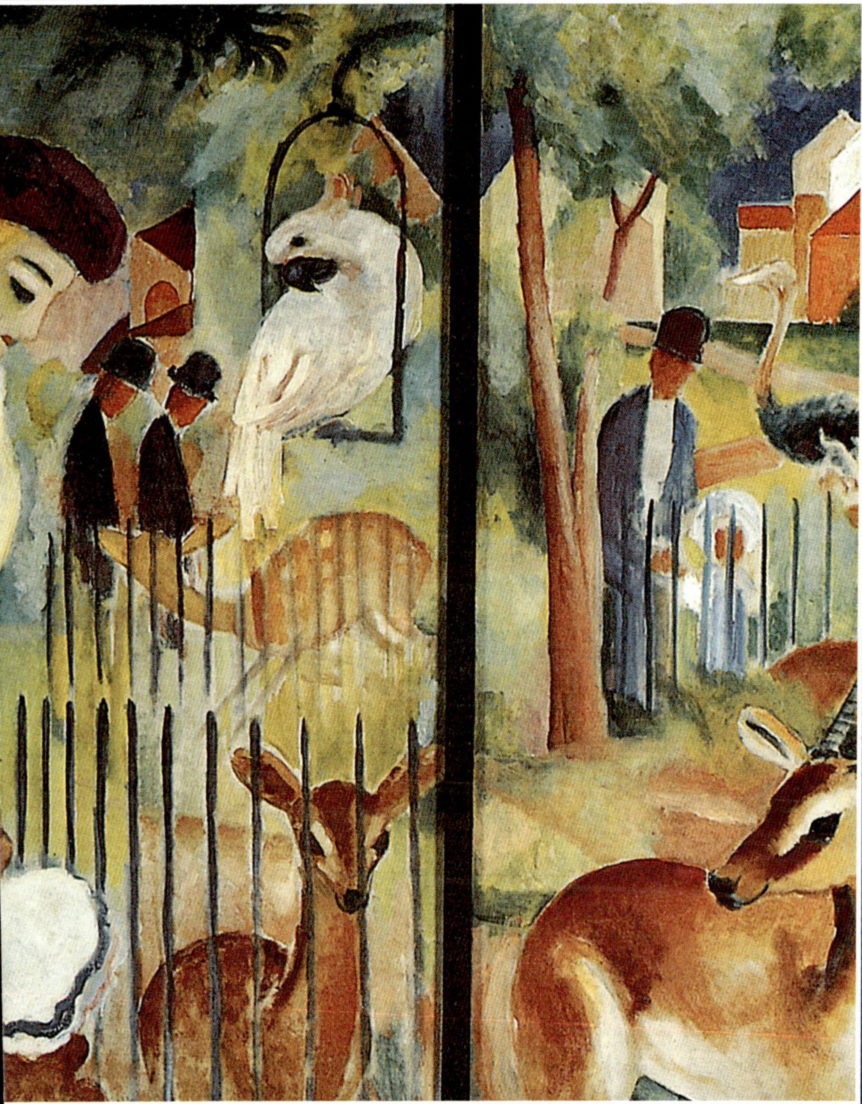

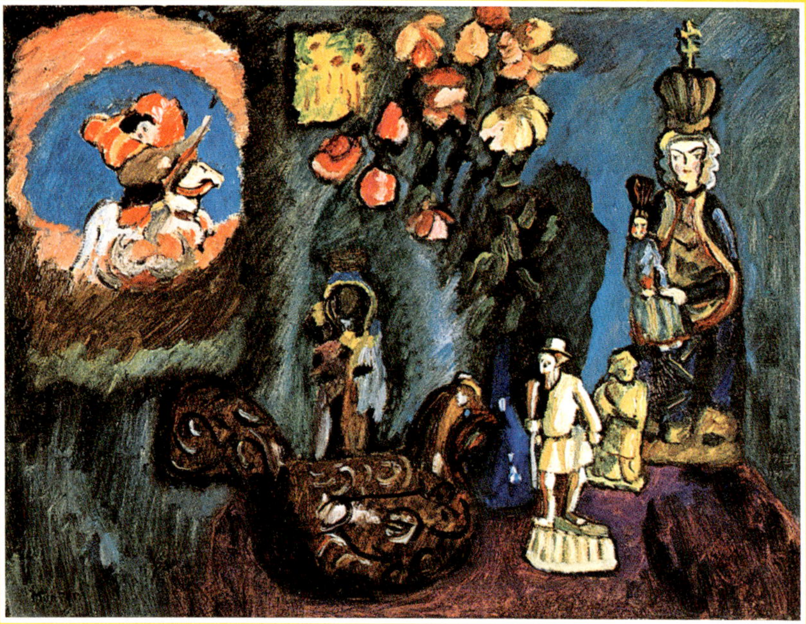

FIRST EXHIBITION OF THE EDITORIAL BOARD OF THE BLUE RIDER

The letter written by Franz Marc to his artist friend Kandinsky in November 1911 supports the conjecture that Kandinsky and Marc had been planning the break with the New Artists' Association of Munich for some time before intentionally provoking it on December 2, 1911: "Have reserved our own room next to that of the Association at Thannhauser for the second half of December, in which the two of us can exhibit what we like. So let's get cracking. [...] My program: the Burliuks, Campendonk, August [Macke], my own glass paintings, Schönberg, Bloch, and if at all possible a Rousseau (not too large). Then Delaunay and possibly two or three old things, travel pictures, glass pictures, votive pictures. It must be good."[28]

The exhibition was held in the Galerie Thannhauser in the Arco-Palais in Theatinerstrasse from December 19, 1911, to January 3, 1912, parallel to that of the New Artists' Association of Munich. Marc and Kandinsky wanted to use the exhibition to show pictorially the ideas they had expressed in words in the almanac. Their aim was for their art, determined by "inner necessity," to provide a strong contrast to the superficial "modernist program" which in their opinion the New Artists' association of Munich, from which they had just separated, now represented.

Gabriele Münter had also been active in the withdrawal from the New Artists' Association of Munich and had asked Alfred Kubin to leave it as well. At the same time she also announced that the former members of the association would be presenting their own exhibitions. Kubin responded at once and sent in his resignation in writing. The composer Thomas von Hartmann, a close friend of Kandinsky's and like him a supporter of synesthesia in painting and music, also joined the secessionists. Contact with the artist Elisabeth Epstein in Paris was important for the group's French connection; Kandinsky purchased one of her paintings and she was to submit two works for inclusion in the exhibition. She had good contacts and established the links with, amongst others, Sonia and Robert Delaunay, the "artist-writer" Wilhelm Uhde, Henri Rousseau, and the Prague-based artist Eugen Kahler, who however died shortly afterwards; Kandinsky included two of his works posthumously.

A total of fourteen artists participated in *The First Exhibition of the Editorial Board of the Blue Rider* – the somewhat pedestrian full title. Although it is not possible to describe in detail all the participants within the framework of this publication, here at least is a full list of their names so that readers can identify them when reading the literature or visiting collections. They are, in alphabetical order: Albert Bloch, David Burliuk, Vladimir Burliuk, Heinrich Campendonk, Robert Delaunay, Elisabeth Epstein, Eugen von Kahler, Wassily Kandinsky, August Macke, Franz Marc, Gabriele Münter, Jean Bloé Niestlé, Henri Rousseau, and Arnold Schönberg.

It is possible to reconstruct the exhibition because six photos by Gabriele Münter have survived in which the hanging of the pictures can be clearly seen. These show that the arrangement was completely in line with the almanac. The various personal artistic styles were combined and contrasted with each other. In the opinion of the creators of the exhibition, this was justified because they all had something in common: the principle of "inner necessity." Opinions differ widely as to whether this was really expressed in the exhibition and also whether it really was fundamentally different from the exhibitions of the New Artists' Association of Munich, or indeed from other modern groups of artists. Visitors and critics alike had difficulties with the new concept; in the *Kölnische Zeitung* one critic noted: "It is evident that this somewhat motley circle lacks the artistic breeding of the Neue Künstlervereinigung. Their theory is running away with them, and one first needs to clear away a lot of dilettantism and artistic nonsense before striking fertile ground. But this horde overrules the innocent visitor, and it is not surprising that a propaganda lecture held in these rooms should have provoked sensational minor clashes."[29]

Paul Klee's comments were critical but basically positive. He wrote about the exhibition in January 1912: "I know that among my readers there may be perhaps three who would have remained serious in those circumstances; so it would be profitable, in some respects even justified, to join in all the ridicule. But I cling to the idea, and [...] try to console those who were unable to find a link to a favorite work in some museum or other, even an El Greco. There are also the very beginnings of art, which we are more likely to find in ethnological museums or at home in the nursery (do not laugh, reader), for children are capable [...] and there is positive truth in this fact. The more helpless the children are, the more instructive is the art they offer us. [...:] Parallel manifestations are the drawings of the mentally ill, and even madness is not an appropriate insult. All that must be taken far more seriously than all art museums when it is a matter of reforming contemporary art." Klee ended the article with the sentence: "The boldest of them all is Kandinsky, who also strives to have an influence through his writings."[30]

HIGHLIGHTS OF THE EXHIBITION

Wassily Kandinsky **COMPOSITION NO.V**
1911, Oil on canvas, 190 x 275 cm,
New York, Private collection

This picture, the largest that Kandinsky had painted at that time, proved to be the reason for his resignation from the New Artists' Association of Munich and the founding of the Blue Rider (see pp. 78-79). He considered this painting, which he also referred to as the *Last Judgment*, to be so important that he reproduced it in the almanac.

Hans K. Roethel describes it as "absolute painting, 'freed' from tradition,"[31] as a space defined by itself. There is no illusion of space which has been arrived at with the help of traditional artistic means – no central perspective, no modulation of light and shade which corresponds to nature, and no atmospheric representation.

And yet we can recognize a pictorial content. The black, curving form looks more or less like the trumpet with which the Archangel Gabriel heralded the Last Judgment (fig. p. 48). Kandinsky found this angel on a reverse-glass picture which is still preserved in the Lenbachhaus in Munich. We can also make out other "remnants of objects" in *Composition V*. On the left in the foreground a boat with three oarsmen is struggling against the watery masses of the Deluge; and at the top edge of the picture, in the middle, we can make out a little walled city with tottering towers. The subject of the Last Judgment is thus clearly defined. The viewer will seek – and find – further associations, such as the green-and-red figure which animates the picture at bottom right. To a certain extent we can walk around within the picture space. As noted above, when he was

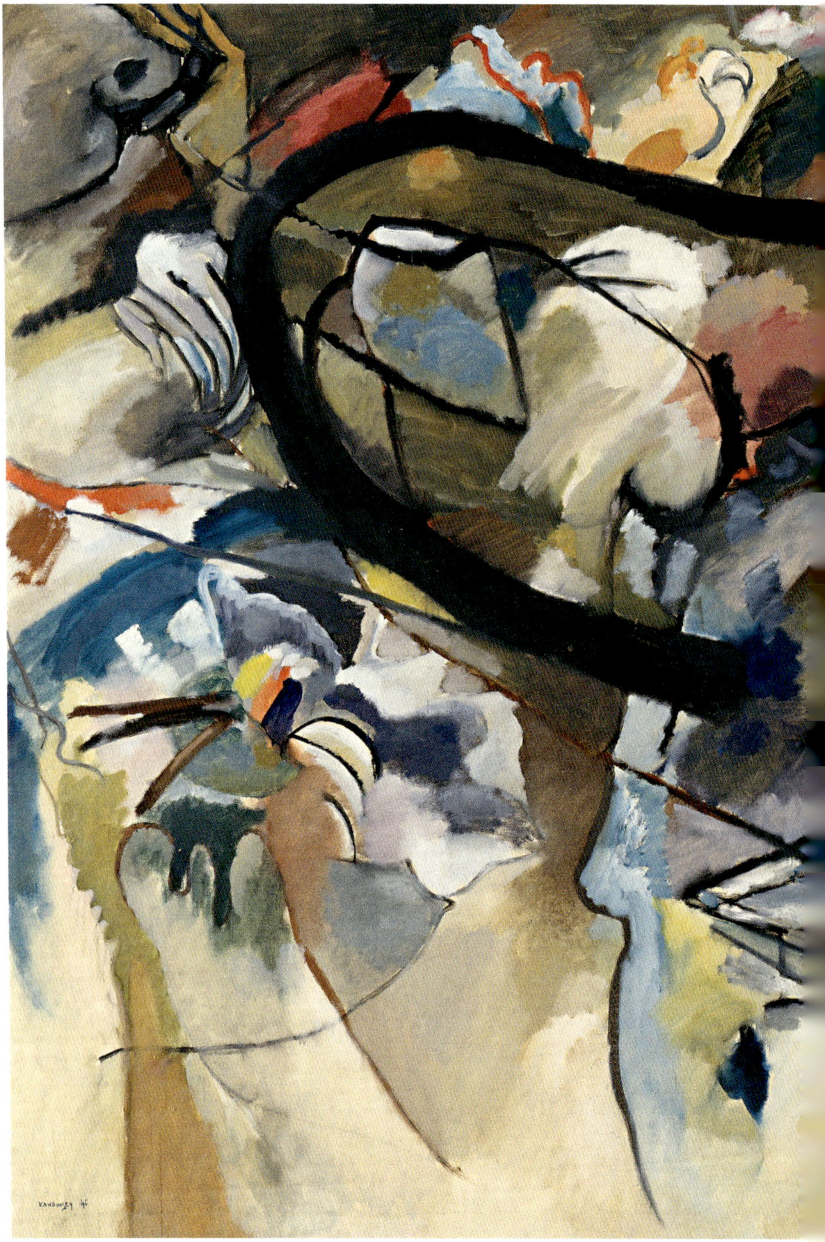
KANDINSKY

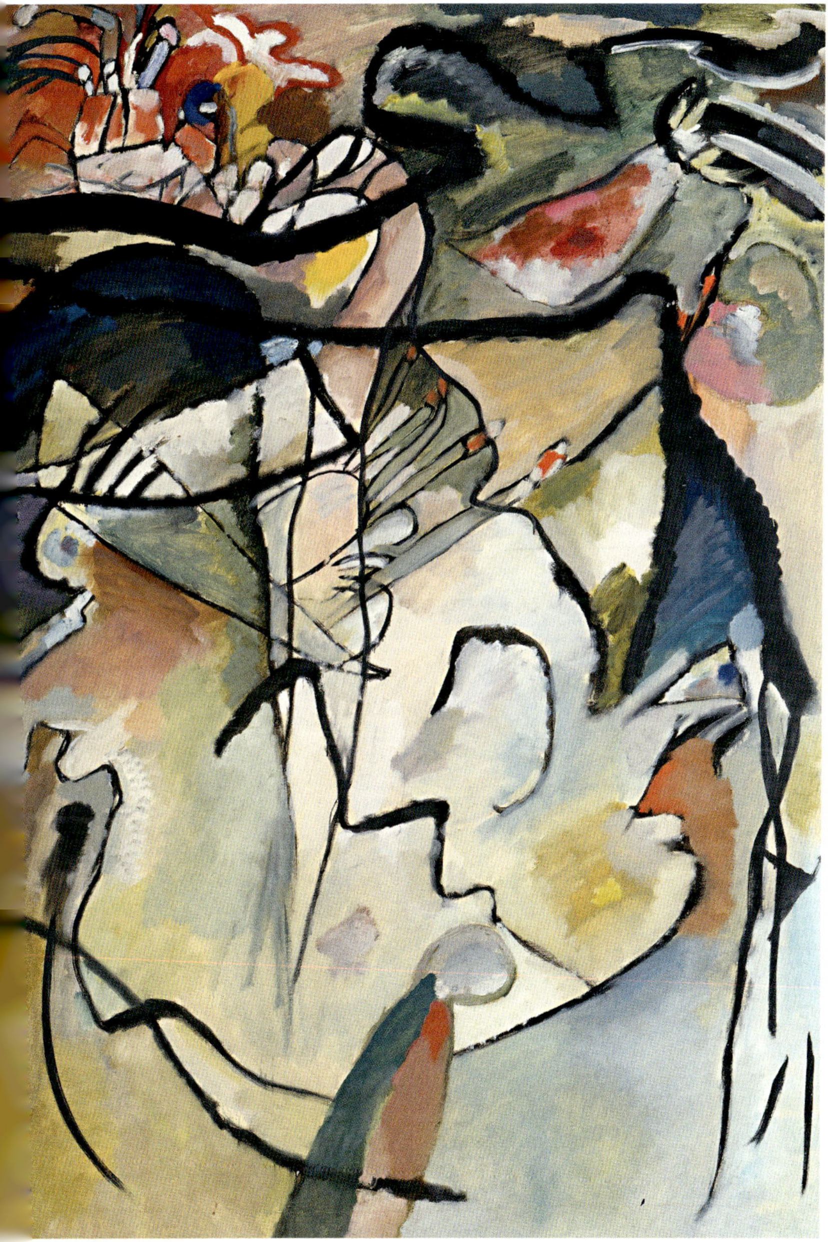

a student in Moscow, Kandinsky had undertaken a study trip to the district of Vologda between May and July 1889. He described it in a diary [32] and later referred back to it. It is worth reading again: "I shall never forget the large wooden houses, covered with wood carvings. In these wonderful houses I experienced something which I have never seen again since that time. They taught me to move within the picture, to live in the picture. The table, the benches [...] the cupboards and every item were all painted with brightly colored, generously proportioned ornaments. There were folk pictures on the walls [...] When I finally entered the room I felt I was surrounded on all sides by the painting into which I had stepped." [33]

Franz Marc **DEER IN THE FOREST I**
1911, Oil on canvas, 130 × 100 cm,
Private collection

While he was working on this picture the artist noted: "I can paint a picture: 'The deer.' Pisanello [34] painted pictures like this. But I can also attempt to paint a picture: 'The deer feels.' How much finer must the senses of a painter be who wants to paint that!" [35] Marc does not aim at a true-to-nature representation; he sees that as the gaze of Man at the animal, which has little to do with the animal's true being. "From now on we must learn not to relate animals and plants to ourselves and to depict our relationships to them in art. Those days are over! [...] We artists, all of us – why are we permanently searching for metamorphous forms? The things as they really are, behind the appearance?" [36]
For Marc, *Deer in the Forest* was an important step away from depicting nature as realistically as possible (for which in any case he had no great talent) to the "spiritual in art" (Kandinsky), to an art of expression, of feeling. Only during the last years before his premature death in 1916 did Marc reduce his language of forms, producing rigorously composed pictures of great emotional depth.

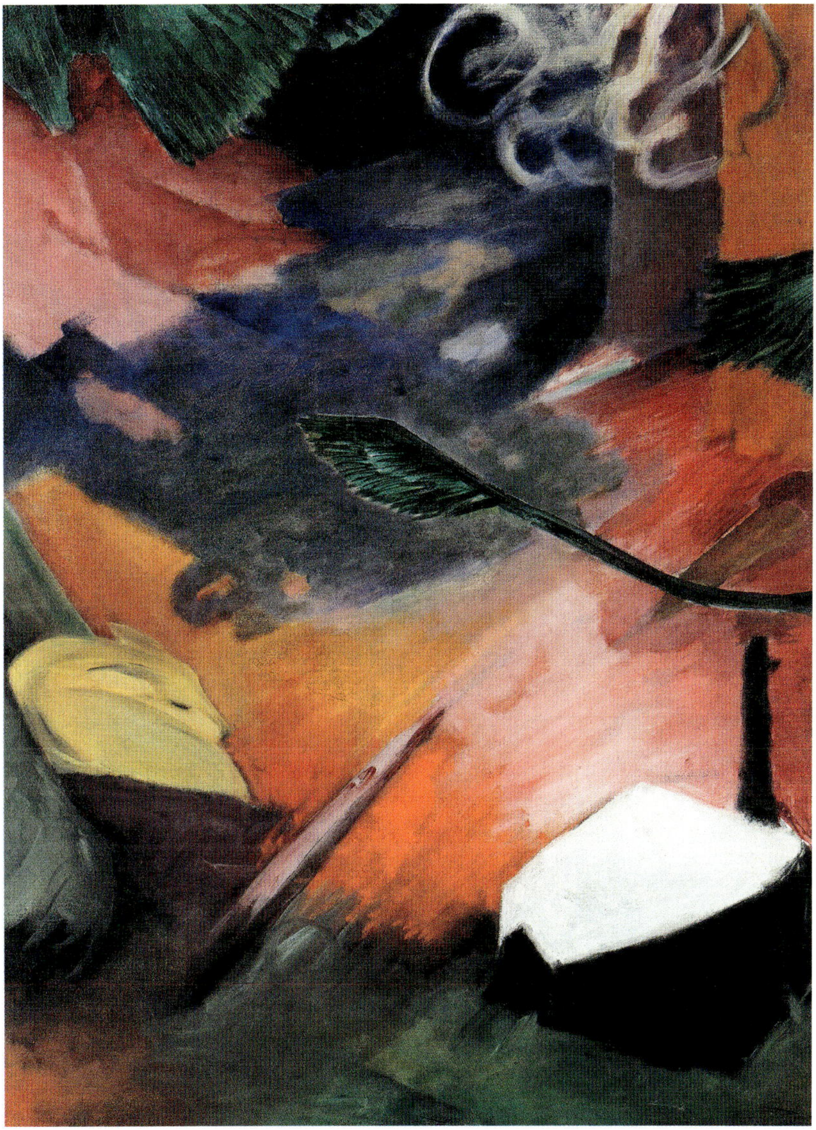

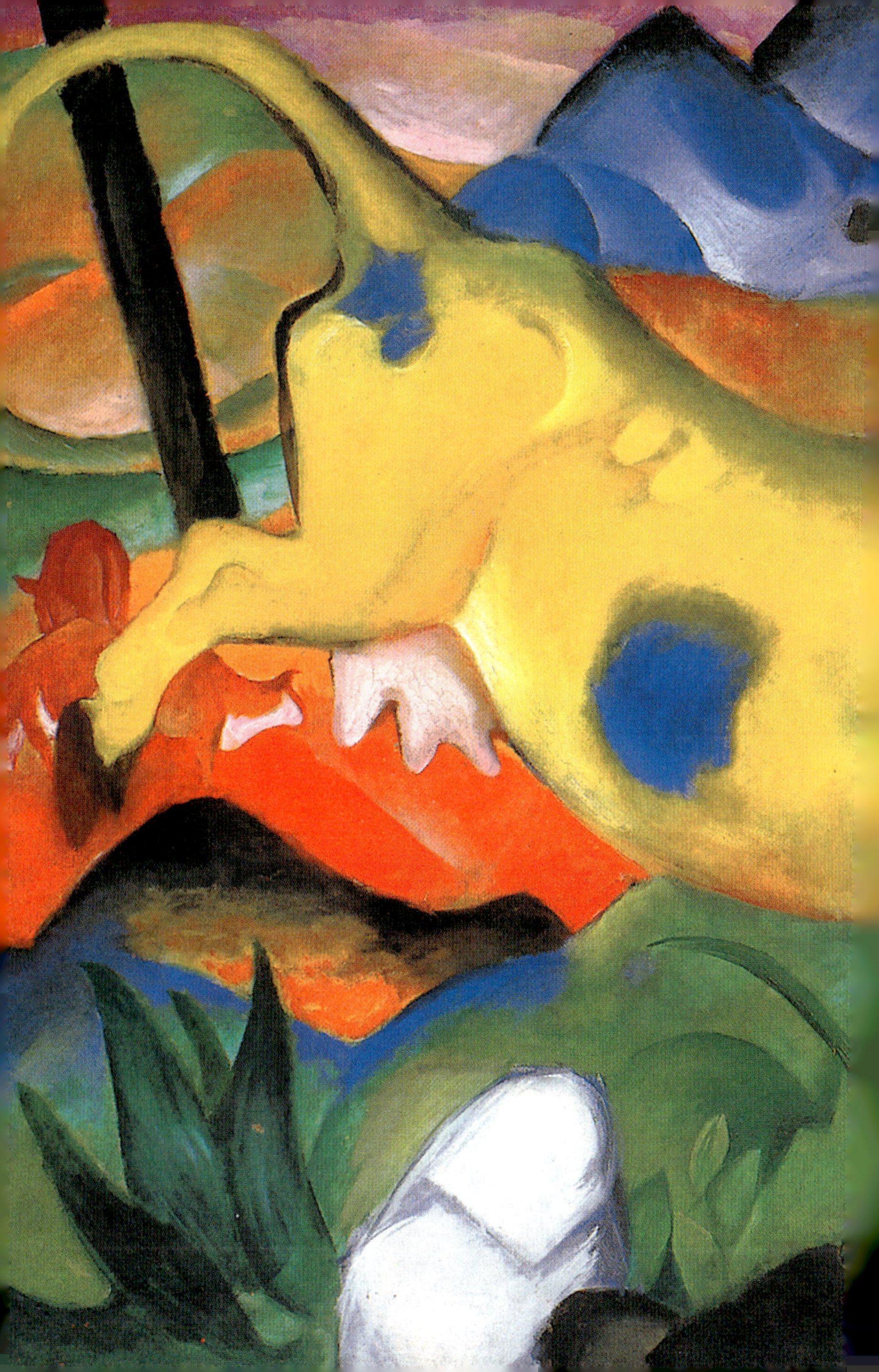

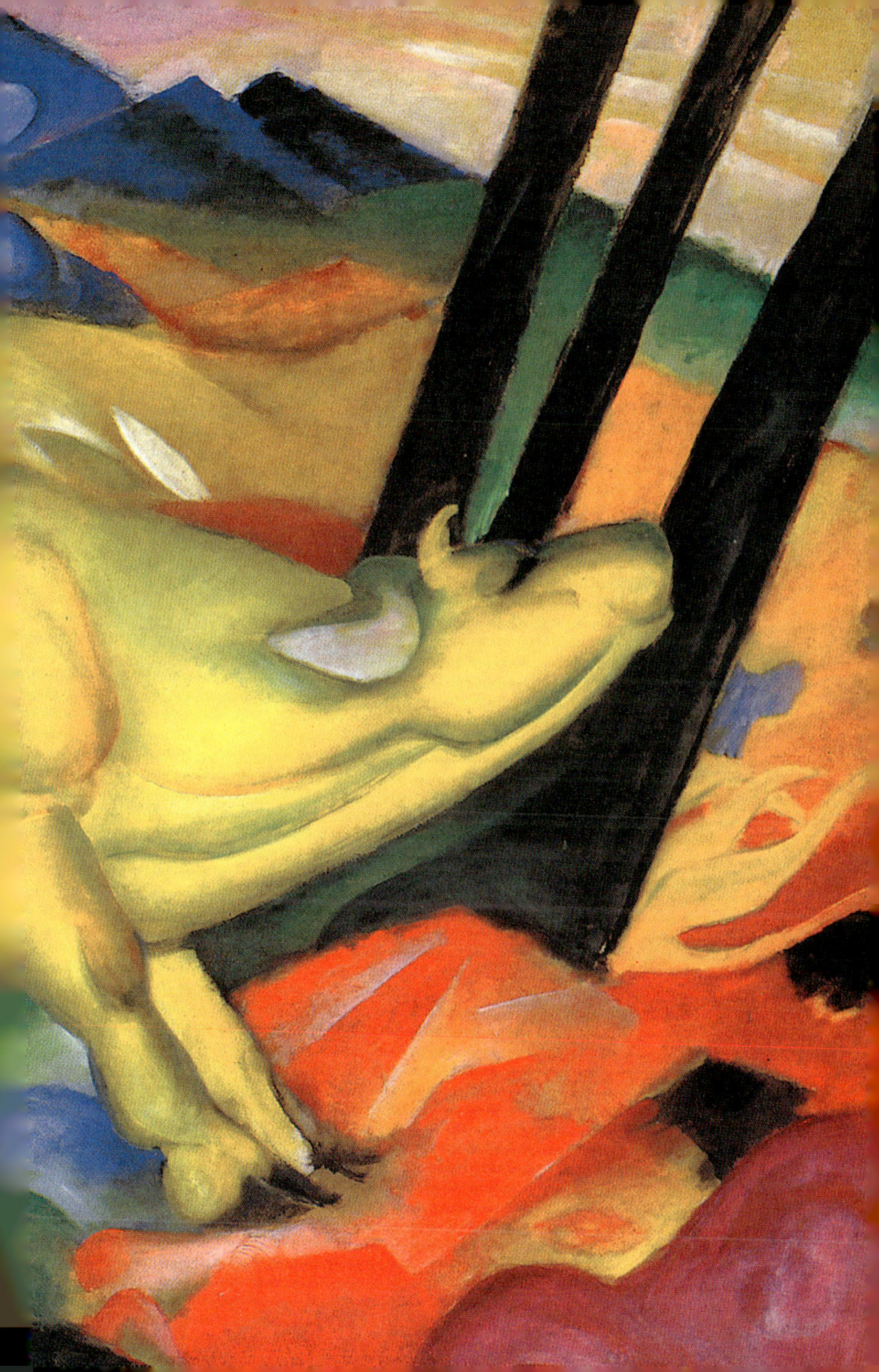

Franz Marc **THE YELLOW COW**
1911, Oil on canvas, 130 × 100 cm,
New York, Guggenheim Museum

The image of this merrily leaping cow somehow radiates cheerfulness, an impression to which the strong, brilliant colors certainly contribute. In essence they are reduced to four colors: yellow, blue, red, and green. White and black have been added to increase the contrasts. The symbolism of colors played an important part for Franz Marc. By 1911 he had already freed himself completely from the "apparent color" of his early works; now he allocates colors to the individual objects within the picture, colors that have symbolic significance, in line with Kandinsky's theory of colors. "Thus, for him, yellow is the 'typical earth color,' which functions like a fanfare and symbolizes 'the leaping over the boundary, the scattering of strength in the surroundings'."[37]
By the term "abstraction," however, Franz Marc understood something quite different from the idea entertained by his artist friend Kandinsky. For Marc, the way led from the idea, in other words the more or less arbitrary form, via constant simplification to a compulsive, expressive form, which extracts the character of what he has portrayed. For Kandinsky, by contrast, "abstraction" means the complete abandonment of the natural model and the creation of autonomous, in other words completely independent pictorial spaces.

Henri Rousseau **THE FARMYARD**
1896–1898, Oil on canvas, 24.6 × 32.9 cm,
Paris, Musée National d'Art Moderne, Centre Pompidou

Kandinsky and Marc had a very high opinion of this naive French artist, who had died in Paris the year before the exhibition. In the pictures of this self-taught artist – he actually worked as a collector of tolls (a douanier) – they saw one of the sources for their strivings towards a new language of forms. They loved his naive, unfussy painting, which lives not by its "craftsmanship" – in other words refine-

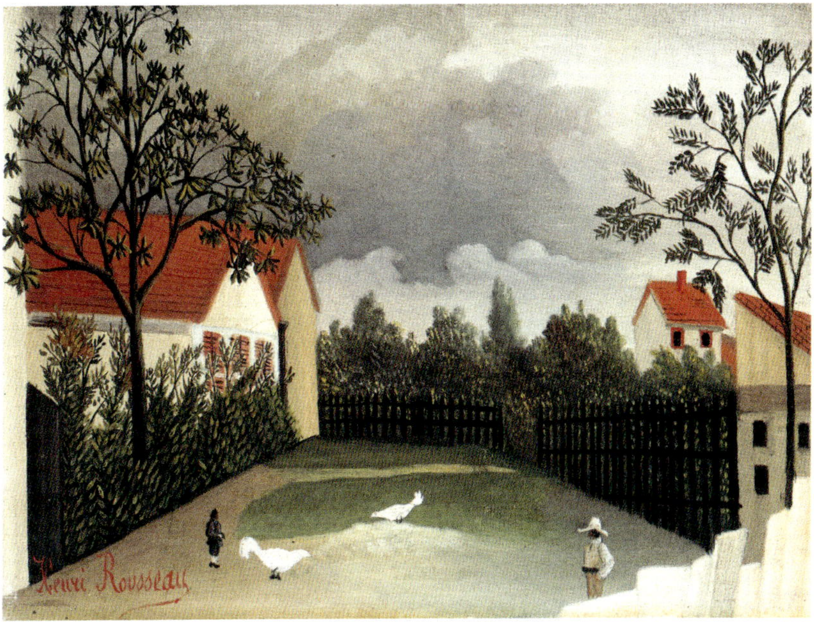

ment and painterly skills – but from simple, honest feeling. As a visible sign of this respect they hung a laurel wreath on the wall underneath the picture of "Douanier" Rousseau.

Franz Marc **PORTRAIT OF HENRI ROUSSEAU**
1911, Reverse-glass painting, 34 × 22 cm,
Munich, Städtische Galerie im Lenbachhaus

It is in this same context that we should see the portrait that Franz Marc painted of Henri Rousseau. It is actually a copy after the *Self-Portrait with Lamp and Glass* by Rousseau and artistically speaking is not typical of Franz Marc's oeuvre, nor is it of particular artistic quality. It was, so to speak, the "funeral portrait" of the deceased, and together with Rousseau's *The Farmyard* and the laurel wreath a posthumous honor for Rousseau.

SALES

Officially nine pictures found buyers, though we should remember that the art patron Bernhard Koehler purchased four of them, and the artists themselves also purchased works from each other; for example, Erbslöh and Jawlensky each purchased a Delaunay; Kandinsky bought two pictures by Rousseau and a portrait by Elisabeth Epstein, which, sadly, has been lost without trace. And so, in fact, not a single picture was sold to a "normal" visitor to the exhibition.

There was instead a great deal of outrage, both from the critics and from the public. When we consider the importance of these artists and especially the exhibition, and see the astronomic prices paid today for works by Marc, Macke, and Kandinsky, it seems very hard to understand. It is, however, a process which has occurred time and time again. Gauguin and the Pont-Aven artists covered the walls of their favorite tavern with their own works because no one wanted to buy them. During his lifetime, Vincent van Gogh was unable to sell even a single picture himself at a reasonable price. Had it not been for the affectionate support of his brother Theo, he would never have been able to lead his poverty-stricken but independent life as an artist.

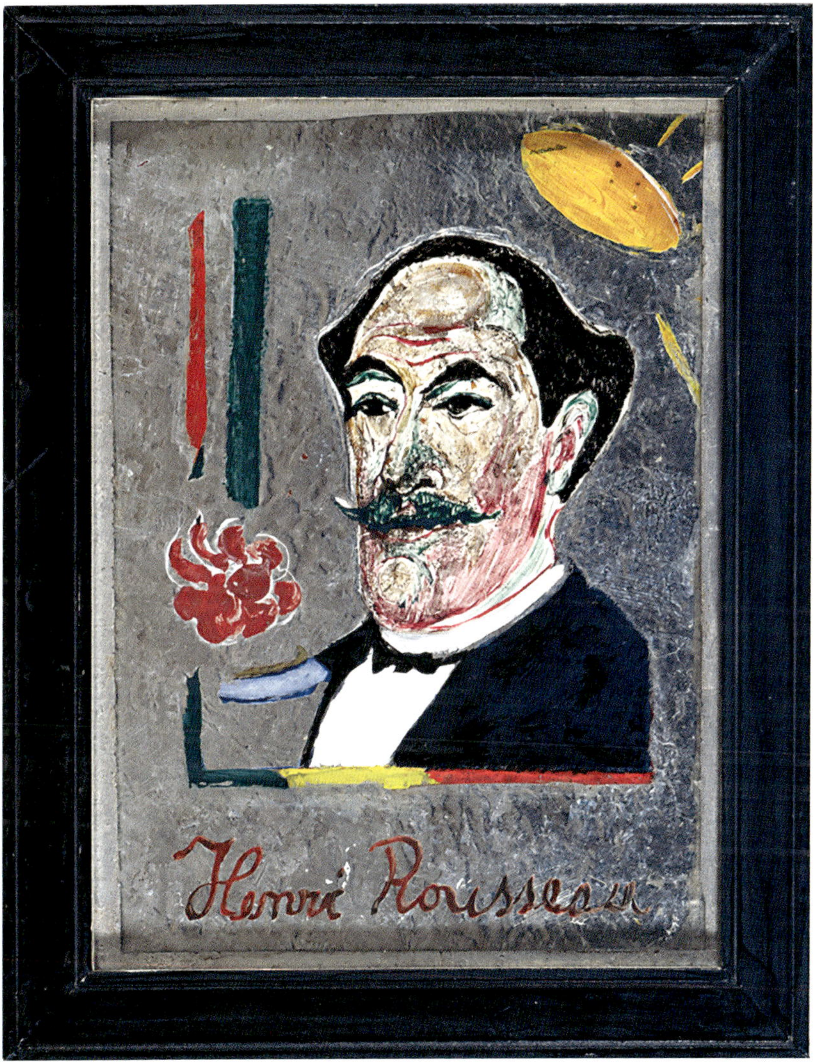
Henri Rousseau

3. PROTAGONISTS

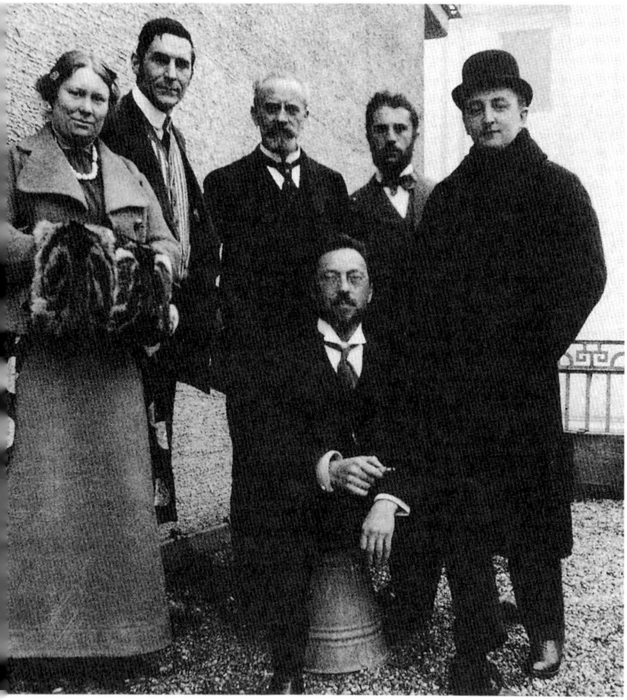

On the balcony of Kandinsky's and Münter's apartment at Ainmillerstrasse 36 (l. to r.: Maria and Franz Marc, Bernard Koehler (senior), Heinrich Campendonk, Thomas von Hartmann; seated: Wassily Kandinsky), *c.* 1911/1912

WASSILY KANDINSKY

16. 12. 1866 Moscow, Russia – 13. 12. 1944 Neuilly-sur-Seine, France

Wassily Kandinsky came from a "good family"; he was the only son of well-to-do parents who moved from Moscow to Odessa in 1871. Soon after that, however, his parents were divorced; Wassily remained with his father and was brought up lovingly by his aunt Elisabeth Ticheeva, to whom he later dedicated his book *Concerning the Spiritual in Art [Über das Geistige in der Kunst]*. From 1885 he studied law and economics in Moscow and completed his studies successfully (with the thesis "Interpretation of the Theories of the Iron Law and the Workers' Fund"). It might have been expected that this well-educated, articulate young academic would pursue a bril-

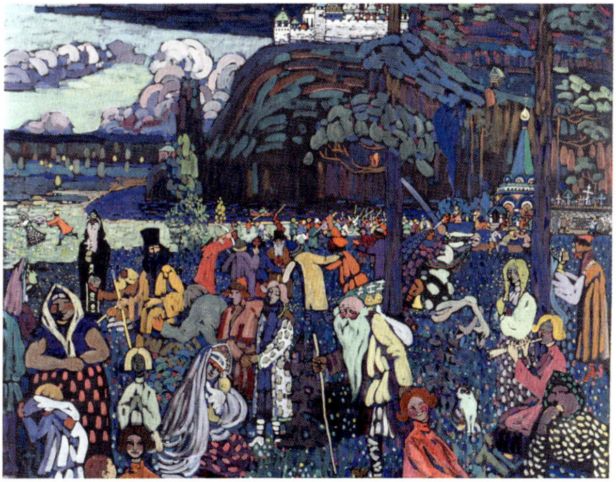

Wassily Kandinsky
MOTLEY LIFE, 1907

liant career in politics or business, but this was not to be. He wanted to become an artist. His father acquiesced and gave him some money, hoping that his son would change his mind. After all, an extended trip to Western Europe would do no harm. His son would no doubt give up his foolish ideas about art given that he was already married and his wife Anya intended to accompany him to Germany. And so in 1897 Kandinsky enrolled at the art school run by the Slovenian artist Anton Ažbé in Munich and (like the artist Paul Klee, who later became his friend) studied under Franz von Stuck at the Akademie der Bildenden Künste (Academy of Fine Arts) in

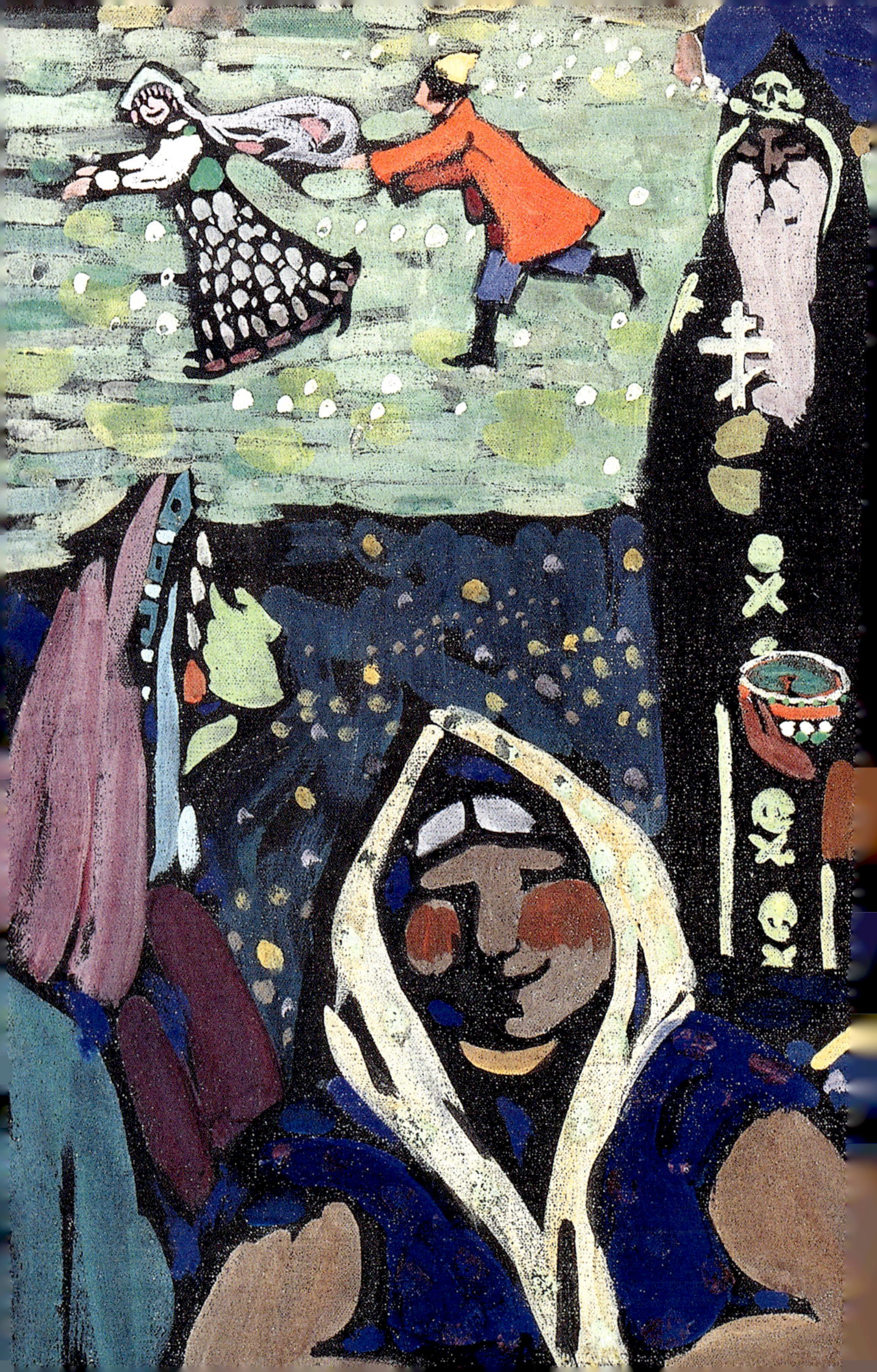

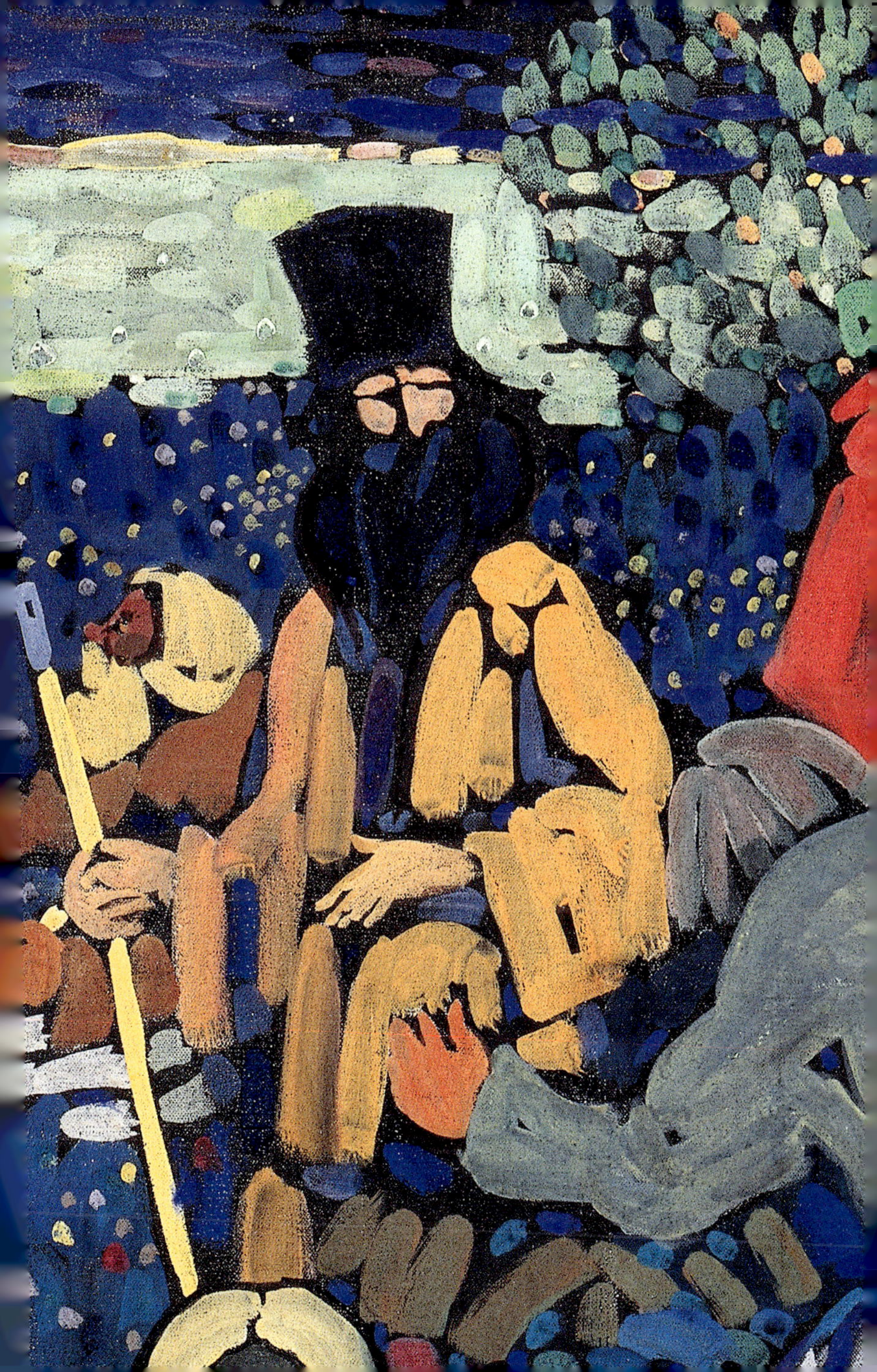

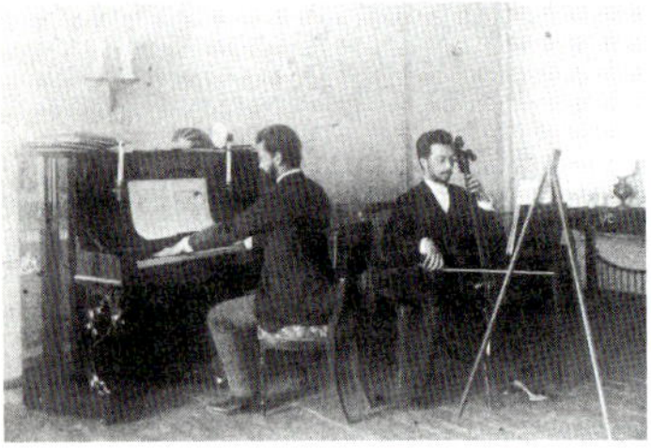

Kandinsky playing the 'cello, c. 1886

1900. Kandinsky, however, preferred to paint landscapes in strong colors using a palette knife, pictures that would "sing out loud." He wanted to leave the academic world and to found his own art association and his own art school, which he achieved in 1901 with the Phalanx (see p. 14).

The Phalanx, however, produced no noteworthy artistic results – we could see it as a sort of "dress rehearsal" for the founding of the New Artists' Association of Munich and then the Blue Rider. But it did result in radical changes in Kandinsky's private life. One of the students was Gabriele Münter, his fellow campaigner and lover during the years 1902 – 1917 (see p. 96). From 1904 the two of them traveled extensively; they spent the winter of 1904 – 1905 in North Africa and the summer of 1905 in Dresden. That same year Kandinsky and his wife Anya separated, and she returned to Moscow.

After lengthy visits to Paris and Berlin, in 1908 Kandinsky and Münter returned to Munich to live. Kandinsky worked with the composer Thomas von Hartmann and the dancer Alexander Sakharoff

Wassily Kandinsky
ST. GEORGE I,
1911

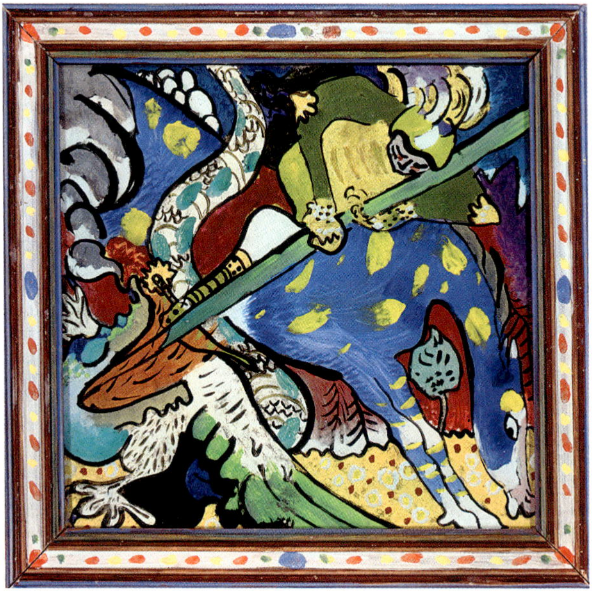

Right page:

Wassily Kandinsky
MURNAU WITH CHURCH I, 1910

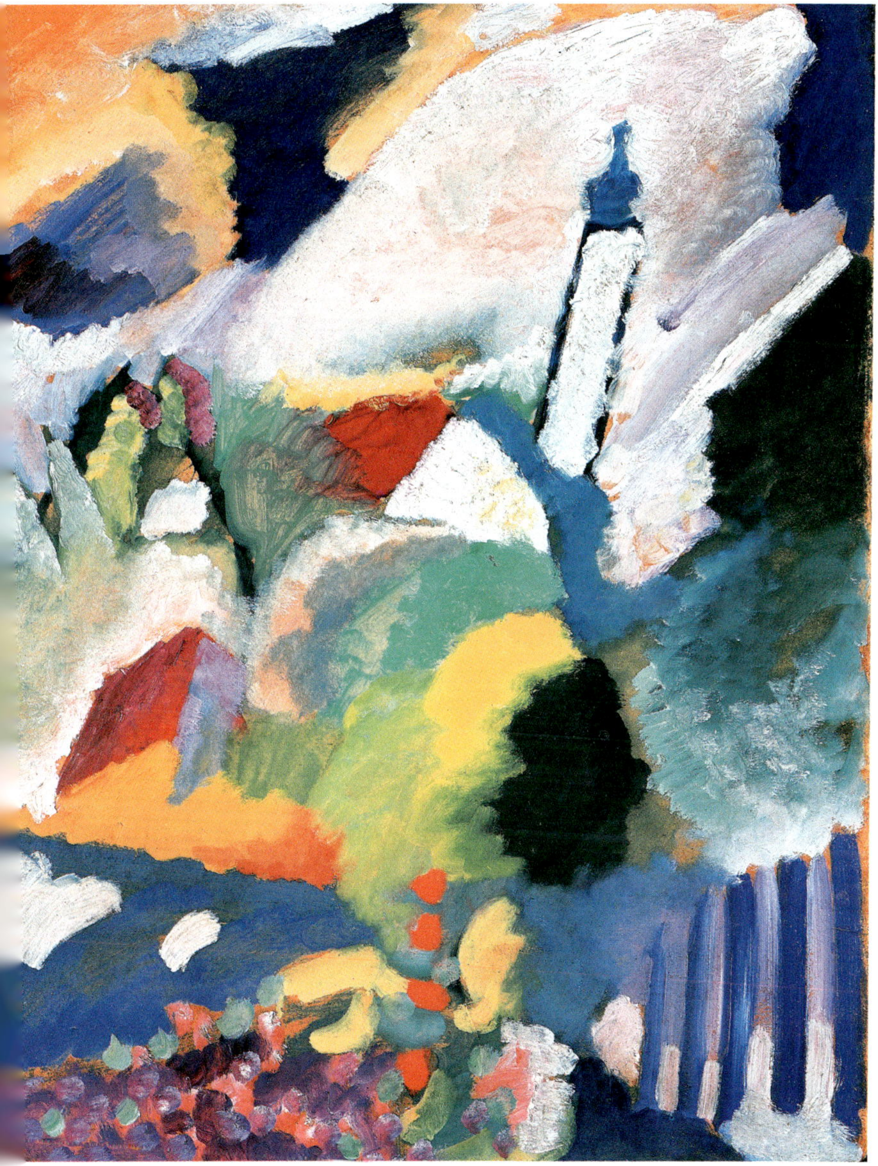

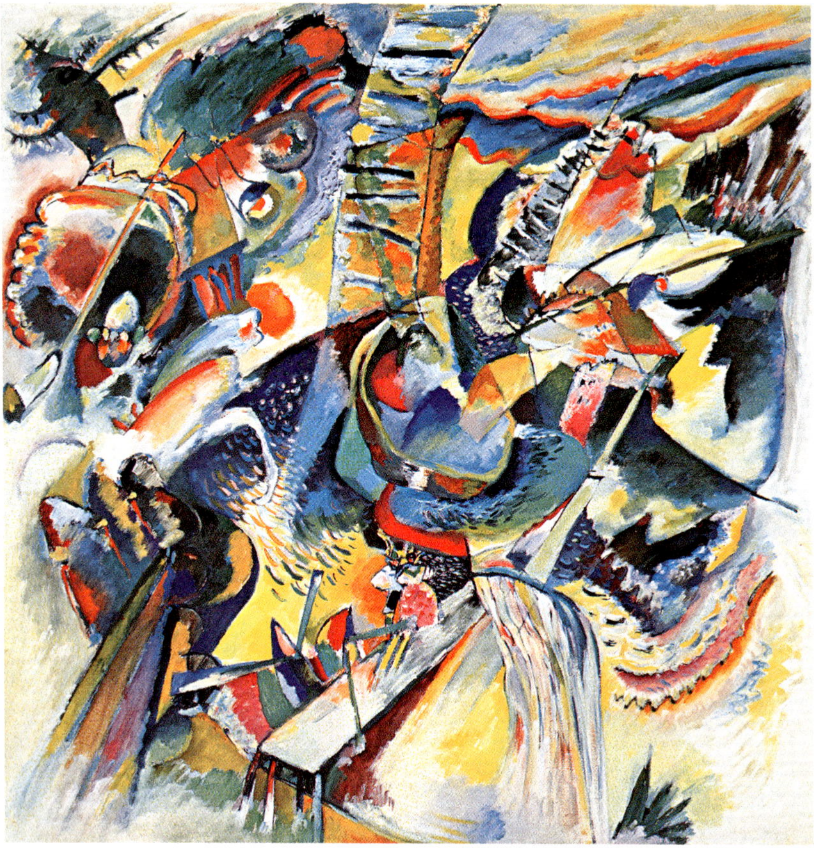

Wassily Kandinsky
IMPROVISATION KLAMM, 1914

(Alexej von Jawlensky painted his famous portrait in 1909, see p. 28) on his stage work *The Yellow Sound*.

During a cycling trip Kandinsky and Münter discovered Murnau, where long painting holidays ensued together with Marianne von Werefkin and Alexej von Jawlensky. All four fell in love with the region in the Alpine foothills around the Staffelsee.

On December 1, 1909, the first exhibition of the New Artists' Association of Munich opened, in which both Kandinsky and Münter were very actively involved.

Kandinsky had never lost contact with his native Russia, and during an extended visit to Moscow and Odessa he made the acquaintance of many of the avant-garde artists there who had joined together

in 1910 to form the Jack of Diamonds (Karo Bube) artists' association; among them was Natalia Goncharova.
The year 1911 saw the meeting of Franz Marc and Wassily Kandinsky and thus the beginning of a celebrated friendship between artists which was to have enormous repercussions for art. Together they founded the Blue Rider and published the almanac of the same name in 1912 (see p. 47). During subsequent years, Kandinsky took part in numerous exhibitions and worked on various publications.
On July 28, 1914, Austria-Hungary declared war on Serbia. This move had been triggered by the refusal of the Serbian government to assist in the investigation into the assassination of Archduke Franz Ferdinand and his wife on June 28, 1914, in Sarajevo. This led to the involvement of all the major European powers, which were linked to each other through a network of mutual assistance pacts. On August 1, 1914, the German Empire declared war on Russia and the First World War began. All foreigners were forced to leave Germany. Kandinsky returned to Russia via Switzerland and Gabriele Münter remained in her house in Murnau. The Blue Rider was a thing of the past.
In 1914 Kandinsky married for the second time in Moscow; thereafter he lived with second wife, Nina, for the rest of his life. After an initial period during which the Soviet administration viewed him favorably, Kandinsky, as a member of the bourgeoisie, had his possessions expropriated, so he was destitute. During the winter of 1921–1922 the couple succeeded in leaving the country for Berlin. Before long Kandinsky was able to establish himself again; he started teaching at the Bauhaus in Weimar, where he became friends with his colleague Paul Klee, and, at the instigation of the art dealer Galka Scheyer, founded with him, Jawlensky, and Lyonel Feininger the group known as Die Blaue Vier (The Blue Four). When the Bauhaus finally closed (in 1933) Nina and Wassily Kandinsky moved to Paris and took up residence in an apartment in the suburb of Neuilly-sur-Seine, where Kandinsky died of a cerebral thrombosis on December 13, 1944.

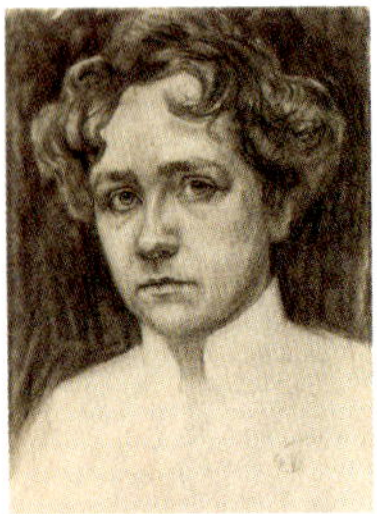

Gabriele Münter
SELF-PORTRAIT,
c. 1901

GABRIELE MÜNTER

19. 2. 1877 Berlin, Germany – 19. 5. 1962 Murnau, Germany

Gabriele Münter's parents had lived in the USA for some years before returning to Germany in 1864, and during her youth Gabriele paid extended visits to her relatives there. Perhaps this is one of the reasons for her self-sufficiency and her modern attitude to life, which manifested itself amongst other things in her long, solitary bicycle tours, unusual for a woman at this time.

From 1902 she studied at the Phalanx art school in Munich (see p. 14). During a painting holiday in Kochel in the summer she went on cycling tours with her teacher Wassily Kandinsky; the relationship between them intensified and they remained together until Kandinsky's enforced return to Russia in 1914. From 1908 onwards they spent increasing periods of time in Murnau, where Gabriele Münter purchased a house in 1909 which they both gradually furnished with loving attention to detail (see p. 166). Marianne von Werefkin and Alexej von Jawlensky (see p. 123), but especially Franz and Maria Marc (see p. 100) were frequent visitors to the "Russenhaus" (Russian House) in Kottmüllerallee.

On September 1, 1911, August Macke described his impressions in a letter to Franz Marc: "I enjoyed seeing Münter. It seems to me that it really is Kandinsky who is very much the intellectual inspiration for her painting as well as his own. I cannot agree at all with her view that she works in a very personal way – any more than I could imagine myself without the strong French influence. Apart from that we got on well. I have the feeling that she has a strong tendency towards the mysterious (see her still lifes, saints, lilies in the corner of the garden, strongly lit thunder clouds, lamps and old grandfather chairs). There's something very 'German' about it, a sort of Romanticism with overtones of religion and family. I like her very, very much. But I still prefer Kandinsky. His pictures radiate for us a permanent aura which is quite wonderful. He is also a romantic, a dreamer, a fantasist, and a story teller."[38]

Gabriele Münter remained firmly at Kandinsky's side until 1914. After his return to Moscow and his marriage with Nina they met only once more. In July 1915 Münter traveled to Sweden, which had remained neutral; Kandinsky was due to join her there. He did not arrive until December, after which they spent almost three months

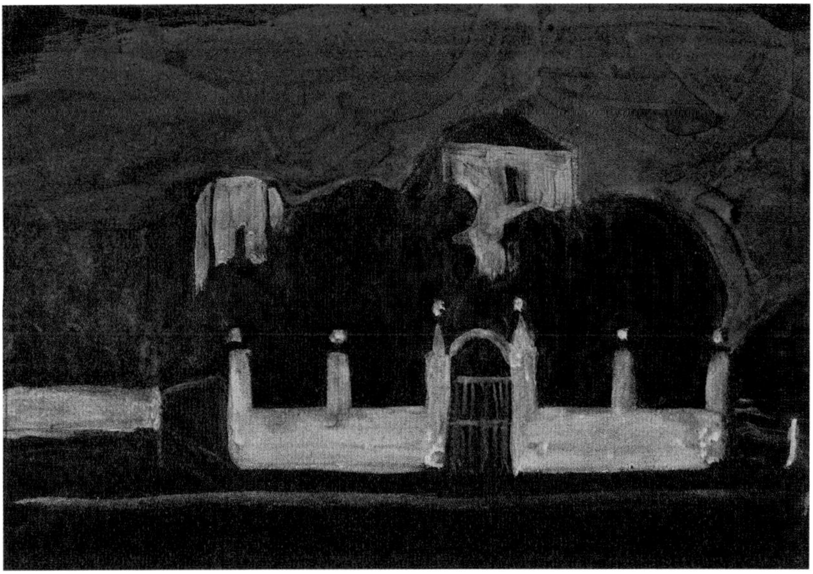

together. On March 16, 1916, Kandinsky returned to Moscow; he and Münter would not see each other again.
Gabriele Münter now lived permanently in Murnau in the "Russian House" and continued to work as an artist. In 1927 she met the art historian Johannes Eichner in Berlin; they lived together until his sudden death in 1958.
On the occasion of her eightieth birthday in 1957, she donated a priceless treasure to the Städtische Galerie im Lenbachhaus in Munich: all Kandinsky's works in her possession, her own paintings, and those of her artist friends. On May 19, 1962, Gabriele Münter died in her house in Murnau. In her will she made provision for the creation of the foundation which bears her name, the Gabriele Münter- und Johannes Eichner-Stiftung; it was established in 1966 with its seat in the Lenbachhaus in Munich. It is dedicated to the administration of the vast legacy and to research.

Gabriele Münter
GARDEN AT NIGHT WITH BUILDINGS, 1905

Next double page:

Gabriele Münter
HAYSTACKS, c. 1909

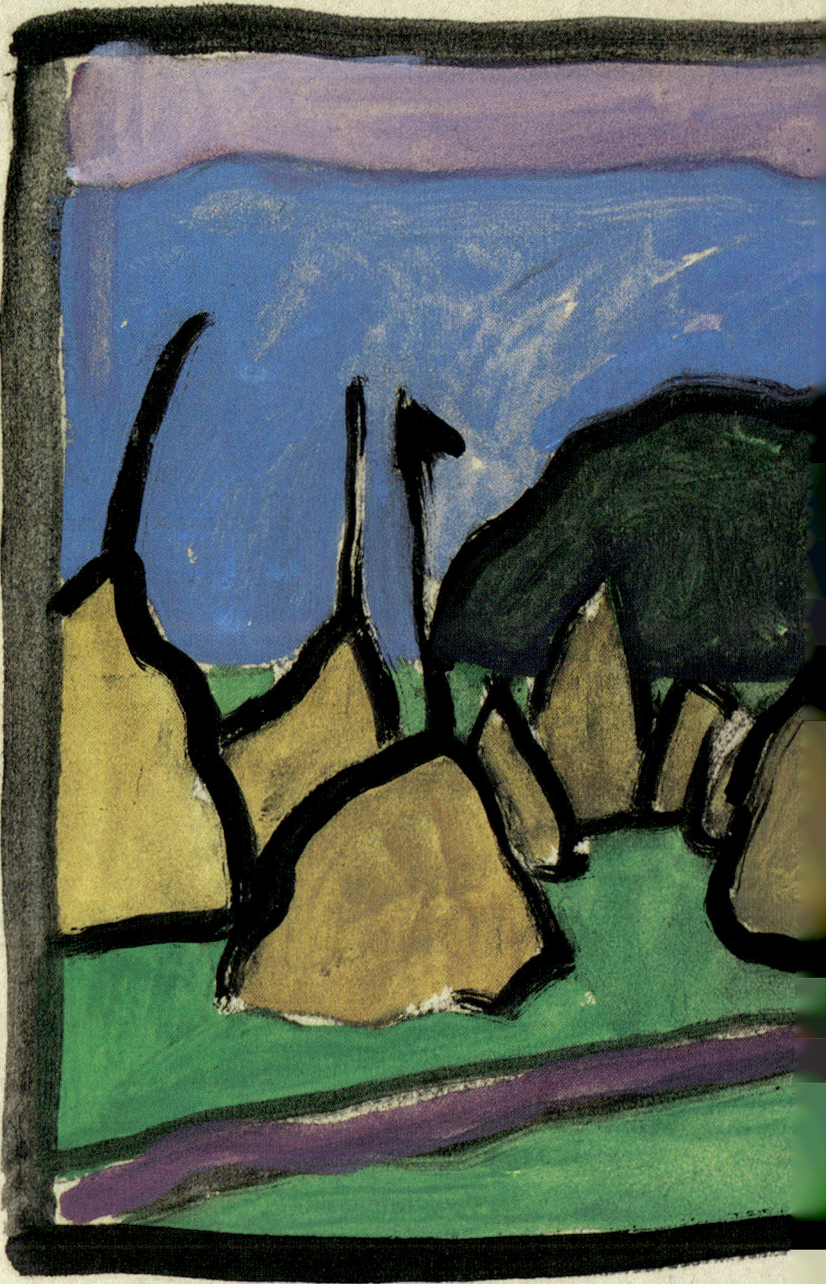

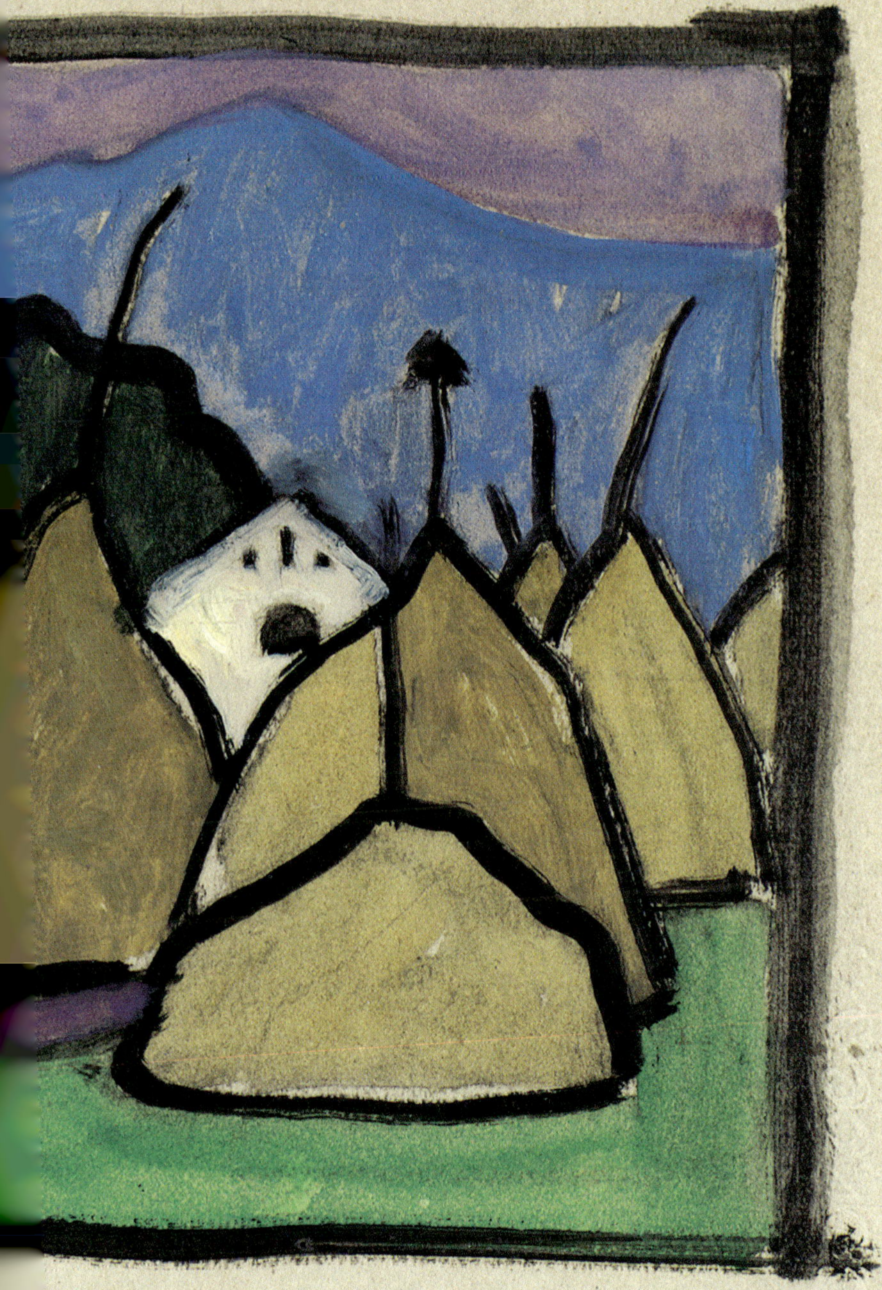

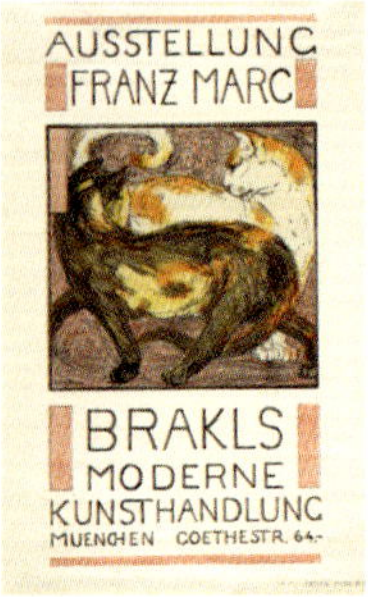

Poster for Franc Marc's first solo exhibition, 1910

FRANZ MARC

8.2.1880 Munich, Germany – 4.3.1916 Braquis near Verdun, France

Franz Marc was born in Munich, the son of the painter Wilhelm Marc and his wife Sophie. After secondary school he did his military service, and from 1900 studied art at the Academy in Munich. From May until September 1903 he was in France. Returning to Munich, he left his parents' home and in 1904 moved into his own studio in Schwabing. He devoted his attention to painting outdoors, repeatedly depicting scenes from nature on the Staffelalm near Kochel and studied the works of Van Gogh.

Around this time he embarked upon a stormy love affair with a married woman, Annette Simon, the wife of a professor, who was nine years older than Marc and who preferred to be called by her maiden name, Annette von Eckardt. He visited the family regularly and drew Annette and her youngest daughter Elisabeth. But before long she put an end to this imprudent relationship.

The following year, when Marc was twenty-five, he met the two who would play critical roles in his life: Maria Franck, an art student, and her teacher, the artist Maria Schnür. Kochel became Marc's retreat, where he lived periodically with his two Marias in a *ménage à trois*. In 1906 he painted a wonderful double portrait of the two women – *Two Women on the Mountain* – almost life-size and flooded with light. Unfortunately, he later destroyed it; an oil sketch can be seen in the museum in Kochel (fig. p. 104).

Haunted by his confused feelings, Marc fled and traveled with his brother Paul to Mount Athos, the Holy Mountain, in Greece. On his return he tried to sort out his life and married Maria Schnür on March 27, 1907, in Munich. The purpose of the marriage was to allow her to have her illegitimate child live with her. But before long Marc turned his attentions back to Maria Franck. On July 19, 1907, he wrote her a long letter in which he described his state of mind: "I loved one woman [Annette von Eckardt] and drove her to distraction; the result was terrible pain – and then you both came along. I know I have been very cruel to you; I dragged you through all my misery until I learned to love you and to love you very much."[39]

Artistically, he devoted his attention increasingly to animal pictures, "which for him increasingly became a metaphor for the purity and innocence of living creatures."[40]

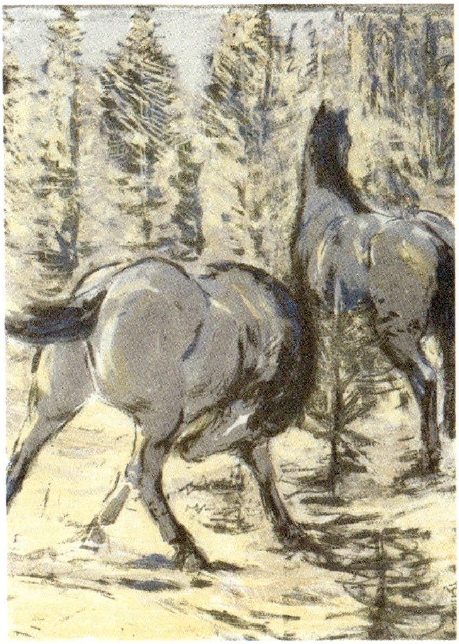

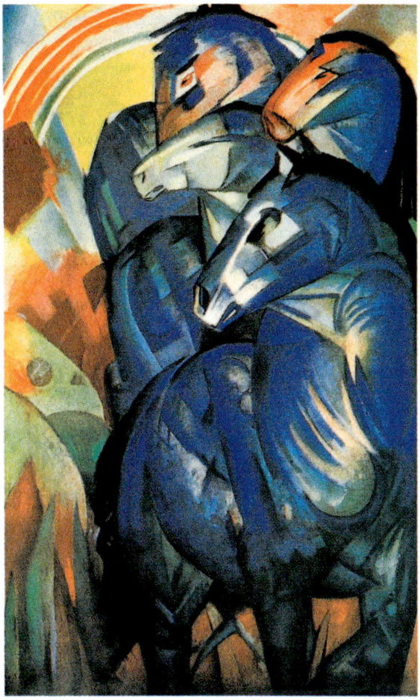

Left:

Franz Marc
HORSES IN THE SUN, 1908

Right:

Franz Marc
TOWER OF THE BLUE HORSES, 1913

On January 6, 1910, some unexpected visitors arrived at Marc's studio in Munich: August Macke, his artist cousin, Helmuth Macke, and Bernhard Koehler, the son of the Berliner industrialist, art patron and collector of the same name. The friendship and lively exchange of ideas with the Rhineland painter would continue until Macke's early death in 1914. In April of the same year, Marc gave up his studio in Munich and moved with Maria Franck to Sindelsdorf on the Kochelsee. They could not marry because Franz Marc would first need to obtain an official "dispensation" from his marriage to Maria Schnür.

In June Franz and Maria traveled to London, hoping that they would be able to marry there. This proved impossible, but Maria assumed the name of Marc. From now on they acted as if they were man and wife. The second exhibition of the New Artists' Association of Munich (see p. 37) filled Franz Marc with great enthusiasm. He noted his reaction in writing and thus established contact with the group surrounding Kandinsky and Münter.

The contact with Kandinsky became more intense; in 1911 he made preparations for the founding of the Blue Rider and the publication

Franz Marc
GIRL WITH CAT, 1910

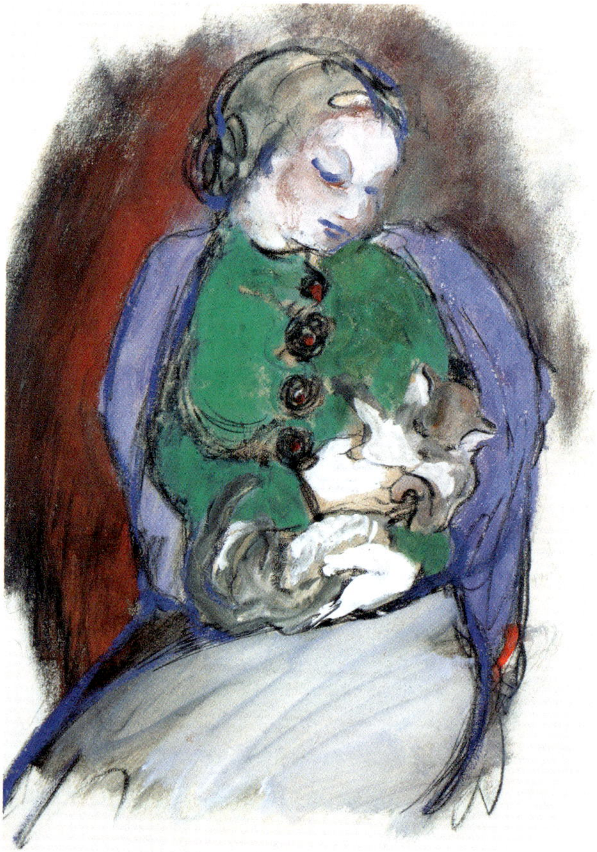

of the group's almanac; both projects were successfully carried through.

Franz Marc sought and found contact with the art scenes of Berlin and the Rhineland and had a number of successful solo exhibitions, including one in September 1912 in the Kunstsalon Schames in Frankfurt. During this time he also met the poet Else Lasker-Schüler, the divorced wife of the owner of the Sturm gallery, Herwarth Walden. She and Marc formed a truly sincere artists' friendship; they sent each other letters and cards they had drawn themselves: she called him "My Dear Blue Rider" or "My Very Dear Half-brother" and signed herself as "Jussuf, Prince of Thebes," or "Your Warrior" or "Your Brother."

On June 3, 1913, Franz Marc and Maria Franck married at the registry office in Munich. Little time remained for a honeymoon, however, because apart from numerous other activities Marc was also actively involved in the preparations for the most important exhibition of modern art to be held in Germany before the First World War. On September 19 the First German Autumn Salon (Erster Deutscher Herbstsalon) opened in Berlin with over 350 works by 75 artists. Franz Marc was well represented with seven paintings.

In April 1914 Franz and Maria Marc moved from Sindelsdorf to a spacious house in Ried near Benediktbeuern, but they did not have long to enjoy their new home. In August Franz Marc volunteered for war service. He was killed on March 4, 1916, at Braquis near Verdun; his body was brought back to Kochel in 1917.

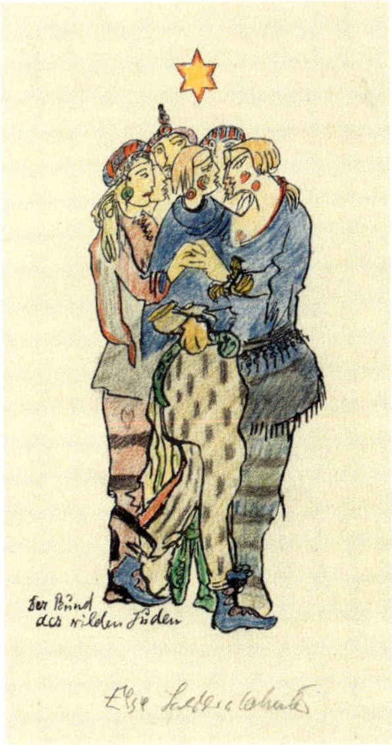

Else Lasker-Schüler
THE GATHERING OF THE WILD JEWS, 1923

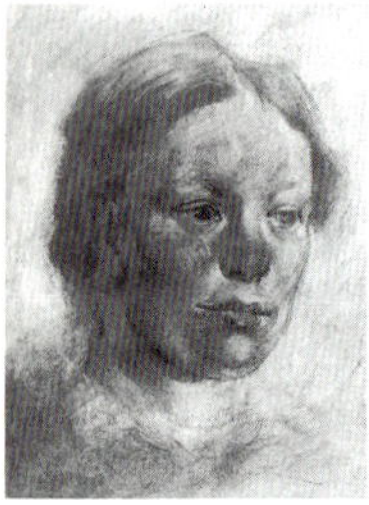

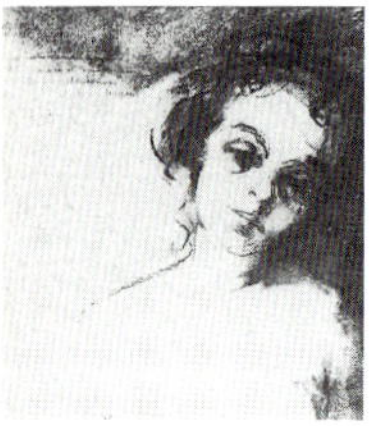

From the top:

Franz Marc
HEAD OF A GIRL (MARIA FRANCK), 1906

Franz Marc
HEAD OF A WOMAN (ANNETTE VON ECKARDT), 1904/1905

MARIA MARC

12. 6. 1876 Berlin, Germany – 25. 1. 1955 Kochel, Germany

Maria Franck grew up in an upper middle-class family in Berlin. She attended the Lyzeum (music school) and took drawing lessons at the Königliche Kunstschule (Royal School of Art). After that she took private art lessons. In 1903, despite the disapproval of her parents, she went to Munich to continue her art studies. One of her teachers was Maria Schnür. In 1905, she met Franz Marc at the parish fair at the brewery in Schwabing; the constellation for the subsequent eternal triangle was now complete. But Maria Franck suffered under the lack of clarity in this relationship. However it happened, she finally succeeded in prevailing against her rival and thenceforth lived permanently with Franz Marc. It could be said that she gradually took over his "organization and communications department"; in any case she deserves praise for her part in the development of the Blue Rider and the almanac, as well as in all activities within the group. As an artist she was unable to keep up in spite of her love of bright colors, which she borrowed from Franz Marc; her pictures remain mawkish representations of an idealized world. After her husband's death she devoted herself to his work, organizing a major memorial exhibition in Munich in 1916 and seeing to his estate and the publication of his writings. In 1955, Maria Marc was buried beside her husband in Kochel.

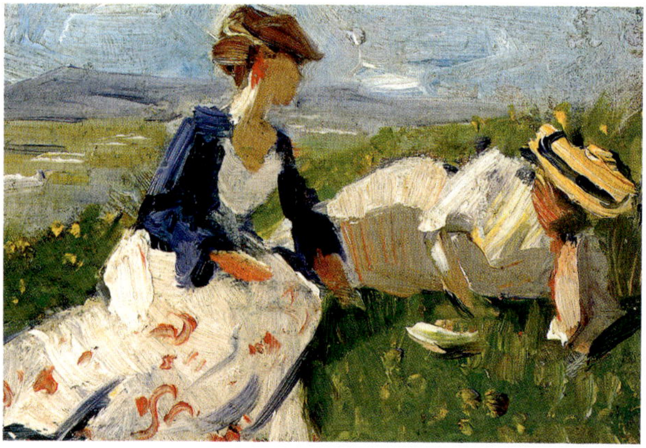

Franz Marc
TWO WOMEN ON THE MOUNTAIN, 1906

ALFRED KUBIN

10. 4. 1877 Leitmeritz, Austro-Hungarian Empire (Litoměřice, Czech Republic) – 20. 8. 1959 Zwickledt (Upper Austria)

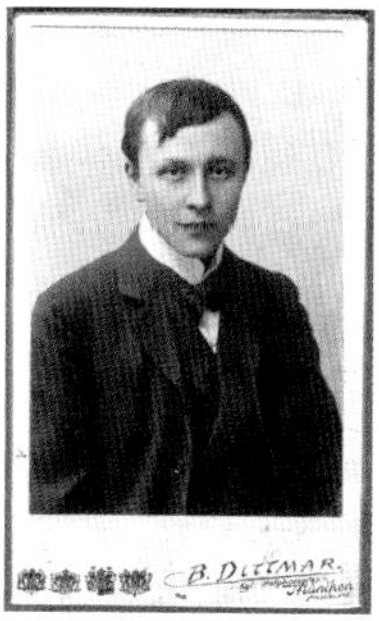

Alfred Kubin during his first year in Munich, 1898

Kubin was born in Leitmeritz in Bohemia, the son of the Austro-Hungarian army officer Franz Kubin and his wife Johanna. The father was often posted to different locations; from 1879 the family lived in Salzburg in Austria and later in Zell am See. When Alfred was ten years old his mother died of consumption shortly after the birth of her second daughter. His father then married his wife's sister, a widow – probably partly in order to provide his three children with a family. But Rosa Kubin also died in 1887, following the birth of a daughter. These traumatic experiences no doubt contributed to the development of Kubin's dark and fantastical personal style. In 1898 he moved to Munich and became a student at the private art school of Ludwig Schmid-Reutte; the following year he transferred to the Academy and established contact with the Munich art scene and the circle around the cabaret *Die Elf Scharfrichter* in the coffeehouses of Schwabing. He discovered the cycle of etchings *Paraphrase on the Finding of a Glove* by the Leipzig artist Max Klinger, which delighted him for its graphic intensity; the harsh black-and-white contrasts and not least its surreal content inspired in him a creative frenzy. In December 1901 he presented his drawings to the general public for the first time; the art dealer Paul Cassirer organized an exhibition for him in Berlin. He took part in exhibitions of the new Secessions in Berlin and Vienna and published a portfolio of drawings. In the spring of 1903 he embarked on a passionate love affair. He had met Emmy Bayer at his father's home in Schärding, but she died of typhoid fever that same year, on December 1, in a Munich hospital. In February of the following year, at the home of the poet Karl Wolfskehl, Kubin made the acquaintance of a young widow named Hedwig Gründler and her little son, and before long asked for her hand in marriage; they married in September. There were two other important events during that year. As a result of his participation in the Phalanx exhibition in Munich (see p. 14) his contact with Kandinsky and his friends intensified; and he met his admired role-model Max Klinger in Leipzig. After various journeys, including trips to Paris and the south of France, Alfred and Hedwig Kubin purchased the country estate of Zwickledt near Wernstein am Inn

Alfred Kubin
PUPATED WORLD,
1906

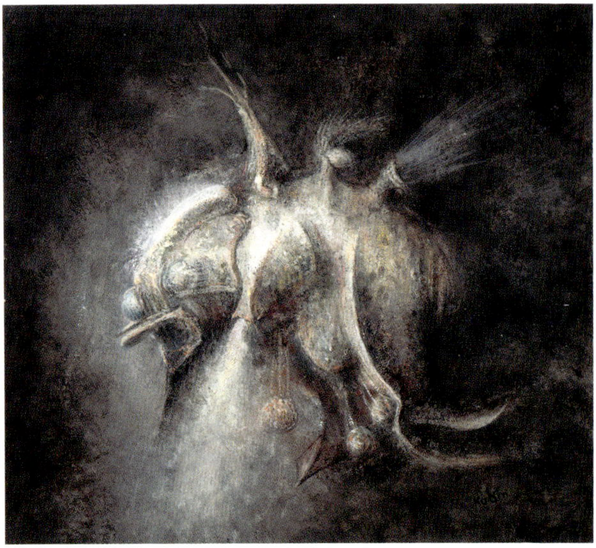

in Austria. They lived here until 1948; after his wife's death Kubin withdrew entirely from public life and took refuge in an almost monk-like seclusion. However, he continued to conduct a lively correspondence with painters and men of letters (including Hans Fronius and Hermann Hesse), and worked with great intensity. The result was a vast graphic oeuvre which focuses almost exclusively on the existential problems: birth, love, violence, the dark powers, and death. In it he developed an inimitable pictorial language. He was associated with the Blue Rider from its beginning, and participated in virtually all the exhibitions which Kandinsky and Marc organized. He wrote and illustrated the fantasy novel *Die andere Seite [The Other Side]* – to this day a highly readable book – and illustrated many works by other writers; the catalogue raisonné of 1977 lists 2,361 illustrations and book illustrations.[41] Between 1933 and 1936 he had an affair with Emmy Haesele. He had met the graphic artist, who was married to a country doctor, through his wife Hedwig. For all three these were years of turmoil, and Kubin ended his relationship with Emmy in a brutal manner. During the National Socialist era, Kubin initially bided his time, but many of his works were defamed as "degenerate." Nonetheless he was not banned entirely from exhibiting. After the war he continued his work undaunted. He died on

Right page:

Alfred Kubin
THE FOREBODING,
1906

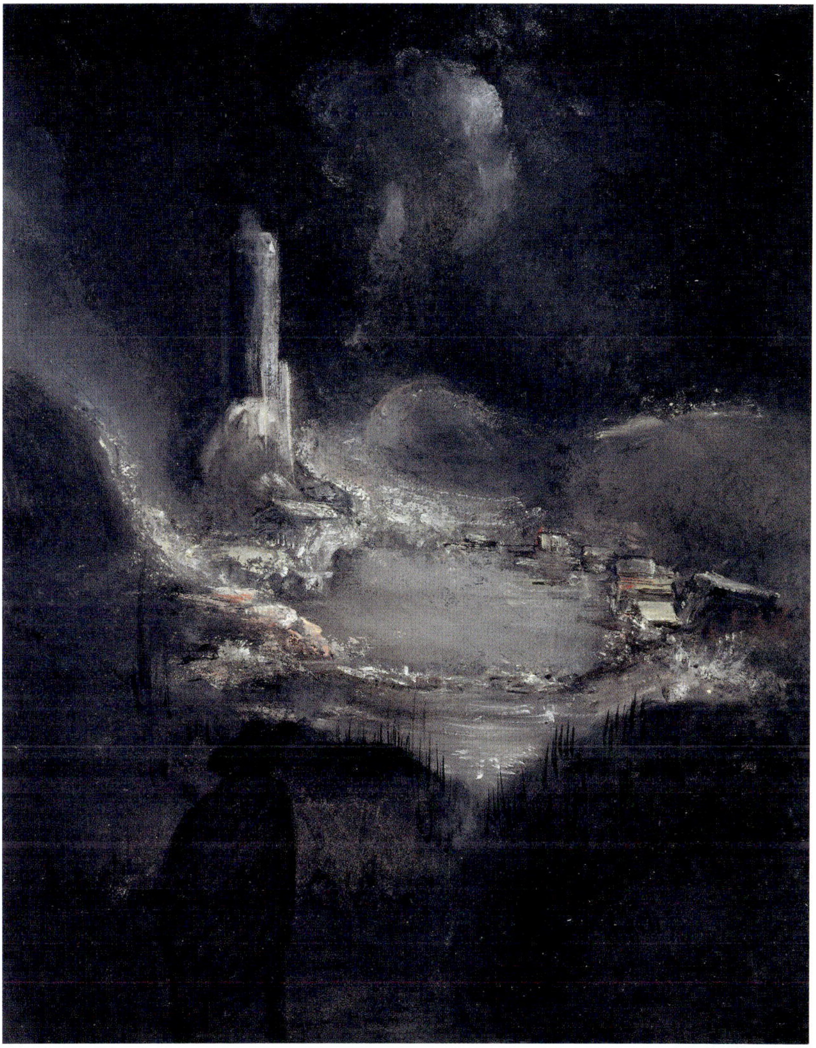

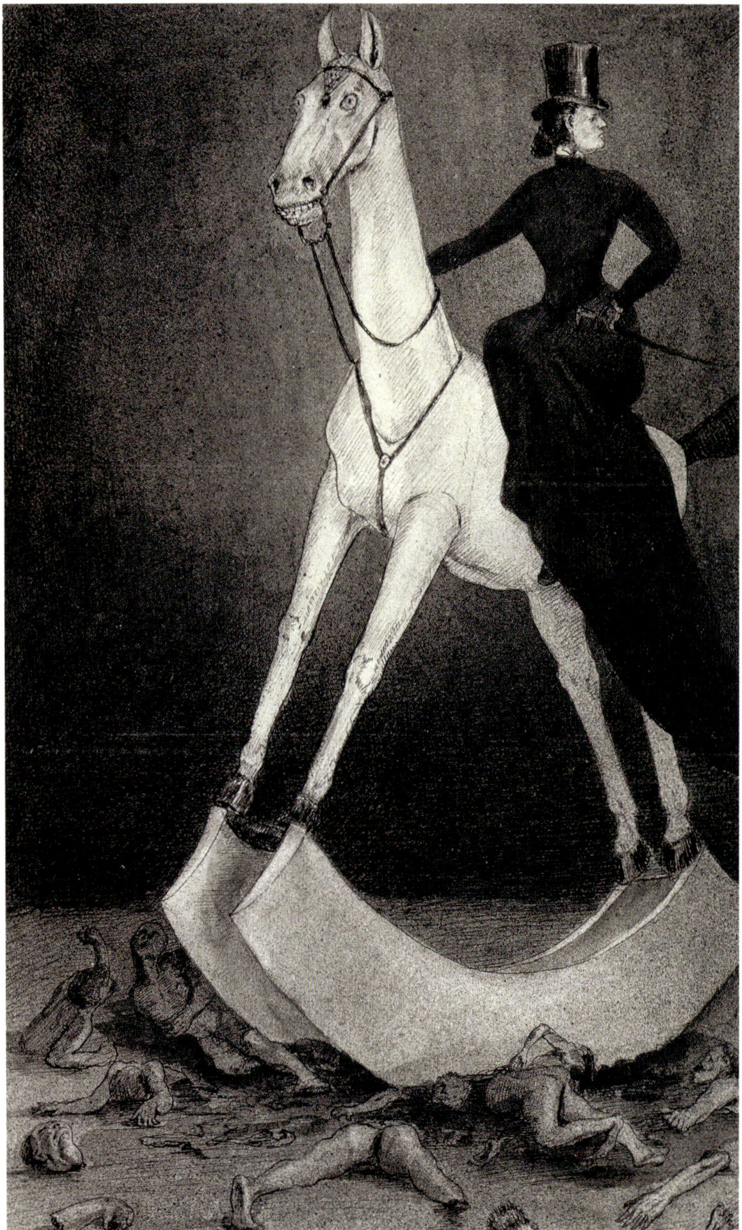

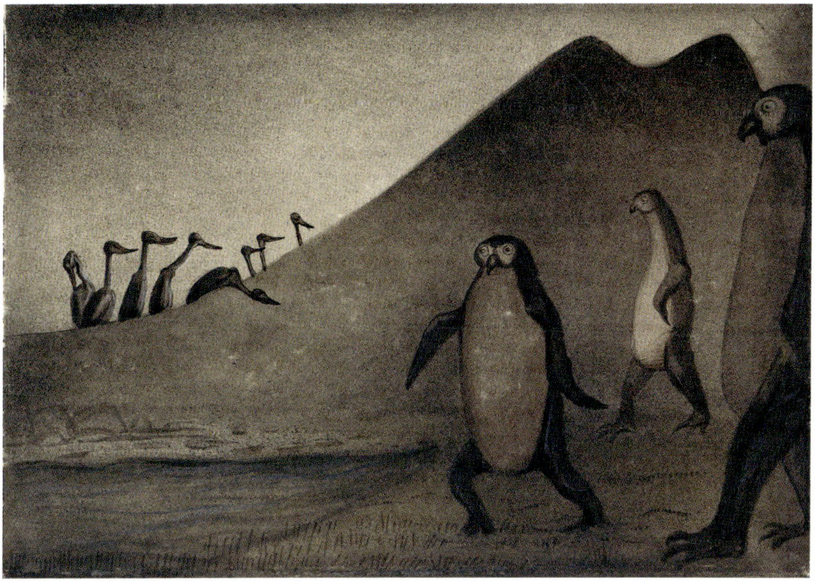

August 20, 1959, in Zwickledt, and was buried in the cemetery at Wernstein (see p. 180). His graphic oeuvre, comprising several thousand sheets, is preserved in the Städtische Galerie im Lenbachhaus Munich, in the Ostdeutsche Galerie Regensburg, in the Staatliche Graphische Sammlung Albertina in Vienna, and in the Provincial Museum Linz. In 1962 the Kubin memorial site was opened in his house in Zwickledt (see p. 179).

Alfred Kubin
THE INVADERS,
c. 1902/1903

Left page:

Alfred Kubin
THE LADY ON THE HORSE,
c. 1900/1901

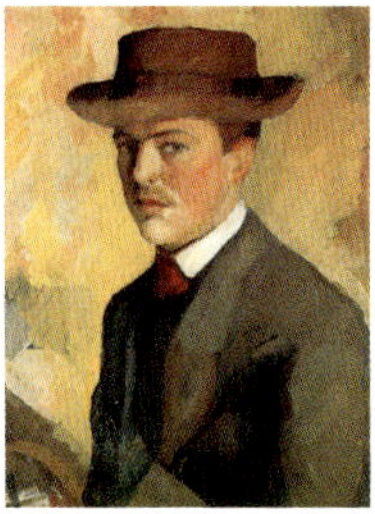

August Macke
SELF-PORTRAIT WITH HAT, 1909

AUGUST MACKE

3. 1. 1887 Meschede (Sauerland), Germany
– 26. 9. 1914 Perthes-lès-Hurlus (Champagne), France

After attending school in Cologne and Bonn, in 1904 August Macke left secondary school early and registered as a student at the Art Academy in Düsseldorf. "School was no more fun, but there were better minds there,"[42] he wrote to his school friend and later wife Elisabeth Gerhardt.

After his father's death he traveled extensively through Holland, England, and especially Italy, where he fell in love with the light of the Mediterranean. In 1907–1908 he studied under Lovis Corinth in Berlin, and in 1909 he married Elisabeth; the couple moved to Tegernsee, in the vicinity of his admired teacher, who had taken lodgings in Urfeld on Walchensee. Their son Walter was born in Tegernsee on April 13, thus strengthening still further the couple's

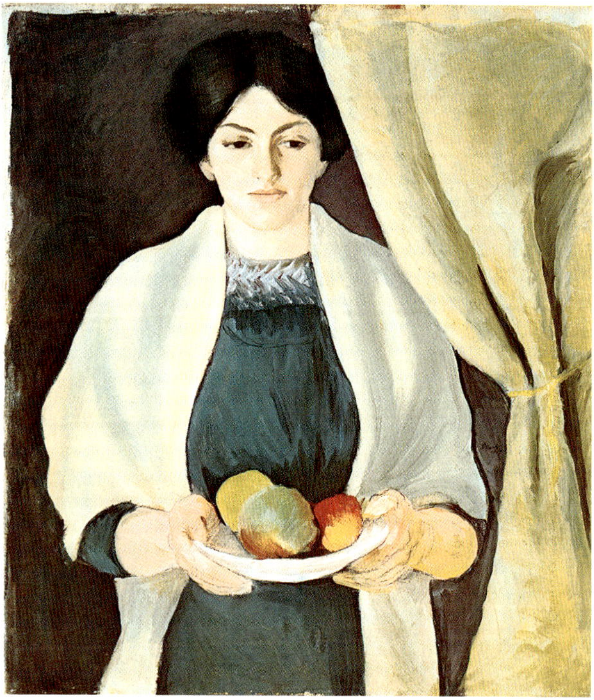

August Macke
PORTRAIT WITH APPLES, 1909

links with Upper Bavaria. Macke made contact with the Munich art scene, especially with the New Artists' Association of Munich and Franz Marc, with whom he maintained a close friendship until his early death. In spite of their frequently expressed liking for their surroundings, the couple returned to Bonn in November 1910, "a real pensioners' town," as August Macke scornfully noted. He hoped for better working conditions in the house with a big studio in Bornheimer Strasse that the couple moved into with their son.

In 1912 Macke became a member of the Blue Rider. He followed the activities of his friend Franz Marc and the Kandinsky circle, including its tensions, with a solidarity that did not shy away from criticism. "I am not arguing against the Blue Rider, but against various lame places on his horse. Ultimately somebody must do it. Otherwise you really will be seeing things in too blue a light,"[43] he wrote to Marc in 1912. His second son, Wolfgang, was born on February 8, 1913. Macke undertook a number of important study trips to France which greatly encouraged his brightly colored, crystalline painting style. He met Robert Delaunay and Henri Matisse in Paris and in April 1914 he traveled with Paul Klee (see p. 114) and Louis Moilliet from Switzerland to Tunisia, where he produ-ced thirty-seven delightful watercolors filled with transparent light and brilliant colors which are among the most beautiful "travel pictures" created during the twentieth century.[44] Macke was conscripted into war service on August 8, 1914; on August 17 he wrote to Elisabeth: "I would be happy if I could come home, into your arms, and could continue painting (for me that seems like a dream at the moment). But when I think of the children I am overcome by despair that I may never see them again [...] My Dear, how happy we shall be when the war is over and we are together again."[45] He had only another forty days to live.

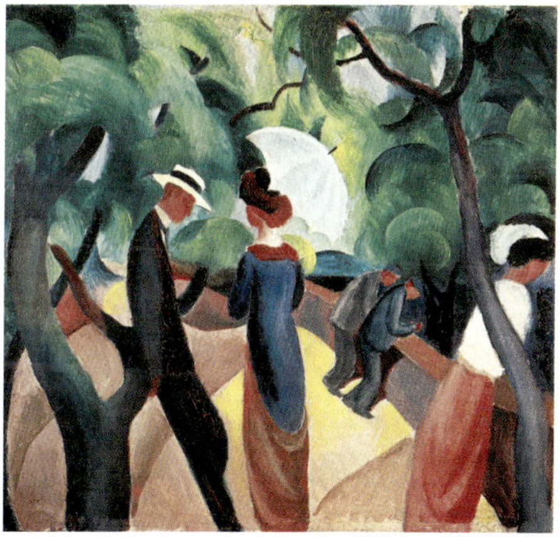

August Macke
PROMENADE, 1913

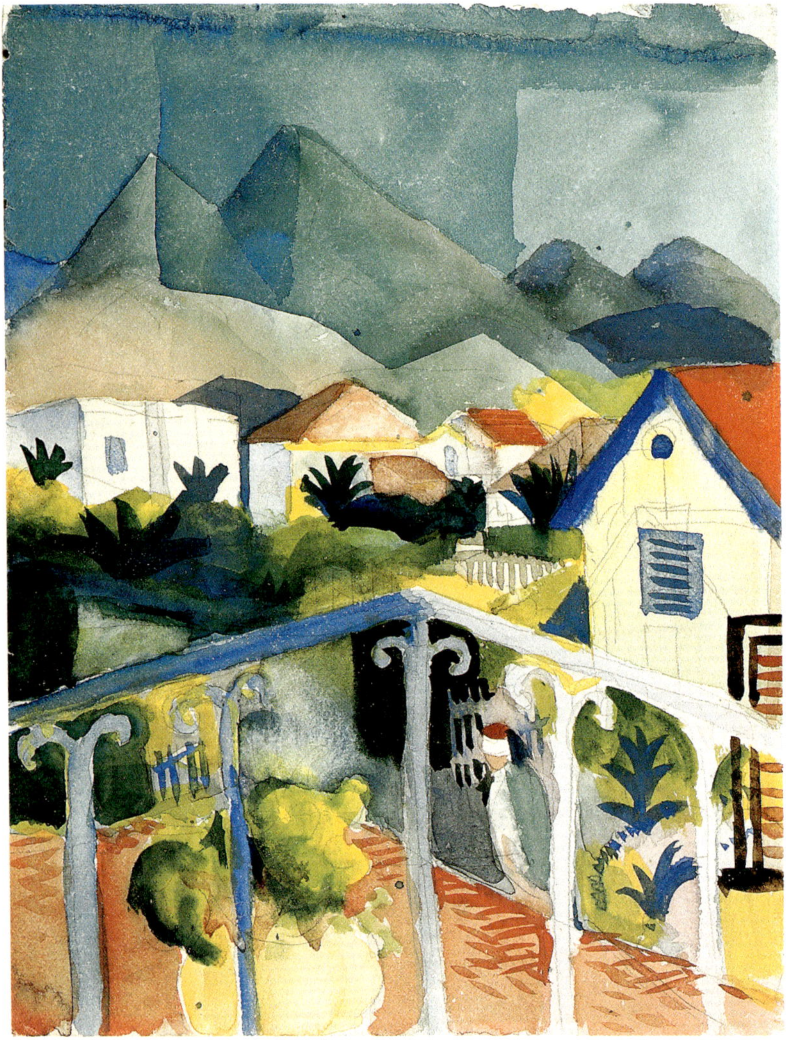

August Macke
ST. GERMAIN NEAR TUNIS, 1914

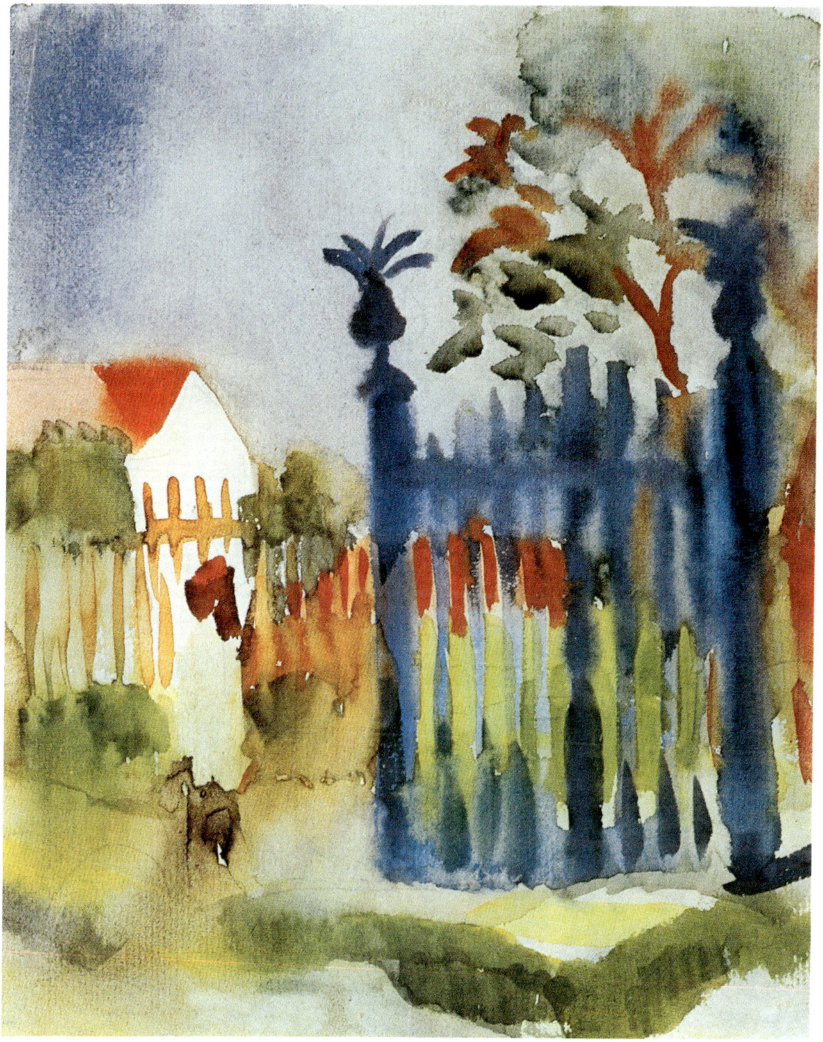

August Macke
GARDEN GATE, 1914

Right page:

Paul Klee
FÖHN WIND IN FRANZ MARC'S GARDEN, 1915

PAUL KLEE

18. 12.1879 Münchenbuchsee near Bern, Switzerland
– 29. 6. 1940 Muralto-Locarno, Switzerland

After attending grammar school in Bern, in 1890 Klee moved to Munich, where he soon met the pianist Lily Stumpf, whom he would marry in 1906; their son Felix was born the following year.

Paul Klee, who from October 1900 had studied under Franz von Stuck at the Academy in Munich and in 1906 showed etchings for the first time, at the Munich Secession, was in urgent need of commercial success, which, however, was slow to materialize. Artistically speaking, Klee's time in Munich was highly productive. He made friends with Alfred Kubin, whom he respected as a highly talented draftsman, and during the winter of 1911–1912 he joined the group surrounding Wassily Kandinsky. "This Kandinsky wants to call together a new association of artists. As a result of our personal acquaintance I have developed a deep-seated confidence in him. He is a personality and has an exceptionally fine, clear head. The first time we met in a public restaurant in the city [...] Then, during the journey home by tram, we agreed to pursue our acquaintance. During the course of that winter I then joined his Blue Rider."[46] In 1913 Klee took part in the exhibition of the First German Autumn Salon in Berlin; a year later he traveled with Macke (see p. 110) to Tunisia and under his influence began to paint with watercolors.

In 1916 Klee was called up to join the Landsturm reserve forces and survived the war without injury. In May 1920 his first solo exhibition, which included 362 works, was held in Munich in the Galerie

Paul Klee
SACRED STONES AND IMAGES OF GODS, 1913

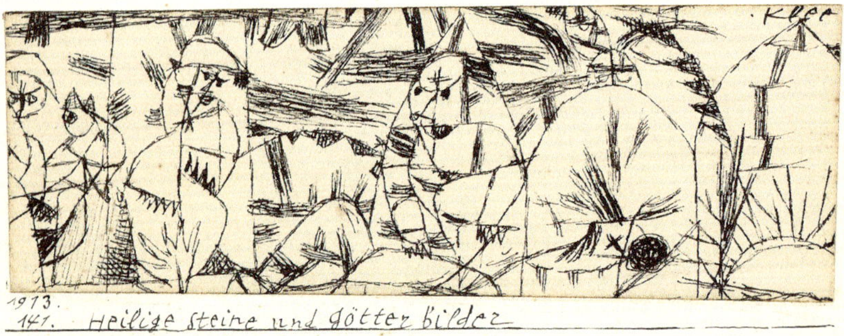

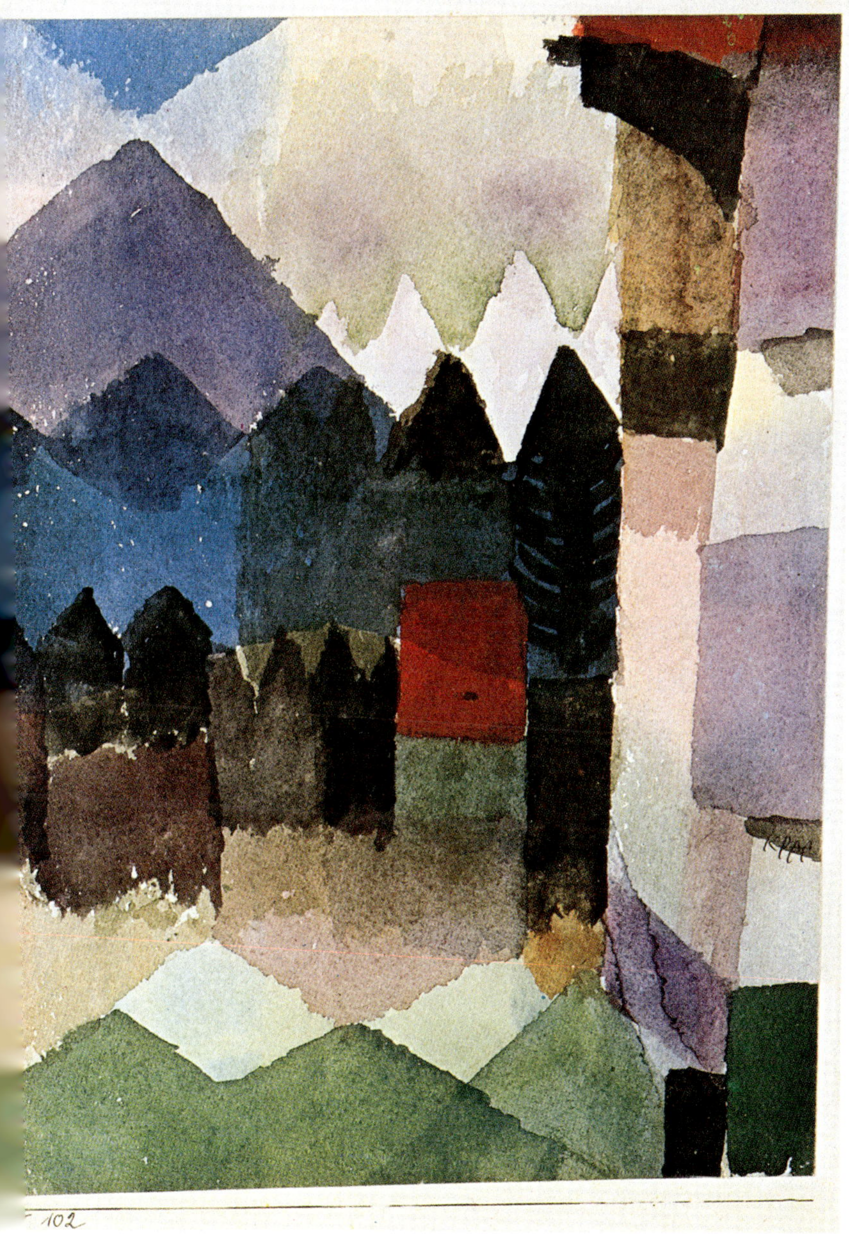
102

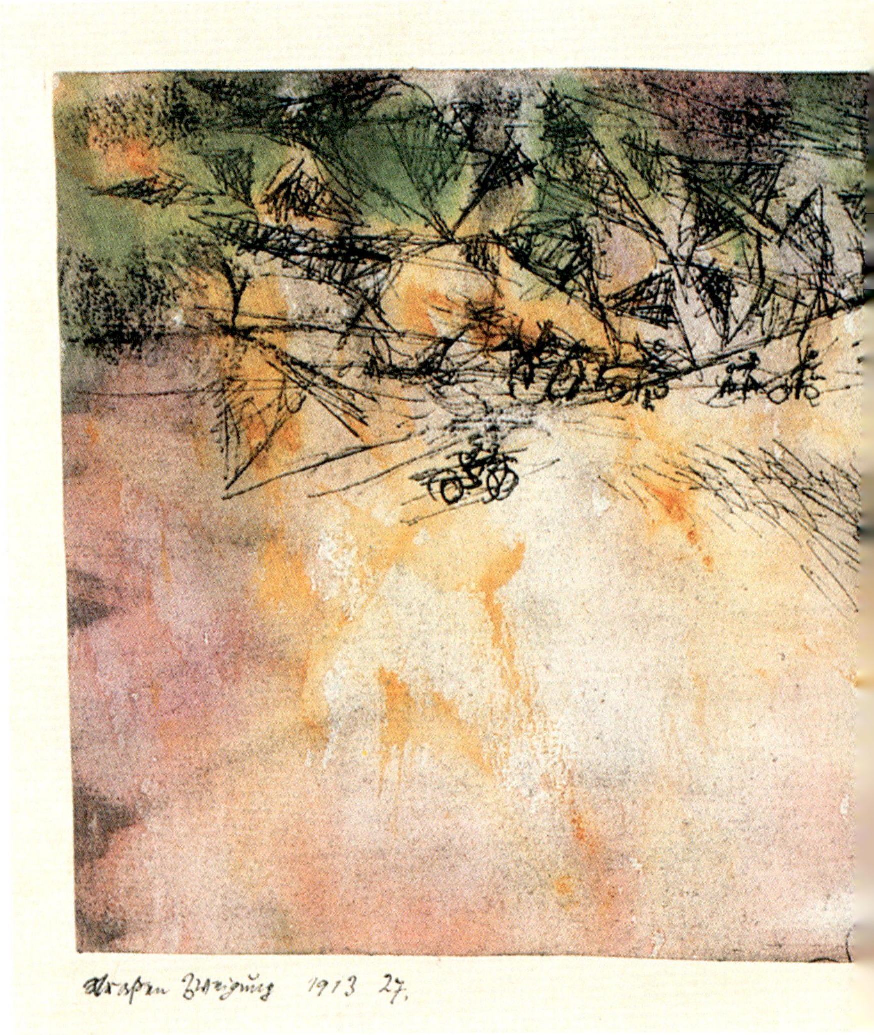

Paul Klee
STREET JUNCTION, 1913

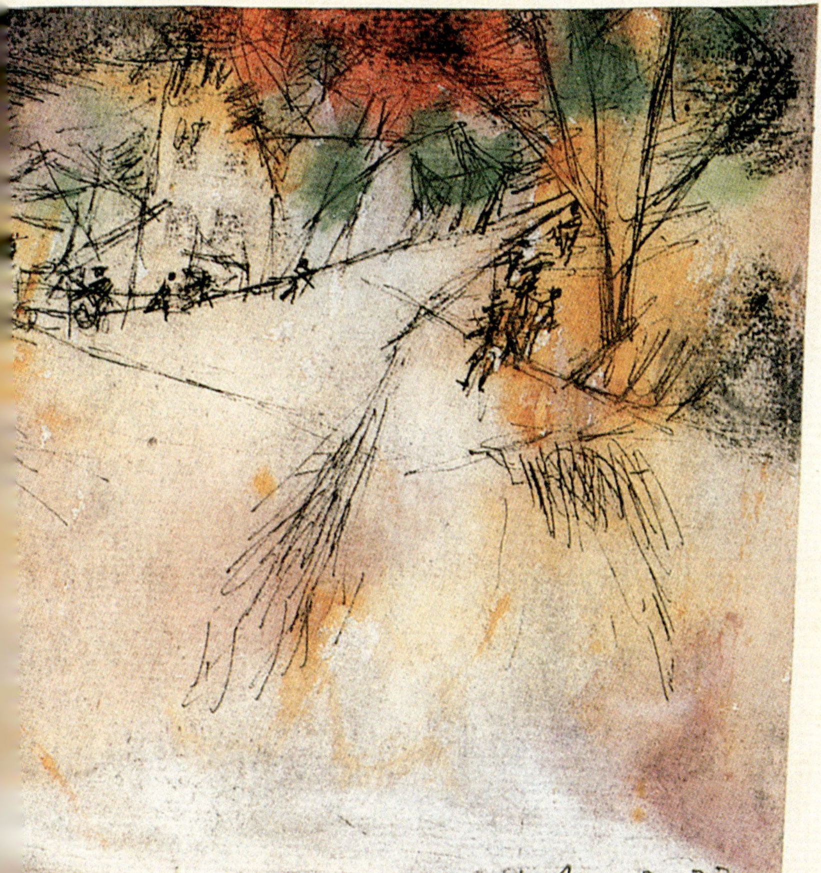
Klee 1913 27

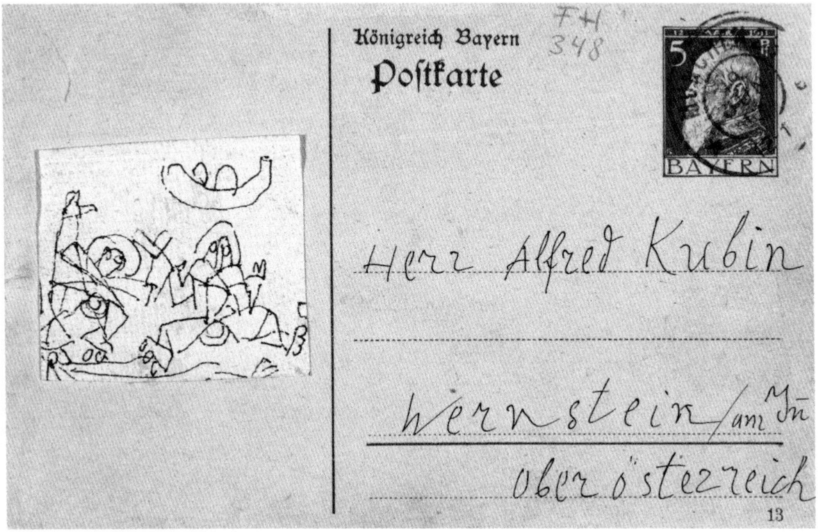
FH
348
Königreich Bayern
Postkarte
5
BAYERN
Herr Alfred Kubin
Wernstein/am Inn
Ober österreich
13

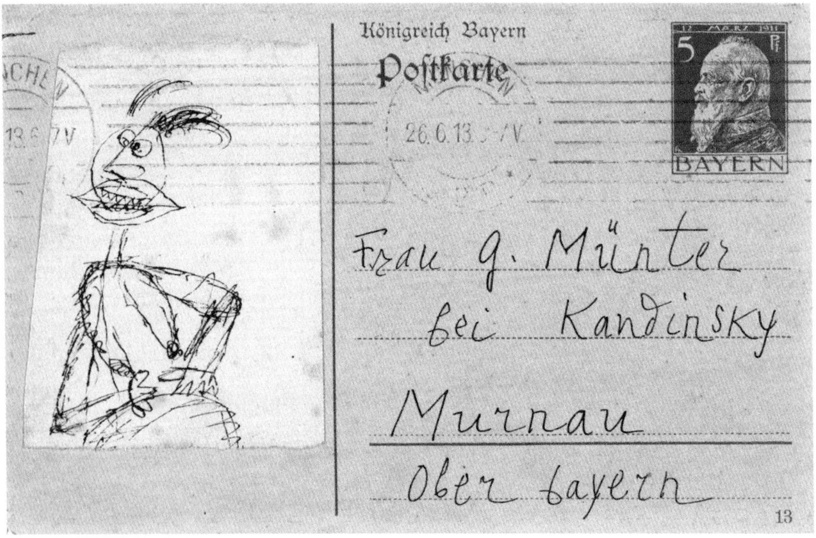
Königreich Bayern
Postkarte
26.6.13
5
BAYERN
Frau G. Münter
bei Kandinsky
Murnau
Ober bayern
13

Goltz, and in October of the same year he was appointed to the Bauhaus in Weimar, where his friendship with Kandinsky deepened. In 1929 a major exhibition opened in the Galerie Flechtheim in Berlin to mark his fiftieth birthday, followed by a second the following year, which was subsequently shown at the Museum of Modern Art in New York. Klee thus reached the summit of the international avant-garde.

Treated with hostility by the National Socialists, he left Germany in 1933 and returned to live in Bern. He maintained his contacts with the international avant-garde. In 1937 he was visited by Pablo Picasso, Georges Braque, Ernst Kirchner, and Kandinsky. In February 1940 the Kunsthaus Zürich dedicated a major exhibition to his works from the years 1935–1940, permitting him to enjoy success once more. On 29 June he died of a heart attack in the Saint Agnese hospital in Locarno, Switzerland.

Left page:

Paul Klee
FIGURES, 1913

Paul Klee
GROTESQUE FEMALE FIGURE, 1913

4. SATELLITES

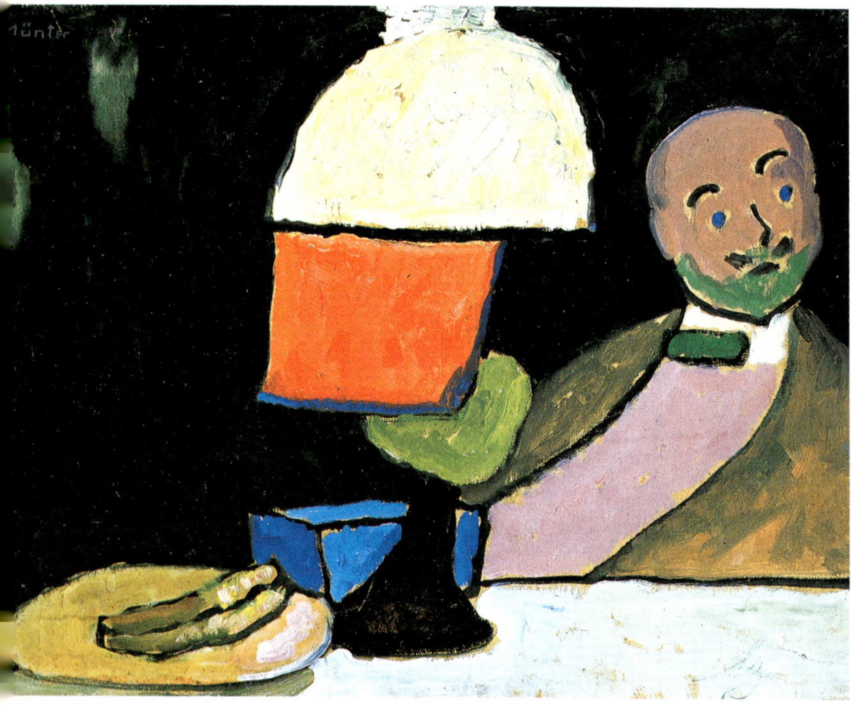

Gabriele Münter
Listening (Portrait of Jawlensky), 1909

MARIANNE VON WEREFKIN

29. 8. 1860 Tula, Russia – 6. 2. 1938 Ascona, Switzerland

Marianne von Werefkin was a member of the Russian aristocracy, the daughter of the commander of the St. Petersburg garrison and an art-loving mother; she grew up surrounded by plenty. Her parents provided her with a solid education based on Western attitudes, including a genteel education in the arts. At the age of twenty-six she became a private pupil of Ilya Repin (1844 – 1930), the most important Russian Realist painter. In circumstances which have not been fully explained to this day, probably a hunting accident, she was shot in the right hand, which was thereafter disabled. In 1891 at Repin's house she met the young lieutenant Alexej von Jawlensky, who was poor but obsessed by art. She actively encouraged him, which however did not prevent his falling in love a few years later with her maid, Helene Neznakomova, who was only eleven years old at the time and whom he would marry in 1918.

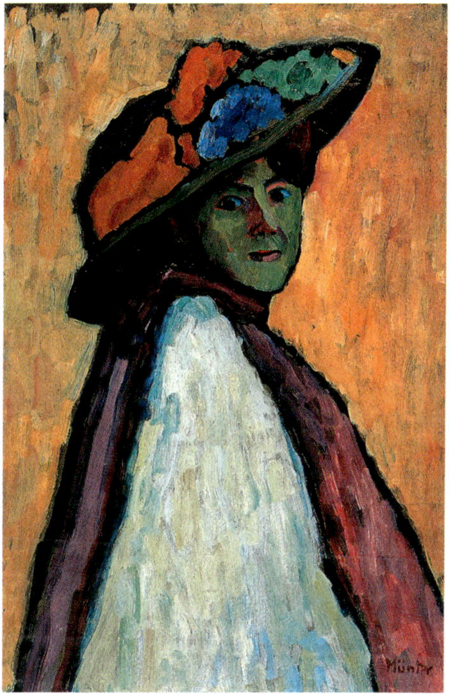

Gabriele Münter
PORTRAIT OF MARIANNE VON WEREFKIN, 1909

The eternal triangle which was to develop from this point onwards would lead to repeated tensions and emotional damage to all the protagonists. Nonetheless, Helene Neznakomova remained in employment in Werefkin's house for almost three decades. This did not change after the birth of her son Andrei in 1902, when Helene was just seventeen years old; Jawlensky was the child's father.

From 1896 Werefkin and Jawlensky lived in an appropriately elegant apartment in Schwabing, the artists' district of Munich, where Maria, the "Baroness," proceeded to establish an artistic and literary salon in Giselastrasse. Among the circle of "Giselisten" were famous names: Henry van de Velde, Hugo von Tschudi, Lovis Corinth, Adolf Erbslöh, Alexander von Kanoldt, Wassily Kandinsky, Gabriele

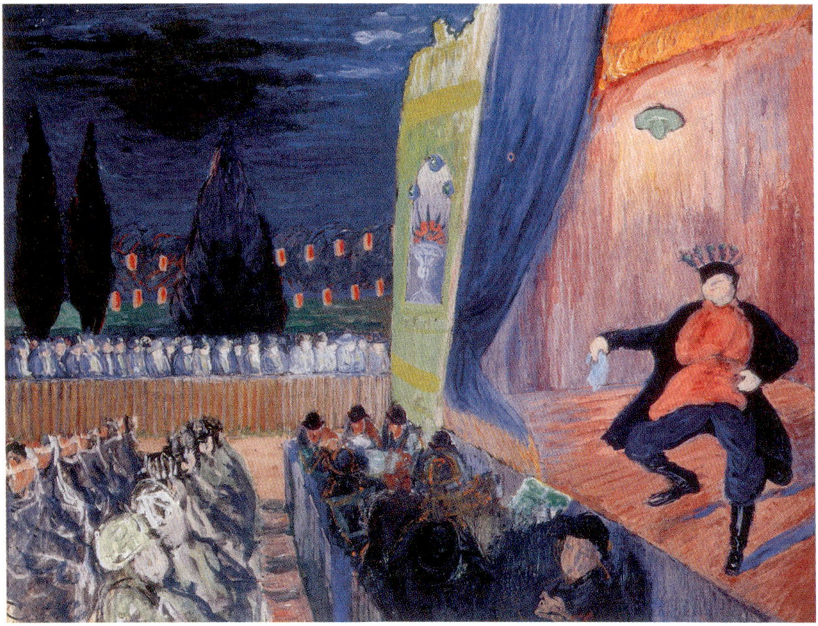

Marianne von Werefkin
SUMMER STAGE, 1910

Münter, and many others. Werefkin was an active supporter of Modernism in Munich, especially of the artists of the Blue Rider, which, however, she did not join personally. She also started painting again herself. After the First World War broke out Marianne von Werefkin, Helene Neznakomova, and the latter's son, Andrei, lived with the child's father in Switzerland. After her possessions were expropriated by the Soviets, Werefkin, by this time separated from Jawlensky, lived in fairly modest circumstances in Ascona, Switzerland, where she died.

ALEXEJ VON JAWLENSKY

13. 3. 1864 Torzhok, Russia – 15. 3. 1941 Wiesbaden, Germany

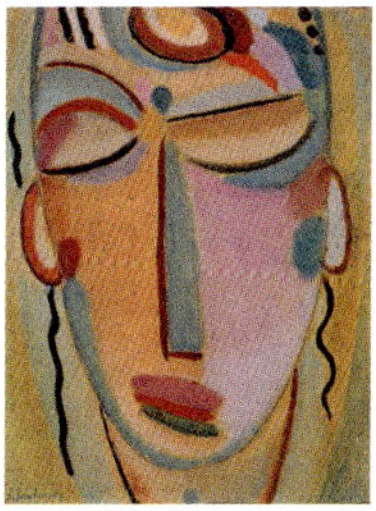

Alexej von Jawlensky
MEDITATION, 1918

From 1877 the young Jawlensky attended the cadet school in Moscow, where he also established contact with the art scene. He studied painting under Ilya Repin, where he also met his later companion, Marianne von Werefkin (see p. 121), who was four years older than he was; in 1896 he moved with her to Munich, accompanied by the young maid Helene Neznakomova, with whom Jawlensky began a relationship and who later gave birth to his son, Andrei. He painted various portraits of her, including *Dark Blue Turban* in 1910. Despite the strains, the triangular relationship was to last for more than two decades; Jawlensky finally separated from Marianne von Werefkin in 1918 in Switzerland, thereafter marrying Helene, with whom he returned to Germany and settled in Wiesbaden.

Jawlensky had met his fellow-countryman Wassily Kandinsky in Munich in 1896 at the painting school run by Anton Ažbé. The artist couples Werefkin and Jawlensky, Münter and Kandinsky, became close friends; they also had a great deal in common artistically. They shared a common enthusiasm for Paul Gauguin, Vincent van Gogh, and Henri Matisse.

In 1908 the four of them spent successful painting holidays together in Murnau; it was during this time that the foundations for the developments leading up to the Blue Rider were laid. But first, in January 1909, they founded the New Artists' Association of Munich. Jawlensky became the second chairman (see p. 20). He now worked hard at developing his painting style, with its strong colors, mostly outlined in a dark color or black. His most important subject remains the portrait, which he increasingly developed from the individual to the almost abstract generalization.

Marianne von Werefkin and Alexej von Jawlensky were close to the Blue Rider but did not become members of the association. On the one hand, their links to Adolf Erbslöh and Alexander Kanoldt, both artists who had remained in the New Artists' Association of Munich, were close; on the other, they also wanted to retain their independence and their position as arbitrators between the various points of view in Werefkin's "salon." After the First World War broke out Jawlensky – together with Marianne von Werefkin, Helene Neznakomova, and her son Andrei – moved to Switzerland. There

Alexej von Jawlensky
DARK BLUE TURBAN,
1910

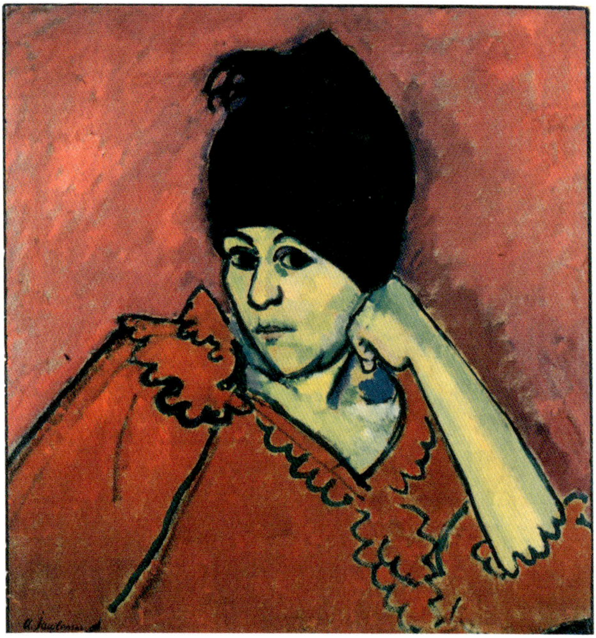

he met Ferdinand Hodler, Rainer Maria Rilke and others, but especially Emilie Esther Scheyer, a young woman from a wealthy Jewish family in Braunschweig, who acted as an art dealer and also painted herself. Jawlensky called her "Galka" (Russian for "Jackdaw") because of her black hair. After emigrating to the United States she adopted the nickname as her official first name. Galka was very enthusiastic about Jawlensky's painting and became his agent, the two of them developing a very close friendship.

In 1918 Jawlensky left Marianne von Werefkin and married Helene Neznakomova, with whom he returned to Germany. From 1921 he lived in Wiesbaden.

Galka Scheyer developed the idea of a group of artists whom she planned to represent and market in the United States. She persuaded Jawlensky, Lyonel Feininger, Kandinsky, and Klee to participate: in 1924 the Blue Four group was founded and by 1944 had arranged thirteen group exhibitions under that name (see p. 153). Jawlensky did not live to see the last of these; he died in 1941 in Wiesbaden.

HEINRICH CAMPENDONK

3. 11. 1889 Krefeld – 3. 5. 1957 Amsterdam

Campendonk began an apprenticeship at the technical college for fabric technology in Krefeld at the age of fifteen and transferred in 1905 to the arts college in the same town, where Johan Thorn-Prikker from the Netherlands became his main teacher and sponsor. It was not long before he met his fellow-student Helmuth Macke, a cousin of August Macke. From 1909 Campendonk continued to work independently under precarious financial circumstances. Through Helmuth and August Macke he came into contact with the New Artists' Association of Munich. During the fall of 1911 Campendonk moved from the Rhineland to Sindelsdorf to live near Franz Marc, whom he greatly admired. His creative work in the next few years was strongly influenced by the artist friends working nearby, primarily Franz Marc, but also Kandinsky. Introducing at the same time ideas from Cubism, Campendonk created an idiosyncratic world of animals and landscapes with scenes of figures, depicted in a transparent, brilliant range of colors, that he transformed into enchanted but fragile idylls. After Franz Marc was killed in action in 1916, Campendonk continued with this style for many years, always incorporating the landscape of Upper Bavaria in which he lived. In May 1916 he moved to Seeshaupt on Lake Starnberg with his wife at that time, Adda Deichmann, and his artist friend, the animal painter Jean Bloé Niestlé, who had also lived in Sindelsdorf and who now moved into a house in Seeshaupt financed by Bernhard Koehler. In 1921 Campendonk returned to Krefeld, where the industrialist and art patron Paul Multhaupt provided him with a house. In October 1926, on the recommendation of Walter Kasebach, he was appointed as teacher for Wall Painting, Glass Painting, Mosaics and Tapestries at the Art Academy in Düsseldorf. In 1933 Campendonk was dismissed from this post by the National Socialists. In 1935 he was appointed Professor for Monumental and Decorative Art at the Rijksakademie in Amsterdam. After the Second World War, in spite of being offered several posts, Campendonk did not return to Germany.

Next page:

Heinrich Campendonk
FOREST, GIRL, GOAT, 1917

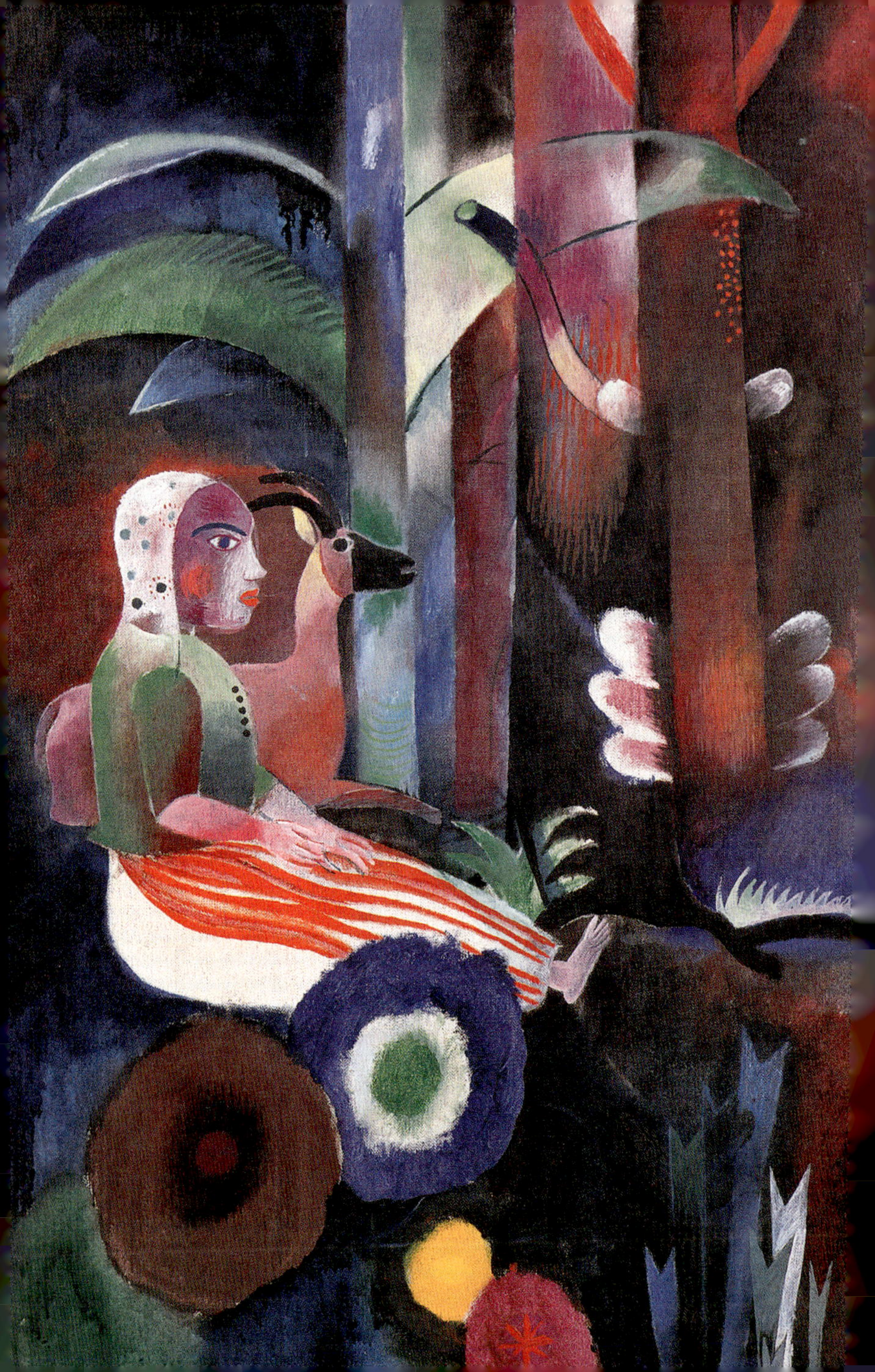

ARNOLD SCHÖNBERG

13. 9. 1874 Vienna – 14. 7. 1951 Los Angeles

Arnold Schönberg, who came from a very modest background, grew up in Vienna. By the age of nine he was an excellent violinist and began to compose music. He completed an apprenticeship as a bank clerk and could only pursue his music in his free time, during which he conducted various amateur orchestras.

Between 1904 and 1914 he also started painting; in 1910 the Galerie Heller in Vienna organized a solo exhibition of his works. He also used the exhibition to perform his own compositions, since he was interested in the relationship between music and painting. For this reason he found the acquaintance of Kandinsky very stimulating; the two artists discussed the question of synesthesia. Schönberg submitted three paintings to the first Blue Rider exhibition and his *Self-Portrait* was also published in the almanac. His talent as an artist remained a subject of controversy, even among the members of the Blue Rider. Franz Marc could see little merit in his paintings, but Kandinsky was enthusiastic about them. They were in agreement, however, about the importance of Schönberg's music. Kandinsky wrote to the composer in 1911: "In your works you have achieved what I greatly longed to do, admittedly in an undetermined form as regards music. The independent walk through their own fate; the independent lives of the various voices in your compositions is precisely what I am trying to find in artistic form."[48] In 1921 Schönberg established a method he described as "composing with twelve tones which are related only with one another" (twelve-tone music), which made him famous. He emigrated to the United States in 1933 and became a US citizen in 1940.

Arnold Schönberg
SELF-PORTRAIT (FROM BEHIND), 1911

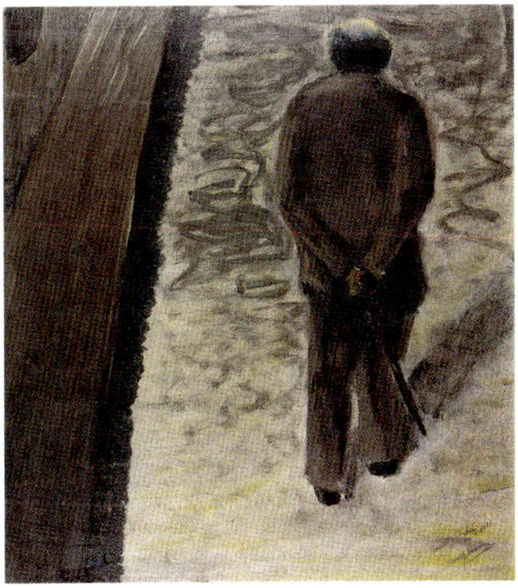

5. EVENTS 1912–1914

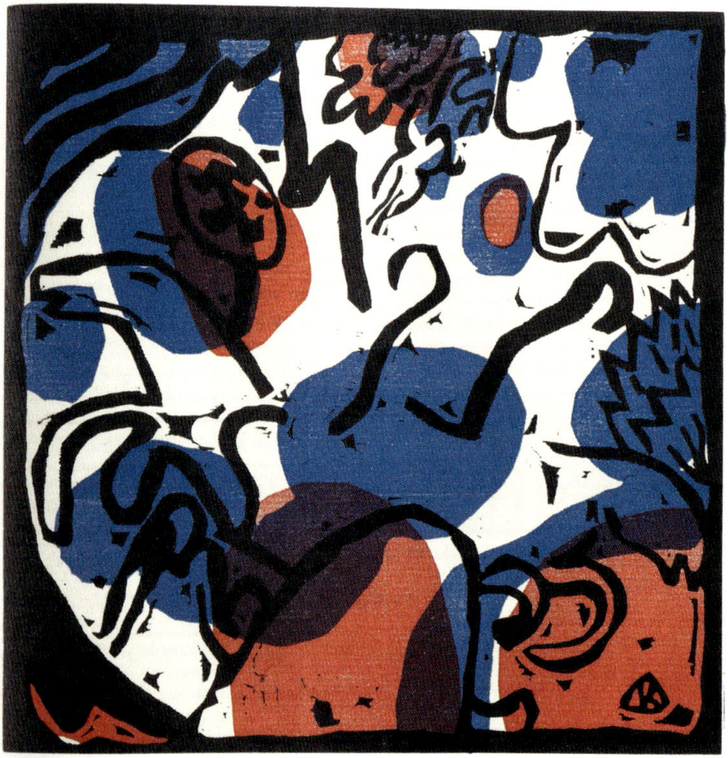

Wassily Kandinsky,
colored woodcut from *Sounds*, 1912

THE YEAR 1912

The year 1912 began very successfully for the friends of the Blue Rider. They had left the New Artists' Association of Munich; the first exhibition of the new group during the winter of 1911–1912 had caused a tremendous stir; and they had successfully completed the work on their programmatic work, the almanac *Der Blaue Reiter*, which was published in March 1912 by Piper Verlag in Munich. Kandinsky published a second important work with the same publishing house: *Concerning the Spiritual in Art*. The opening sentences make clear beyond any doubt his reasons for writing it: "Every work of art is the child of its age and, in many cases, the mother of our emotions. So each cultural period gives birth to its own art, which can never be repeated. An attempt to revive the principles of art of a past age can at best produce works of art which resemble a stillborn child."[49]

For Kandinsky, artistic styles of the past are above all academic painting, then Impressionism and Jugendstil. They were important once, but now they are exhausted by repetition and variations. A new language of colors had to be found.

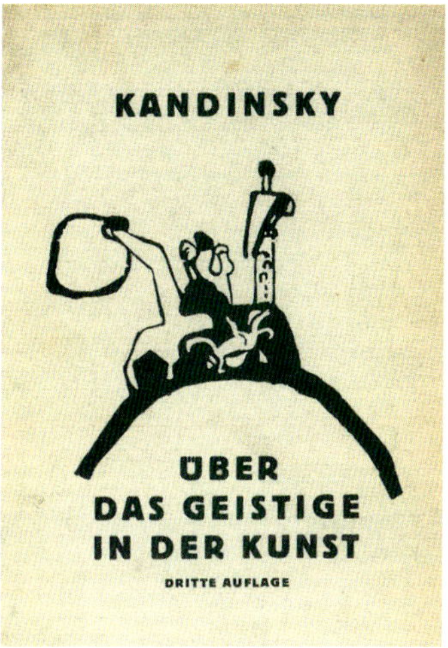

Wassily Kandinsky,
Cover of *On the Spiritual in Art*, 1911/1912

THE BLUE RIDER IN THE GEREONS CLUB IN COLOGNE

The artist friends refused to rest on their laurels; they wanted to take advantage of the fact that in Munich they were the talk of the town. Their first task was to prepare the second showing of the Blue Rider exhibition, in the Gereons Club in Cologne.

Two women artists, Olga Oppenheimer and Emmy Worringer, ran a private art school in the office and atelier building in Gereonstrasse. They also used the rooms for exhibitions, lectures, and discussions on the subject of modern art. Founded in 1911, the club had rapidly become an important meeting point for the progressive art scene in Cologne; August Macke was a member. In his house he showed club members works by Kandinsky, Marc, Münter, and

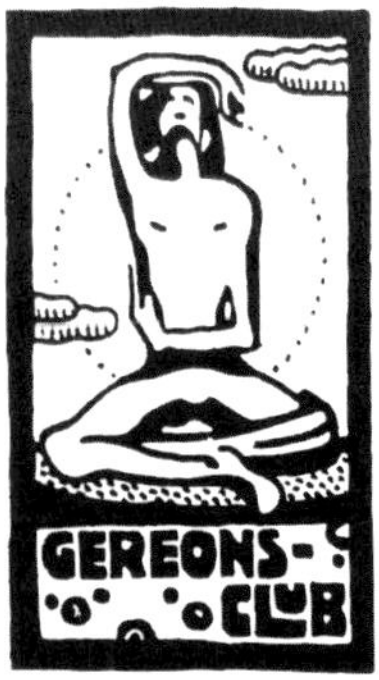

Franz M. Jansen, Invitation to the first exhibition at the Gereons Club, 1911

Kubin, which all enjoyed a very positive reception. An invitation was therefore issued to the members of the Blue Rider to show their Munich exhibition in Cologne. Franz Marc, who had met the members of the Brücke group in Berlin, encouraged them to take part in the exhibition. On January 2, 1912, he wrote to Kandinsky: "I am sending you at the same time by registered post a picture by Pechstein that I should like to include as a highlight in the Bl. R. [Blauer Reiter] exhibition in Cologne ... And I am also sending directly from here to Cologne a wooden figure by Kirchner for the exhibition. It's very lively, a bit African, but that doesn't matter."[50] Kandinsky was not very enthusiastic; in the works by the "Wild Ones" from

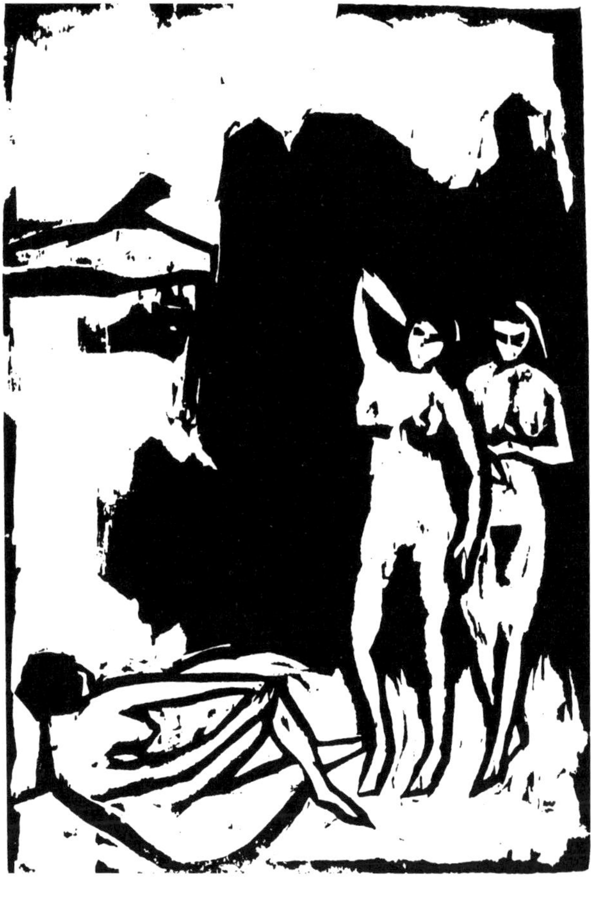

Ernst Ludwig Kirchner
THREE BATHERS (MORITZBURG), 1910

Dresden he was unable to recognize the spiritual element, the subjectivity that he saw as essential for real art. Nonetheless, he initially agreed, since there was no time for discussion; the second Blue Rider exhibition was already approaching fast, this time on the premises of the art dealer Hans Goltz in Munich.

THE SECOND BLUE RIDER EXHIBITION

The second exhibition, which was given the somewhat awkward title of *Die zweite Ausstellung der Redaktion Der Blaue Reiter Schwarz-Weiß [The Second Exhibition of the Editorial Team the Blue Rider Black-White]* opened on February 12, 1912, and included over 350 exhibits. Its title is open to misinterpretation, because apart from monochrome drawings and prints *(Black-White)* it also included watercolors and other colored works on paper. In addition to members of the Blue Rider, who now also included Paul Klee, this time the artists of the Dresden Brücke group were also well represented, as was the international avant-garde. Apart from sheets by French artists, especially Derain and Picasso, works by Russian artists such as Natalia Goncharova and Kazimir Malevich were also on view.
The exhibition was well-attended but was once again largely rejected by the public. Franz Marc wrote to his friend August Macke: "It is certainly good that the people in Munich are reacting with such vehemence. Maybe we have lost touch with the public; I often wonder about that. But I ask myself even more frequently whether all these people are simply blind because they cannot even see the honest attempt to produce art!"[51]
Marc was also troubled because Kandinsky indicated that he was annoyed with him. In a letter dated March 22, 1912, Marc justifies himself towards his friend: "You seem cross and are making a mountain out of a molehill – forgive the expression and do not think that I am not taking your letter seriously, or that I am pretending there is nothing wrong. I personally do not feel anything of the changed tone which you claim I am using towards you. You even emphasize at the beginning specifically that it is not necessary for us

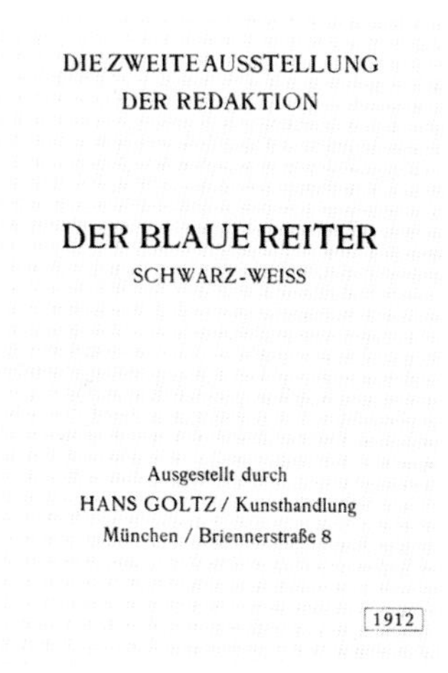
DIE ZWEITE AUSSTELLUNG
DER REDAKTION

DER BLAUE REITER
SCHWARZ-WEISS

Ausgestellt durch
HANS GOLTZ / Kunsthandlung
München / Briennerstraße 8

1912

Cover page of the Blue Rider exhibition catalogue of 1912

Right Page:

Albert Bloch
PRIZE FIGHT,
c. 1912/1913

always to be of the same opinion. [...] However, in a relationship of this nature our working together is based on mutual trust – trust in the quality of the other; as far as I am concerned, at any rate, this trust remains unshaken." Then he comes to the point: "You admit that you often don't like to say anything and that afterwards you always regret your compliance – here I can only think of a single case – my assessment of the Brücke. [...] As regards Heckel, Kirchner, and Pechstein (and especially Heckel), in the end our opinions really do differ, but is that a tragedy? I see it as an incentive, and certainly not as a dead end." He then describes other possible reasons for the bad blood between the two of them: "[...] that I do not regard Schönberg as a painter with the same appreciation and love as you do – maybe I will one day, but I won't do it to order. And the same applies to Fräulein Münter's current works."[52]

These are candid statements! We can imagine that they made a deep impression on the sensitive Kandinsky; there is no record of a written reply. The fact remains, however, that the two friends were able to put their differences of opinion to one side, and that the joint plans and joint work continued.

THE SONDERBUND AND STURM

In May 1912 the Munich artists took part in the international art exhibition of the Sonderbund westdeutscher Kunstfreunde und Künstler (Separate League of West German Art Lovers and Artists) in Cologne, the most comprehensive and important exhibition of the international avant-garde before the First World War. More than 600 works were shown in 29 rooms; for the first time in Germany it was possible to study large numbers of works by Vincent van Gogh, Paul Cézanne, Paul Gauguin, Pablo Picasso, Henri Matisse, Georges Braque, André Derain, Piet Mondrian, Ferdinand Hodler, Oskar Kokoschka, Egon Schiele, Edvard Munch, and others. The members of the Brücke artists' association, and some of the artists in the group surrounding the Blue Rider – including Wassily Kandinsky, Franz Marc, and Alexej von Jawlensky – were represented. However, they were not satisfied with the result, because they were not permitted to exhibit as a single group and some of the pictures they submitted were rejected by the jury.

Title page for the catalogue for the Blue Rider exhibition at the Sturm gallery, 1912

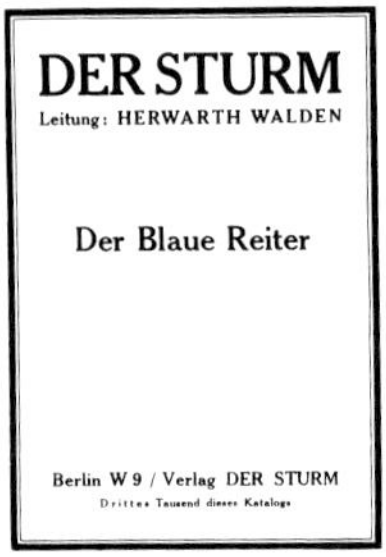
DER STURM
Leitung: HERWARTH WALDEN

Der Blaue Reiter

Berlin W 9 / Verlag DER STURM
Drittes Tausend dieses Katalogs

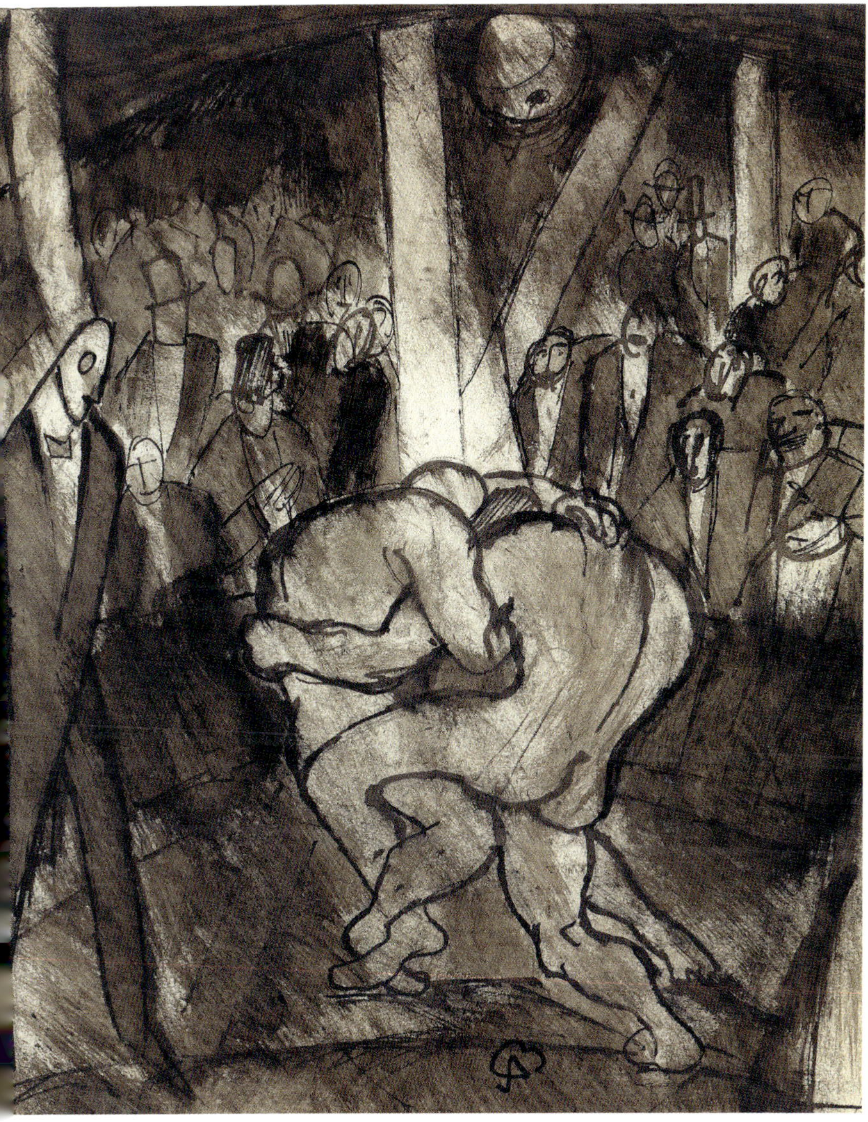

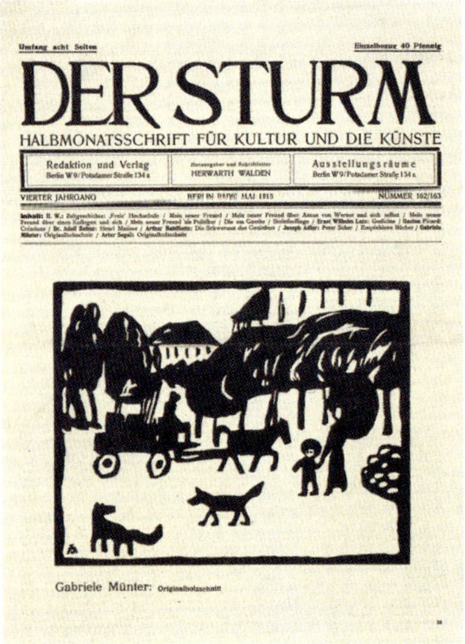

Umfang acht Seiten

Einzelbezug 40 Pfennig

DER STURM

HALBMONATSSCHRIFT FÜR KULTUR UND DIE KÜNSTE

Redaktion und Verlag
Berlin W 9/Potsdamer Straße 134 a

Herausgeber und Schriftleiter
HERWARTH WALDEN

Ausstellungsräume
Berlin W 9/Potsdamer Straße 134 a

VIERTER JAHRGANG

MAI 1913

NUMMER 162/163

Gabriele Münter: Originalholzschnitt

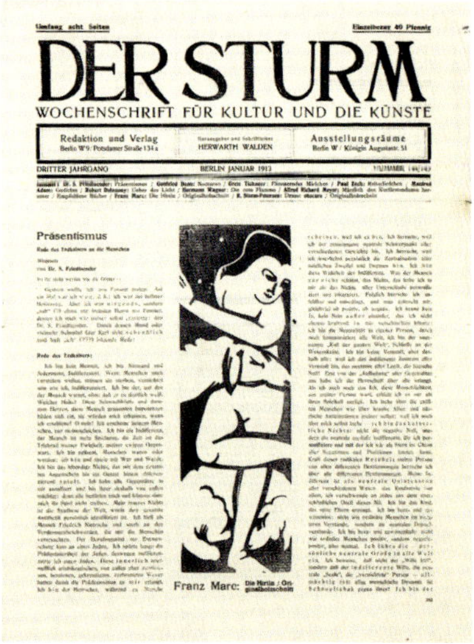

Umfang acht Seiten

Einzelbezug 40 Pfennig

DER STURM

WOCHENSCHRIFT FÜR KULTUR UND DIE KÜNSTE

Redaktion und Verlag
Berlin W 9/Potsdamer Straße 134 a

HERWARTH WALDEN

Ausstellungsräume

DRITTER JAHRGANG

BERLIN JANUAR 1913

Präsentismus

Franz Marc: Originalholzschnitt

Left:

Gabriele Münter,
Woodcut for the cover of the periodical *Der Sturm*, May 1913

Right:

Franz Marc,
Woodcut for the cover of the periodical *Der Sturm*, January 1913

It was decided – following the French model of the Salon des Refusés – to stage an exhibition by the artists who had been rejected by the Sonderbund, the "refused ones." The exhibition was to be held in the *Sturm* gallery in Berlin. Since 1910 the musician, critic, and journalist Herwarth Walden had published the magazine *Der Sturm*. His first wife, Else Lasker-Schüler, was one of the main contributors. She established and maintained friendships with writers, actors, and also a large number of artists, including Franz Marc. The artist's postcards, which she signed "Prince Jussuf" and addressed to "My Dear Blue Rider" [Franz Marc], are among the loveliest and most intimate records of a friendship between artists during the Expressionist era.[53] Herwarth Walden (1878–1941) belonged to a Jewish family living in Berlin – his real name was Georg Lewin – but had little contact with his relations. The painter Nell Walden, his second wife, wrote: "He never felt himself to be a Jew, but he did not see himself as a German either. He loved Berlin, not because he was born there, but rather because he liked the way the Berliners were."[54]

A clear expression of his affinity with art – inspired by Nell Walden – was the founding of his Sturm gallery, which opened in June 1912 with the exhibition *The Blue Rider*. On March 1, 1912, Franz Marc wrote to his friend August Macke: "Yesterday we were thrown into confusion by a sudden invitation from the Sturm-Redaktion, which requested us (at their cost) to send the Blue Rider collection from Cologne to Berlin for an exhibition which the editorial team will be putting on from March 12 in a rented villa at Tiergartenstrasse 34a, mainly with Kokoschka and some young French artists. After thinking about it for a while and exchanging telegrams with Kandinsky, I finally agreed [...] Now you must at all costs give us something good, a largish work if possible, so that the three of us in particular [Kandinsky, Marc, and Macke] are extensively and well represented."[55] Marianne von Werefkin, Alexej von Jawlensky, and Paul Klee also took part and thus became still more closely involved in the Blue Rider.

THE FIRST GERMAN AUTUMN SALON 1913

"Seen through the perspective of history, today it is beyond doubt that the First German Autumn Salon in 1913 was a beacon for twentieth-century art."[56] Herwarth Walden demonstrated not only an admirable instinct for sensing quality within the avant-garde art scene of the time, but also proved himself to be a skilled organizer. He succeeded in bringing together artists, writers, patrons, and his own many-sided activities to form a widely branching and highly effective network. Seventy-five artists from twelve countries took part in the Autumn Salon at the Sturm gallery, exhibiting more than 300 works. However, Walden turned down the request of Marc and Kandinsky to present their works and those of their artist friends together as the artists' group the Blue Rider within the exhibition. His main concern was the international philosophy of his gallery and he was not prepared to permit any independent approaches by a group of artists which might compromise his independence. He was also aware of the disagreements between the Munich artists and the gallery owner Paul Cassirer and the influential art critic Julius Meier-Graefe, who in a lecture in Munich had described the Blue Rider artists as "business-minded." That was harsh but accurate inasmuch as Kandinsky in particular knew very well how to organize the business interests of the group and how to represent them. Thus on March 4, 1912, in a letter to Arnold Schönberg he claimed: "I should really like to travel to Prague for the concert, but how could I have done so – I, a poor slave of the Blue Rider. Day after day is spent completely attending to it: book, exhibitions, etc; I have no time for anything else [...] If only you knew how I long to get back to my work, how I should like to draw, draw, draw, paint, paint, paint." Then he pushes his complaints to one side: "But that is enough sentiment; let's get down to serious business. Der Sturm is putting on what promises to be a really fantastic exhibition (French artists, Hodler, Munch, Kokoschka), and it has invited our first exhibition as a whole: freight, own rooms. We have accepted."[57]

Within the Blue Rider there were also tensions and differences of opinion, especially between Kandinsky and Macke. As an "accompaniment" to the Autumn Salon, so to speak, the Rhineland artist painted a watercolor in which he made fun of the group in a satirical

August Macke
SATIRE ON THE BLUE RIDER, 1913

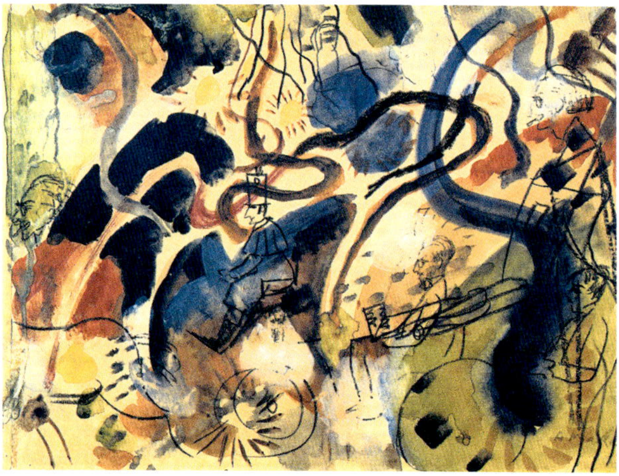

manner by making a clear reference to the language of forms in Kandinsky's painting *Composition V* – the "founding picture" of the Blue Rider. It shows "Franz Marc on the coachman's seat [...] Kandinsky sitting elegantly in the coach, and behind the nervous profile of Herwarth Walden, but with Macke himself small and insignificant at the edge of the picture."[58] (above).

Nonetheless, Macke still felt himself to be closely linked to the Blue Rider as an artist, and he also clearly recognized the importance of the Autumn Salon for the further development of modern art. In a later dated October 16, 1913, he consoles his wife Elisabeth's uncle, Bernhard Koehler, a staunch supporter of the Blue Rider, who had

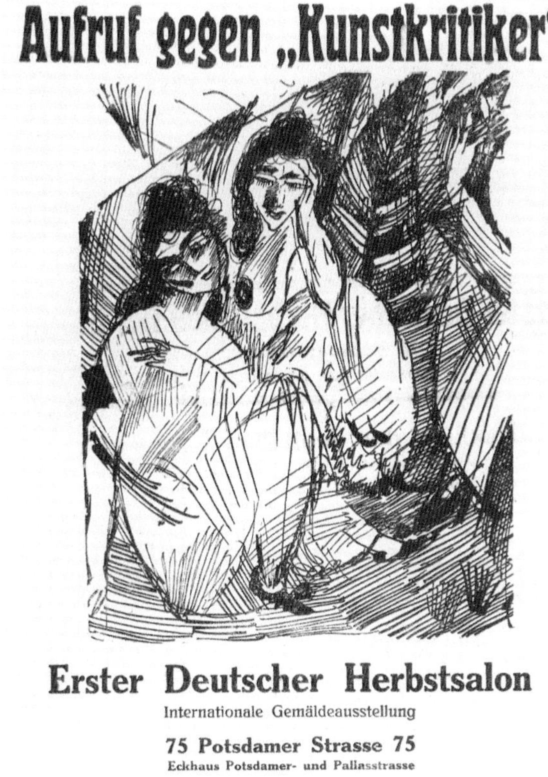

Title page of the leaflet *Aufruf gegen Kunstkritiker* [*Appeal against Art Critics*]

indicated his horror at the rejection of the Autumn Salon in the official media. "In your letter I can detect a quiet bitterness at the evils of the world, which I can well understand. It is simply incomprehensible to me how a city like Berlin can behave in this manner towards such an event. I see things as follows: Walden is a very naive person on the one hand, who always wants to rush in on behalf of what is right and who actually then does so. But the motivation of others allows them to laugh at his behavior, they are annoyed, and feel themselves impeded in their work by methods which are nothing less than inspirational. He will always have most of the art world against him, because they are not prepared to allow him to be right ... I

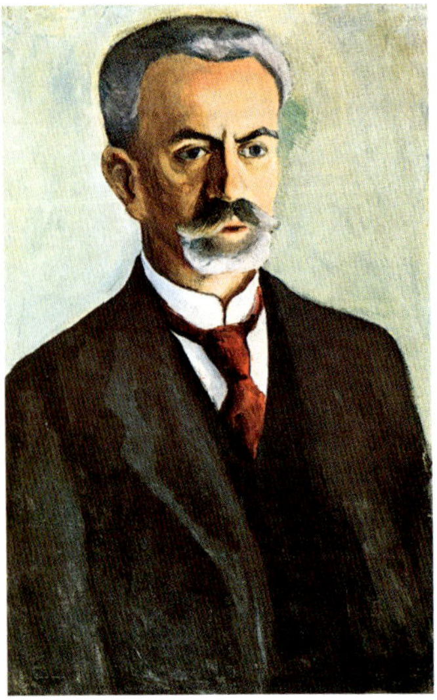

August Macke
PORTRAIT OF BERNHARD KOEHLER, 1910

have a moral hangover, because I advised you to do something that has proved more of a financial burden for you than I or anyone else could possibly have guessed. And yet, wait until the exhibition is over; then people are bound to think of the entire affair with pleasure and will no longer remember which members of Berlin's society did not attend. People will think instead that it was an important event in our brief lives. The worst thing of all, and what annoys us most of all, is that one can lose so much optimism, which is so positive and so justified, and for which these bastards, this wretched rabble of journalists, show so much contempt. Under no circumstances should one allow art and optimism, which is linked to pure art, to be determined by money matters. Art is life, and life is something that we should never – indeed we never can – buy and sell."[59]

PUBLISHING PLANS

For Franz Marc the continuation of the almanac was a matter of great importance. He discussed its possible content with Kandinsky and started to work on the foreword. But Kandinsky hesitated and could not find the topic that would rouse interest, complaining that there were no important new pictures. As the introduction of the art of the primitive peoples and naive painting had already occurred in the first almanac, he now searched for new ways of widening the scope of his search to find support for his doctrine of the "inner necessity" of art. He suggested going "to the very borders of kitsch" and portraying fairground painting and similar works. And in a letter to Franz Marc dated May 14, 1912, he wrote: "In this respect my egoistic wish is that I may retain a certain amount of time (at least the summer) in order to allow my further thoughts to mature. I am completely out of the routine!"[60] Marc suggested publishing panel paintings from the Orthodox monasteries on Mount Athos; to this day only men are allowed to set foot there.
In 1906 he had gone on a pilgrimage to the Holy Mountain together with his brother Paul and had been deeply impressed by the

medieval monasteries and their art treasures. Kandinsky continued to react in a non-committal way to Marc's activities. Marc finally drew his own conclusions, writing to August Macke: "It is there [in Ried on the Kochelsee, where Marc lived] that the birth of the second Blue Rider volume will take place – laugh if you like; it really will! I'm sitting over it like a broody hen; I shall publish this second volume alone, that is to say with helpers, of course, among whom I hope I can include you. And then Kandinsky will take over a later one. This division of work is the only way of continuing with the volumes and producing something uniform."[61] But the second and third volume of the almanac would never be published; the outbreak of the First World War put an end to all publishing ideas.

These also included a project which Franz Marc had supported very actively: a work with texts from the Bible, illustrated by artists of the Blue Rider and some painter friends, consisting of six individual volumes "so that we do not run out of steam on one of the volumes."[62] As a precaution, Marc the diligent publisher determined the format as 23 x 30 cm (9 x 11.8 in.) and decreed that all the pictures should be portrait format, so that readers would not have to turn a book on its side in order to see an image. Paul Klee wanted to work on the Psalms, Kubin was to produce drawings to illustrate the Book of Daniel, and Kandinsky's topic was the Apocalypse. Oskar Kokoschka selected for his subject the Book of Job, and Erich Heckel chose

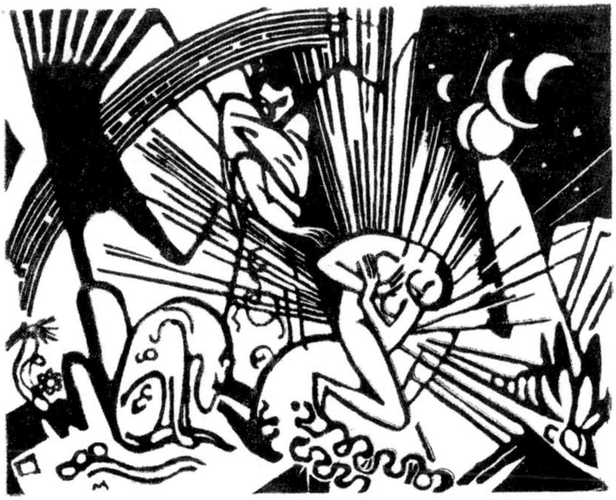

Franz Marc
RECONCILIATION, 1912

the Gospels. Marc himself wanted to work on the First Book of Moses. But work progressed very slowly, and only Kubin announced, at the end of June 1914, that he had finished working on the "Prophet." In fact, the work was never finished. Franz Marc's last written report reached the publisher, Reinhard Piper, in September 1914: "After I, too, have been called up, all the work on the Bible will have to be put on one side – who knows how long the "interval in art" will be."[63]

From 1912 until 1914 the young writer Hugo Ball (1886–1927) worked at the Münchner Kammerspiele theater. He felt an affinity with the artists of the Blue Rider, especially Kandinsky. Together they planned to perform Expressionist dramatic art in Munich and to publish a sort of sequel to the almanac entitled *Das Neue Theater [The New Theater]*, a book which was to be devoted entirely to the synthesis of drama and fine art. Hugo Ball – whose first and only play, *Die Nase des Michelangelo [Michelangelo's Nose]*, was published in 1910 by Reclam, also had ideas of founding an international society for new art, which was to further drama, painting, music, and dance equally. He agreed with Piper Verlag that a book entitled *Expressionistische Theaterkunst (Expressionist Dramatic Art)* would be published, on which the revered Kandinsky, as well as Marc and Kokoschka, were to co-operate. The German Empire's declaration of war on Russia on August 1, 1914, put an end to all these fine plans.

Wassily Kandinsky
LARGE RESURRECTION, 1911

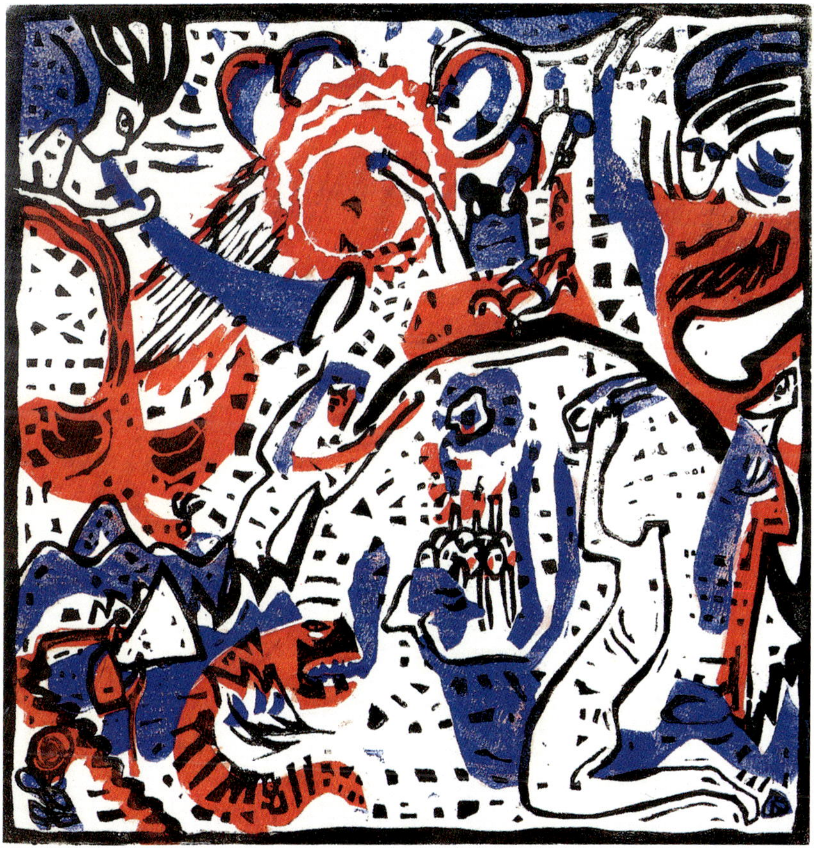

6. INNOVATIONS

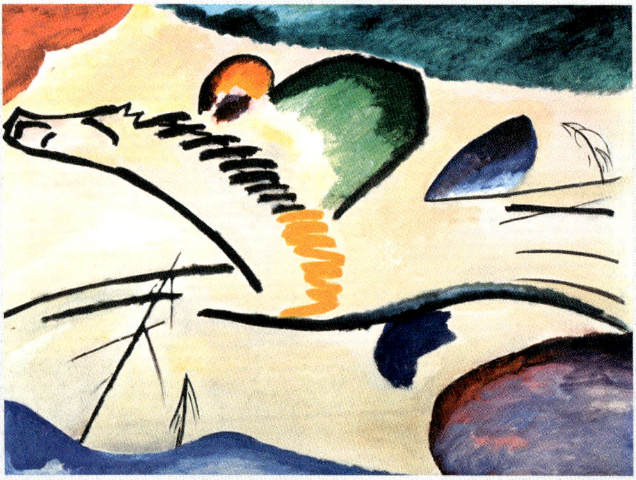

Wassily Kandinsky, *Lyrical*, 1911

THE PRIMACY OF THE SPIRITUAL AND THE DEVELOPMENT OF A CULTURAL THEORY

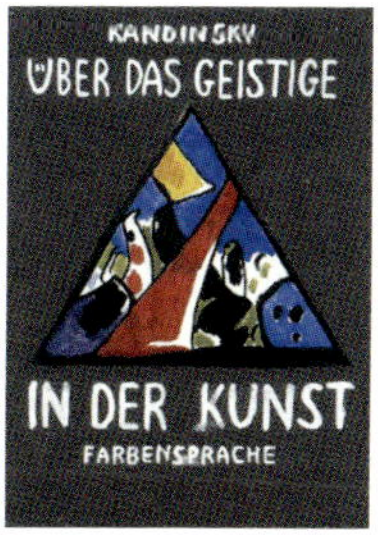

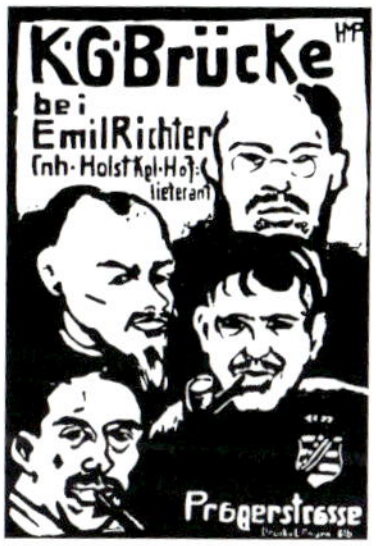

Wassily Kandinsky, Cover design for *On the Spiritual in Art*, c. 1910

Hermann Max Pechstein, Poster for the exhibition of the artists' association the Brücke in the Galerie Richter, 1908

There were two main currents in German Expressionism which represented very different approaches to the theory of art, although they were, artistically speaking, on a comparable level. The Brücke was established in Dresden and Berlin, the Blue Rider in Munich. In their aim – to bring about a fundamental renewal of art – they were definitely in agreement, but the two groups made different assumptions and went different ways.

The program of the Brücke was contained in a few sentences: "In the belief in development, in a new generation of those who create and those who enjoy, we call together the youth of today. As the youth who will be responsible for the future, we want to create for ourselves freedom of movement and freedom in life compared with the complacent older powers. Everyone belongs to us who reproduces directly and authentically that which drives them to be creative."[64] The Brücke was a true artists' association which survived for for several years. They spent a lot of time together and painted and drew together, for example beside the Moritzburg Lakes near Dresden. In the conversations and writings of Erich Heckel, Ernst Ludwig Kirchner, Otto Mueller, Emil Nolde, Max Pechstein, and Karl Schmidt-Rottluff, it was not so much a question of philosophical concepts or questions of art theory, but more a matter of motifs and subjects for pictures from everyday life, and also issues of picture design. In their approach to art four main subject complexes predominate: the human figure, usually female and naked; expressive portraits (such as Kirchner's *Self-Portrait* of 1906); landscapes, especially townscapes in all their facets; and the representation of social life, with strongly socio-critical tendencies. Of course these subjects imply the retention of representational art. Abstraction can be found here only in the sense of the simplification of forms and the intensification of expression. The artists' styles converged to a large extent; in the field of prints this effect was heightened above all because they chose to work with the relief printing techniques of woodcuts and lino cuts, which generally have bold effects.

The attitudes which Wassily Kandinsky and Franz Marc expressed in their almanac *Der Blaue Reiter* represent the very opposite view. "He [Kandinsky] confronted the feeling for reality in the works of the

Brücke artists [...] with the freeing of the soul from all references to reality. The only guideline for the artist is the 'inner necessity' [...] Here the ancestral history reached back much further than that of the Brücke artists. It extends from Russian folk art to the French naive painters and includes old Bavarian glass painting as well as Egyptian shadow puppets. [...] Anyway, it is just as impossible to speak of stylistic agreement like that found in the case of the artists of the Brücke, as it is to talk of an agreement over the choice of subject. In view of this fact, we are justified in asking the question as to exactly what it was that linked the artists of the Blue Rider. To a greater or lesser degree they all aimed at the spiritual in art, but at the same time their views as to how it was to be realized diverged greatly. So the program of abstraction was drawn up in a very different way in Kandinsky's work than it was, for example, in Klee's metamorphoses and in Marc's animal meditations. We experience a very different re-structuring of the world of things [...] until they are entirely dematerialized [...] This wide palette of artistic conceptions of form, which were achieved within the space of a few years, not least through a broad range of foreign influences [...] lends the south German group its specific character."[65] And more than that: only in the deliberate internationalism of the group and the constant study of the spiritual dimension of art, only through the (at least theoretical) surmounting of the barriers between the genres in art, theater, and music was it possible to succeed in the most important step in the continued development of painting during the twentieth century: the complete overcoming of representationalism in painting.

PATHS TOWARDS ABSTRACTION

As early as 1912 Kandinsky had astutely formulated the prerequisites for a new art and his path toward achieving it. "In general, therefore, color is a means of exerting a direct influence on the soul. Color is the key and the eye is the hammer. The soul is the piano with its many strings. The artist is the hand, which through one key or another intentionally makes the human soul vibrate. And so it is clear that the harmony of colors can only be based on the principle of the intentional touching of the human soul. This basis should be designated as the principle of inner necessity."[66]

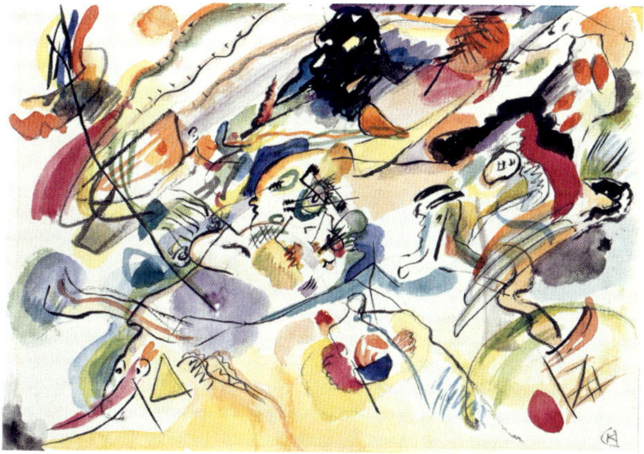

Wassily Kandinsky,
Study for
COMPOSITION VII,
1913

There follows a very detailed, at times a seemingly over-intellectual, study of the artistic principles with the help of which "inner necessity" can be expressed. "I have supplied reproductions of my pictures as examples of the new symphonic compositions, in which the melodic element is used only sometimes and as one of the subordinate aspects, but when it does so is given a new form. These reproductions are examples of three different sources of origin:

1. A direct impression derived from 'external nature,' which is expressed in the form of a drawing or painting. I call these pictures *Impressions;*
2. Mainly unconscious, largely suddenly created expressions of the processes of the inner character, in other words impressions derived from 'internal nature,' which I call *Improvisations;*
3. In a similar way (but especially slowly) expressions are formed in me which I then examine and work on for a long time, in an almost pedantic manner. This type of picture I call *Compositions*. Here reason, consciousness, and intention, the purposeful, play the dominant role."[67]

With these three examples Kandinsky described very precisely his creative process. In fact virtually all his pictures from the pre-war period can be allocated to one of these rubrics, though in the nature of things there are more cases of doubt than there are clear allocations. Although Kandinsky was an artistic intellectual who possessed

Next page:

Franz Marc
FIGHTING FORMS (ABSTRACT FORMS I),
1914

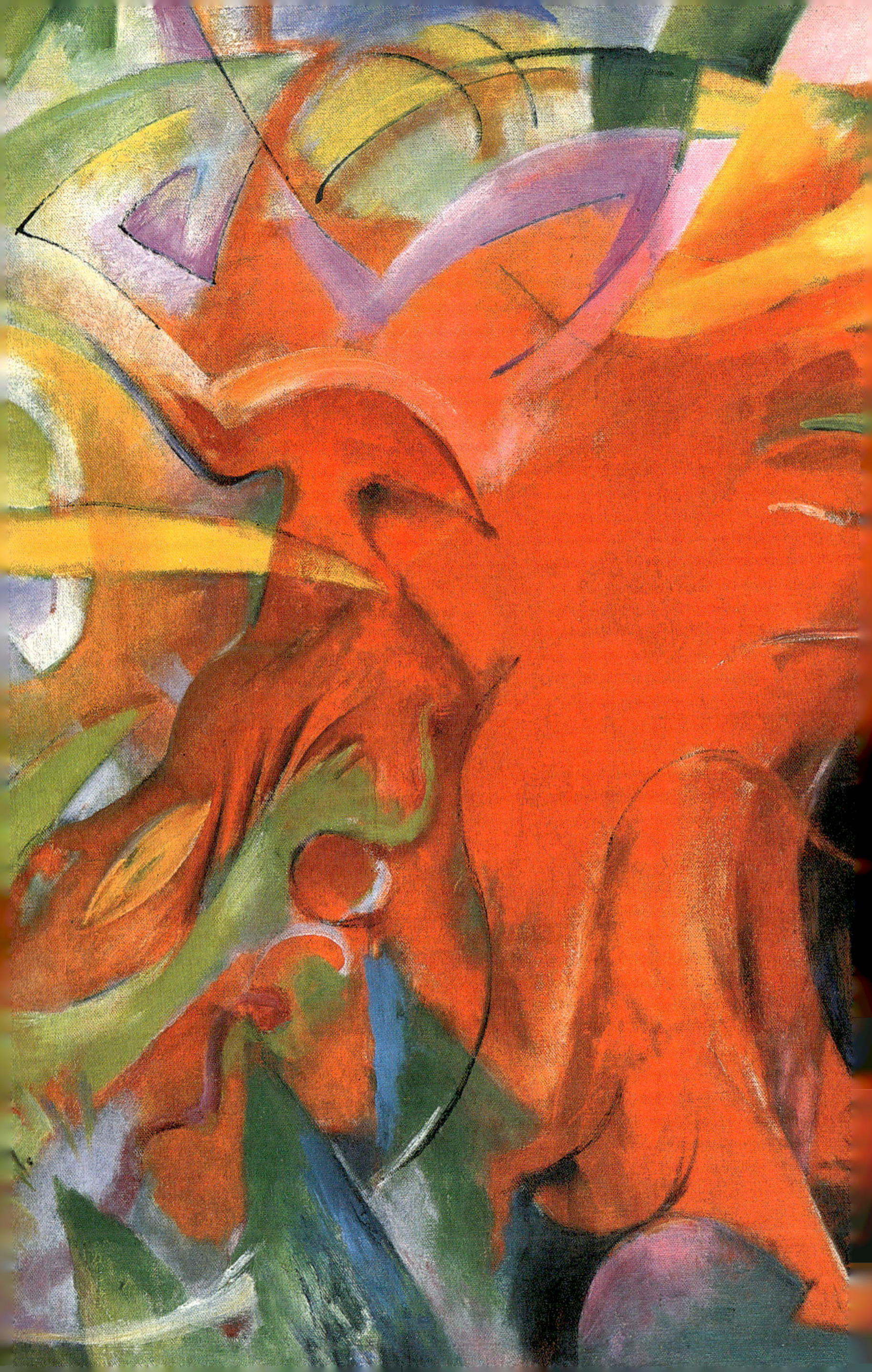

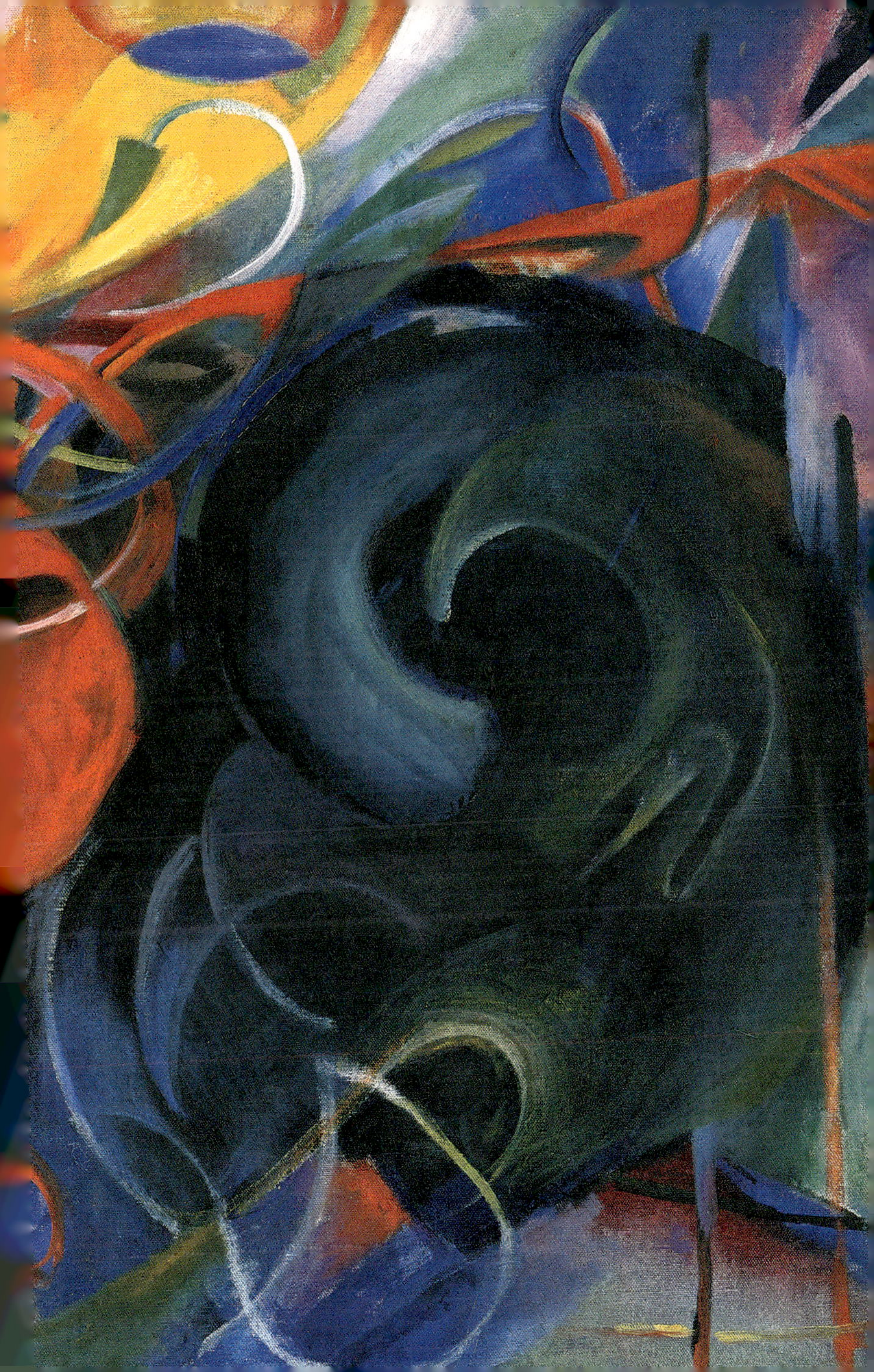

Wassily Kandinsky
UNTITLED (FIRST ABSTRACT WATER-COLOR), 1910

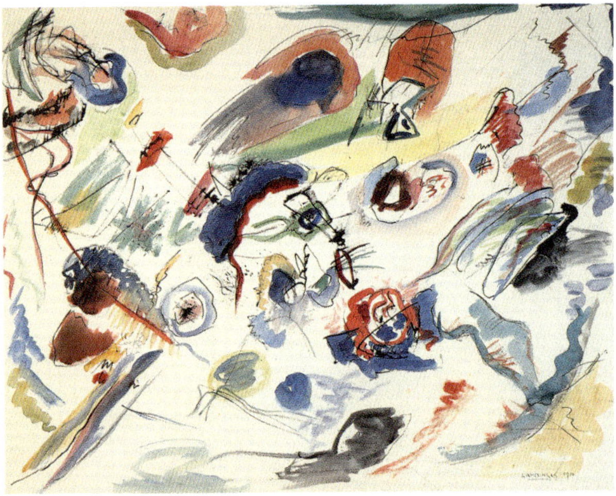

a highly developed sense of order, he is far removed from painting according to a set scheme. This characteristic will only emerge during the late works of the 1920s and 1930s.
Kandinsky was a painter, and his paintings during the years 1908–1912 are of epochal significance. They would have been that too if he had never published his thoughts. However, with the publication of his works on art theory he underlined his claim to leadership in the process of artistic renewal.
In various statements from a later time Kandinsky explained that he had effected his transition to abstraction through three steps: "the overcoming of perspective, the transfer of graphic elements into oil painting, and the freeing of color from its role describing objects."[68]

SYNESTHESIA AND CHROMATIC HARMONY

Kandinsky's affinity with music and his attempt to understand music and painting as essentially similar, as two arts which can be fused together, goes back to his Moscow years. He loved the music of Richard Wagner and remembered a particular evening mood in Moscow: "*Lohengrin* seemed to me to be a perfect realization of this Moscow. The violins, the deep bass notes, and above all the bass instruments embodied for me at that time the full power of the early evening hour. I saw all my colors in my mind's eye; they stood before my eyes. Wild, almost insane lines were drawn before me [...] But suddenly it was clear to me that art in general is much more powerful than I had thought it was, and that on the other hand painting could develop the same powers as music possesses."[69] Kandinsky was firmly convinced that it was possible to hear colors and developed a system that allocated the primary colors to individual instruments. A key picture in these endeavors is *Impression III (Concert)* of 1911. It was created after attending a concert of Schönberg's works that filled Kandinsky with inspiration. Strong, brilliant colors dominate the picture, especially yellow and black. The black shape still recalls a grand piano, but the picture is the translation of Schönberg's music into painting.[70]

THE YELLOW SOUND

But painting music was not Kandinsky's sole aim; he wanted to achieve nothing less than the creation of a total work of art of a completely new kind that would unite painting, music, language, movement, and dance. He not only referred to this concept several times in his theoretical writings, he also developed several "stage compositions," the most famous of which he called *The Yellow Sound.* In it he was even further ahead of his time than he was in his painting. Admittedly there are still people on stage (shadowy figures, five giants, people in flowing robes, etc.) but there is no continuous plot based on logic, and no dialogue which could explain this. Instead, all means which the stage has to offer are employed, feelings and associations aroused, and "mysterious things are said by mysterious events," moods are created and emotions triggered. Colored light, blue mist, pictorial elements (large yellow flower), movement and singing by individual figures and by the choir, incomprehensible onomatopoeia ... a century ago it was an atrocity, a boundless provocation. Today we are used to these complex art forms, which we refer to under the name "performance."

Wassily Kandinsky,
The Yellow Sound, 1912

DER GELBE KLANG

Eine Bühnenkomposition[1])

Mitwirkende:

Fünf Riesen

*

Undeutliche Wesen

*

Tenor
(hinter der Bühne)

*

Ein Kind

*

Ein Mann

*

Menschen im losen Gewand

*

Menschen in Trikots

*

Chor
(hinter der Bühne)

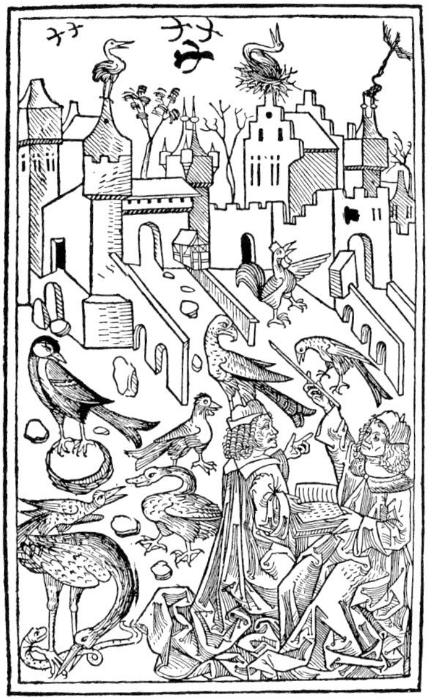

[1]) Der musikalische Teil wurde von Thomas v. Hartmann übernommen.

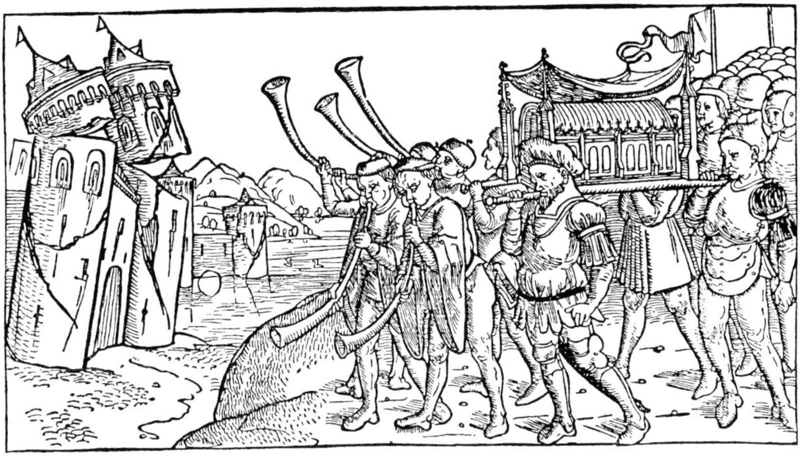

EINLEITUNG

Im Orchester einige unbestimmte Akkorde.

V o r h a n g.

Auf der Bühne dunkelblaue Dämmerung, die erst weisslich ist und später intensiv dunkelblau wird. Nach einer Zeit wird in der Mitte ein kleines Licht sichtbar, welches mit der Vertiefung der Farbe heller wird. Nach einer Zeit Orchestermusik. Pause.

Hinter der Bühne wird ein Chor hörbar, welcher so eingerichtet werden muss, dass die Quelle des Gesanges nicht zu erkennen ist. Hauptsächlich sind die Bassstimmen zu hören. Das Singen ist gleichmässig, ohne Temperament, mit Unterbrechungen, die durch Punkte bezeichnet sind.

7. RECEPTION AFTER 1918

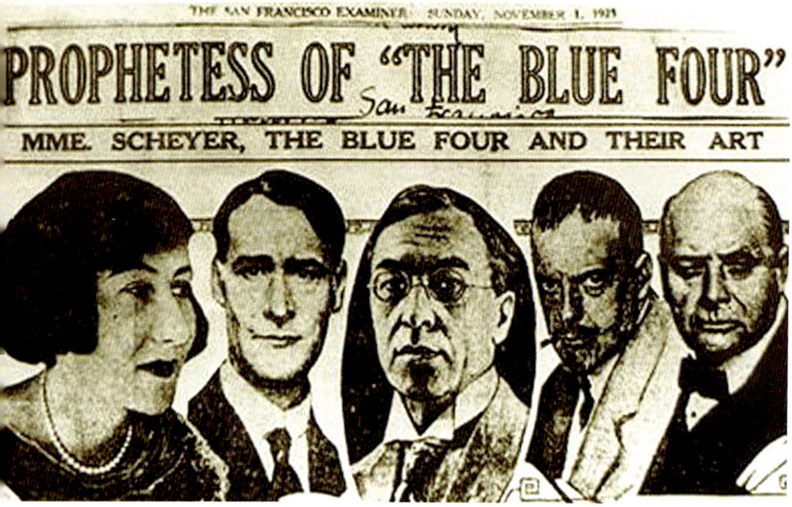

"Prophetess of 'The Blue Four'," 1925
L. to r.: Galka Scheyer, Lyonel Feininger, Wassily Kandinsky, Paul Klee, Alexej von Jawlensky

After the end of the cataclysm of war the economic situation in Germany changed overnight. "The Empire collapsed like a house of cards. It left behind a scene of devastation, not only on the battlefields [...] but also in the hopes and expectations of a nation that for four years had clung to the deceptive illusion of a future Germany with the status of a great power and that now stood facing a heap of shards."[71] This also applied, of course, to the arts and cultural scene. Revolutionary groups of artists formed, such as the Novembergruppe (November Group) in Berlin; class warfare and social criticism were the order of the day. But the conservatives organized themselves again, too, and between them lay a wide range of people searching for meaning in a demoralized society. The Bauhaus in Weimar, founded by Walter Gropius in 1919, presented itself as modern and forward looking, willing to try out new things. It demanded that people look to the past, but to traditional crafts rather than outdated, reactionary forms of art. "Holistic" and "sustainable" would be the modern expressions for the work of the Bauhaus, which not only propagated but also realized a synthesis of architecture, fine art, applied art, and crafts.[72]

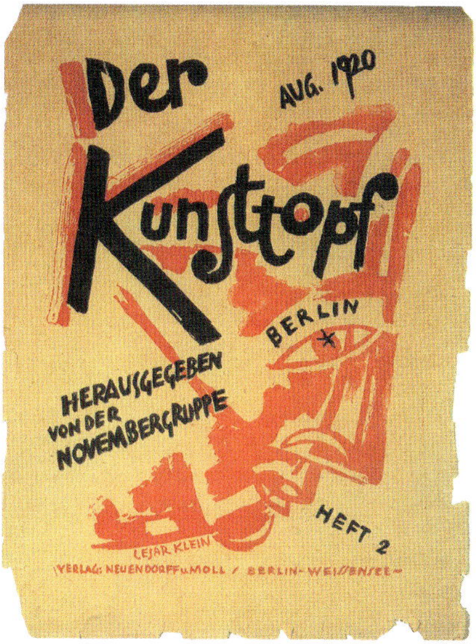

Cover of the magazine *Der Kunsttopf*, César Klein, August 1920

And so it is not surprising that two former members of the Blue Rider were to be found among the teaching staff at the Bauhaus: Wassily Kandinsky and Paul Klee. There was also an attempt to revive the Blue Rider as a group. In 1924, on the initiative of the gallery owner and painter Galka Scheyer, the artists Kandinsky, Klee, Feininger, and Jawlensky founded the group the Blue Four. Although numerous exhibitions took place, especially in the United States, the artists failed to take over where the pre-war successes of the Blue Rider had left off.

The proclamation of Adolf Hitler as Chancellor of the German Reich by President Paul von Hindenburg in 1933 marked the end of the republic and cleared the path for the National Socialists and their reign of terror.

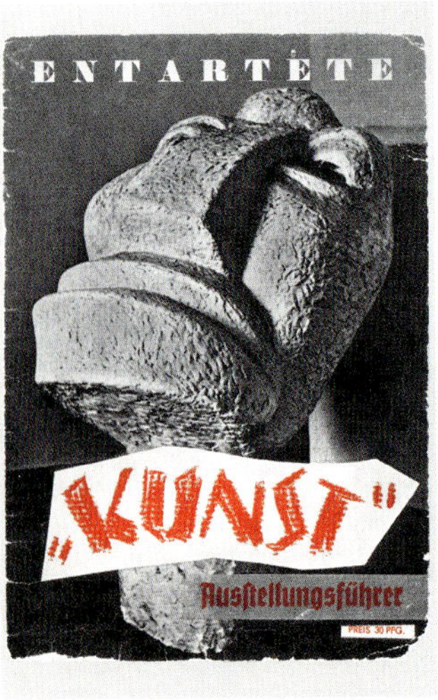

Cover of the guide to the *Degenerate Art* exhibition, 1937

Race and ethnic community, the Fatherland, loyalty, and valor were now the watchwords to which everyone was subject. The book-burnings of 1933 and the exhibition *Entartete Kunst [Degenerate Art]* prescribed the course which literature and art were required to follow. The location of this infamous exhibition was the Galeriegebäude am Hofgarten in Munich (now the Deutsche Theatermuseum). It was held at the same time as the *Grosse deutsche Kunstausstellung [Great German Art Exhibition]*, which was opened on July 18, 1937, in the Haus der Deutsche Kunst zu München, and which formed, as it were, a contrasting program. The exhibition was divided up according to themes. The official exhibition catalogue of the exhibition made its purpose abundantly clear. "What is the aim of the exhibition *Degenerate Art?* At the start of a new era for the German people the exhibition aims by means of original examples to provide a general insight into the gruesome final chapter of the cultural decline of the most recent decades before the great change." The list of works in the exhibition sounds today like a who's who of German contemporary art during the twentieth century.[73] The artists of the Blue Rider were represented. Kandinsky's works were shown with a scornful comment attached: "Mad at any price: works by Kandinsky, a teacher at the communist Bauhaus in Dessau until 1933." Works by Heinrich Campendonk, Alexej von Jawlensky, Paul Klee and Franz Marc (who was still categorized as "dangerous," even though he had already been dead for twenty-one years) were also on show. There was so much hatred to be seen here! And what a sense of satisfaction it must have given the survivors that the Blue Rider was honored with an exhibition in the Haus der Kunst in Munich as early as 1949. Important stages in the rehabilitation and fitting presentation of the Blue Rider were provided by Gabriele Münter's donation to the Städtische Galerie im Lenbachhaus in 1957 of numerous pictures by Kandinsky and by herself; by the Bernhard Koehler Foundation of 1965; by the founding of the Gabriele Münter and Johannes Eichner Foundation in 1966; and by the acquisition of the Kubin archive of the Hamburg collector Kurt Otte in 1971.

This made the Lenbachhaus *the* institution for the research into and care and presentation of the Blue Rider (see p. 157).
To mark Kandinsky's one hundredth birthday, Will Grohmann, the indefatigable champion of abstract art, delivered a celebratory lecture on December 4, 1966, in Berlin, in the presence of Nina Kandinsky, which he ended as follows: "Kandinsky always believed in the future of his works, and no rejection was ever able to make him doubt this. We are happy that you at least, dear Frau Kandinsky, are able to witness what Kandinsky hoped for in the happiest moments of his life: that the world would comprehend his pictures, and that their significance would not be restricted to their artistic merit alone. Art like Kandinsky's is one of the fundamentals of our existence."[74] This assessment can surely be applied to all the artists of the Blue Rider.

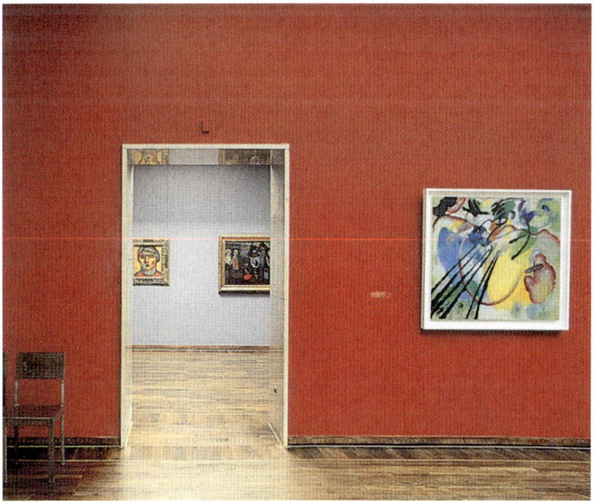

Städtische Galerie im Lenbachhaus, Munich. View of Room 25 showing a work by Kandinsky, and of Room 24 with works by Jawlenksy and Münter

8. DISCOVERIES

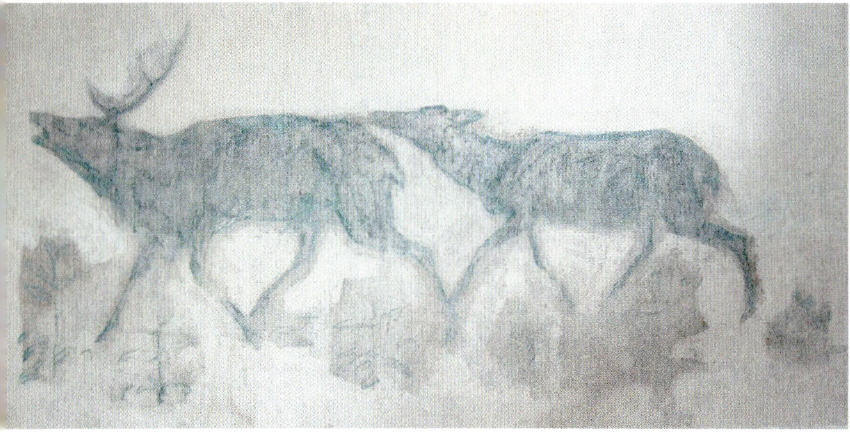

Staffelalm beneath the Rabenkopf with a wall painting by Franz Marc

MUNICH

STÄDTISCHE GALERIE IM LENBACHHAUS

Luisenstrasse 33
80333 München
Tel.: +49 (0) 89 233 32 00 0

In 1885, Franz von Lenbach wrote in a letter: "I am thinking of building myself a palazzo which will put everything to date in the shade; in it, the powerful centers of great European art should be linked with the present."[75]

This Tuscan-style villa, built between 1887 and 1891, was designed by Gabriel von Seidl, a famous German architect of the time. The result was an architectural jewel, distinguished and yet intimate, bright and filled with Southern flair. The master painter's former living accommodation on the upper floor gives a hint of the glamour of the nineteenth-century Gründerzeit (period of prosperity), as do the lovely gardens, which are framed by the three wings of the house and are open to visitors.

The highlights of the collection, which extends from the nineteenth century to the present day, are and remain the works of the Blue Rider and the circle surrounding it. Helmut Friedel rearranged the collection in 1994, since when the pictures have been hung on brightly colored walls, as they did in some cases during the original exhibitions of the artists' group. With this bold and justified decision, however, the director of the museum started a veritable avalanche: today there is hardly an exhibition that is not hung on brightly colored walls, whether it suits the works or not!

In the colorful world of the Blue Rider, we are quite justified in speaking of "icons" in the modern sense. Wassily Kandinsky's "key picture," *Impression III* of 1911, his *Study for Composition VII* of 1913, and his *Improvisation Klamm* of 1914 are representatives of the three design principles which Kandinsky claims to have followed during the years 1911–1914 (see p. 145). Gabriele Münter's early landscapes are just as impressive as her dark still lifes and the graveyard crosses. Franz Marc is

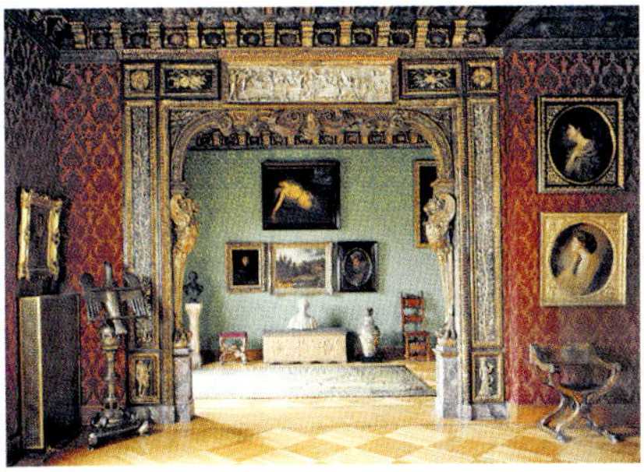

The historical rooms in the Lenbach Villa

View of the Kandinsky room 25 and of Room 24

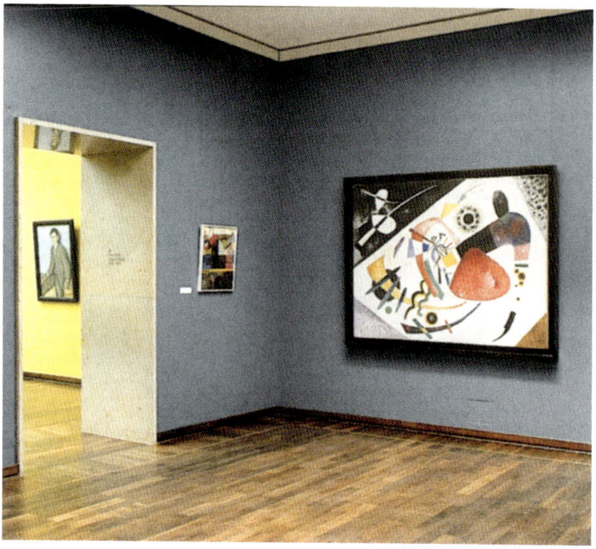

represented by some brilliant pictures which have become immensely popular: *Blue Horse* of 1911, *The Tiger* of 1912, and *The Yellow Cow* of 1911.

The suggestive expression of the dancer Alexander Sakharoff, painted by Alexej Jawlensky in 1909, is simply irresistible. And we should be just as happy to go for a walk in Paul Klee's *Rose Garden* as in August Macke's *Zoological Garden I*. You should allow at least two hours for this feast for the senses in this charmingly beautiful building, which one always leaves relaxed and happy.

But we must be patient. The rebuilding of the house according to the plans drawn up by Sir Norman Foster will not be completed until 2013. Let's hope that they are successful in linking together the historical and contemporary elements as planned, and that the building gains extra space and practicality without losing anything of its intimate atmosphere and individuality.

PHALANX SCHOOL

Hohenzollernstrasse 7a

Wassily Kandinsky was one of the principal founders of the art school, which was established in 1901. Most of the students were women, who at that time were still prohibited from taking part in classes at the Academy. One of them was Gabriele Münter, who attended a sculpture class under Wilhelm Hüsgen during the winter of 1901/02 which also included Wassily Kandinsky's "Abendakt" evening nude painting classes. The young student's admiration of her teacher was to have far-reaching consequences.

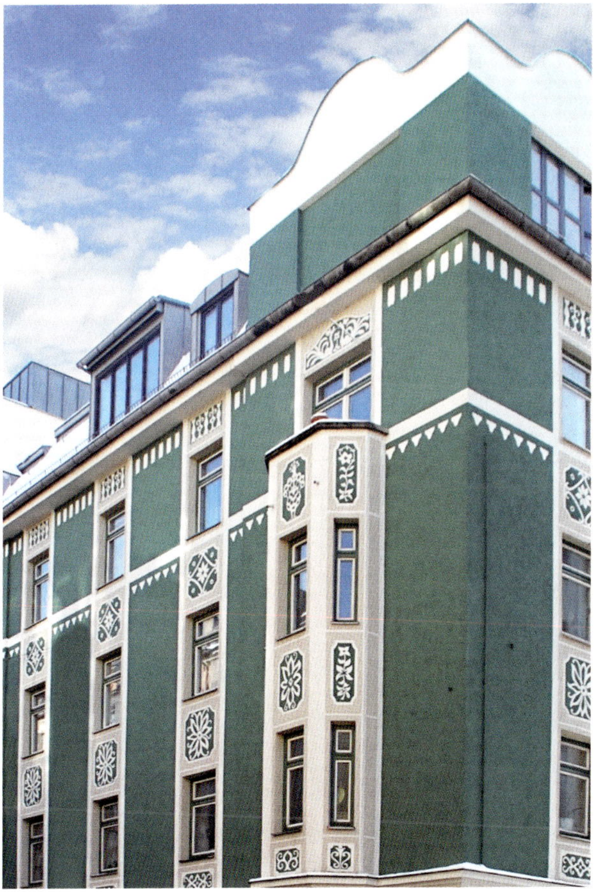

PHALANX EXHIBITIONS 1902-1904

Finkenstrasse 3

It was here that the group staged exhibitions of its own works and invited progressive artists to take part. Lovis Corinth, Claude Monet, Alfred Kubin, Paul Signac, Wilhelm Trübner, Felix Vallotton, Henri de Toulouse-Lautrec and Albert Weisgerber all showed their works here.

GALERIE THANNHAUSER

(Site of the First Exhibition of the New Artists' Association of Munich in 1909) Theatinerstrasse 7 (entrance on Maffeistrasse)

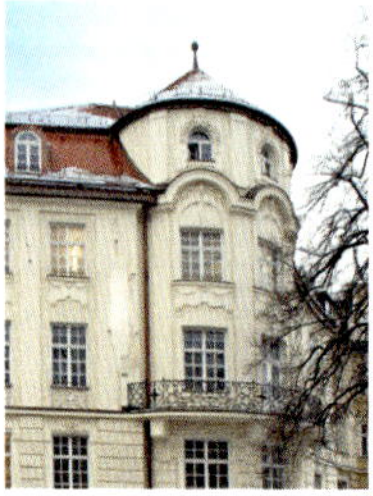

BRAKLS MODERNE KUNSTHANDLUNG

Goethestrasse 64

This was the location for the first major solo exhibition of Franz Marc's works in Munich in 1910. The Hungarian-born singer Franz Josef Brakl had been appointed director of the Gärtnerplatztheater in 1899. In 1905 he retired from active involvement with the theater and founded the Kunsthaus Brakl, which soon acquired a fine reputation. Franz Josef Brakl's gallery moved to Beethovenplatz 1 in 1913 and continued to operate until 1930.

KUNSTHANDLUNG GOLTZ

Brienner Strasse 8

The Buchhandlung Goltz, to this day a famous art bookshop with premises at Türkenstrasse 36, was a leading institution in the field of "modern art" in the years before the First World War in Munich. Its founder, Hans Goltz, was born on August 11, 1873, in Elbing in East Prussia. He learned the bookseller's trade in Bamberg and moved to Munich in 1904, where he founded a book and art shop in 1911 which became a remarkable center of art. It was here that *The Second Exhibition of the Editorial Team the Blue Rider Black-White* was held in 1912 (see p. 131).

In the same year, Goltz extended his business at the same location with the addition of the Galerie Neue Kunst on the second floor, which introduced the international avant-garde in more than 150 exhibitions.

Hans Goltz died unexpectedly in the fall of 1927 during a trip to the Oostal near Baden-Baden. The author Oskar Maria Graf paid him

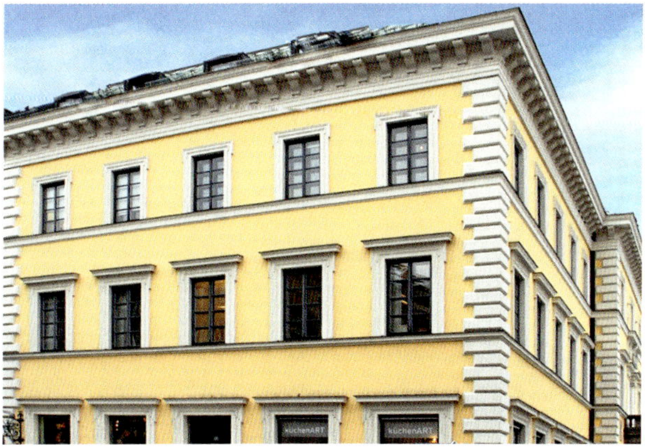

his respects in his autobiography *Gelächter von aussen (Laughter from Outside)* as the "most famous pioneer of modern art" in Munich.

PIPER VERLAG

Hohenzollernstrasse 23

This was the first home of the publishing house. It was founded in 1904 by Reinhard Piper, who was only 25 years old at the time. He built up an attractive art program and published the almanac "Der Blaue Reiter" in 1912.

APARTMENTS OF WASSILY KANDINSKY AND HIS WIFE ANJA

Georgenstrasse 62, 1897
Giselastrasse 28, 1897 – 1899 (below left)
Georgenstrasse 35, 1899
Friedrichstrasse 1, 1901 – 1905 (below right)

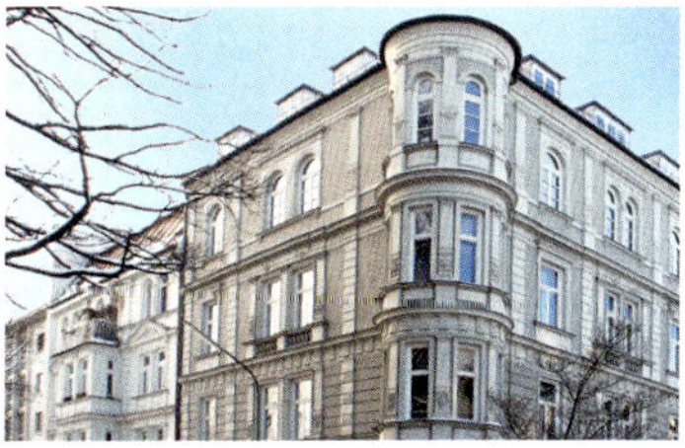

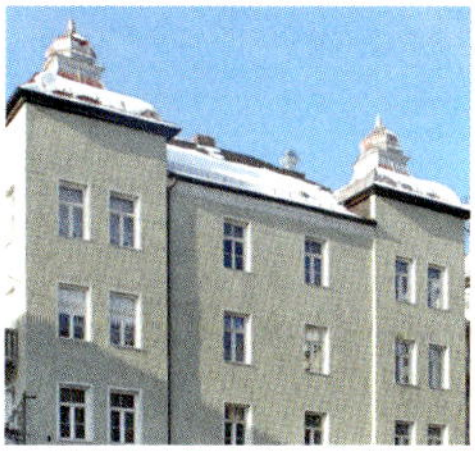

WASSILY KANDINSKY'S APARTMENT

Ainmillerstrasse 72, 1905. Kandinsky lived here alone after his separation from his wife Anja.

FIRST APARTMENT OF GABRIELE MÜNTER IN MUNICH

Schackstrasse 4

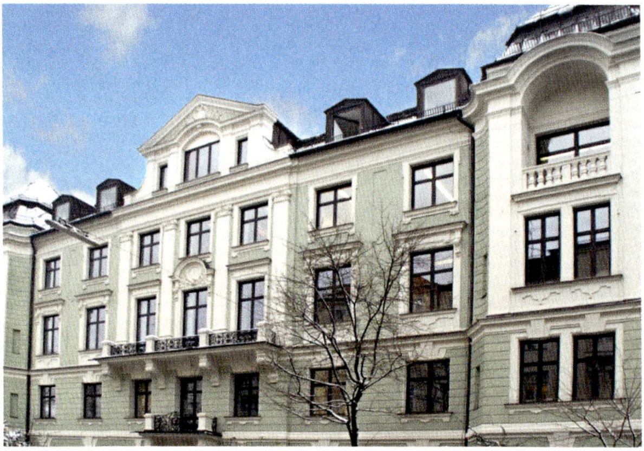

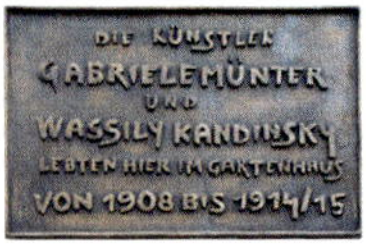

THE APARTMENT OF WASSILY KANDINSKY AND GABRIELE MÜNTER

Ainmillerstrasse 36, from 1908 on the second floor, from 1909–1914 on the fourth floor

TWIN APARTMENT, STUDIO AND SALON OF MARIANNE VON WEREFKIN AND ALEXEJ VON JAWLENSKY

Giselastrasse 23

RESIDENCE OF THE MARC FAMILY

München-Pasing, Flossmannstrasse 30 (formerly Luisenstrasse)

FRANZ MARC'S FIRST STUDIO

Schellingstrasse 23, back building, from June 1907

FRANZ MARC'S SECOND STUDIO

Schellingstrasse 23, back building, from June 1907

COMMEMORATIVE PLAQUE FOR FRANZ MARC

Marks his birthplace in Schillerstrasse

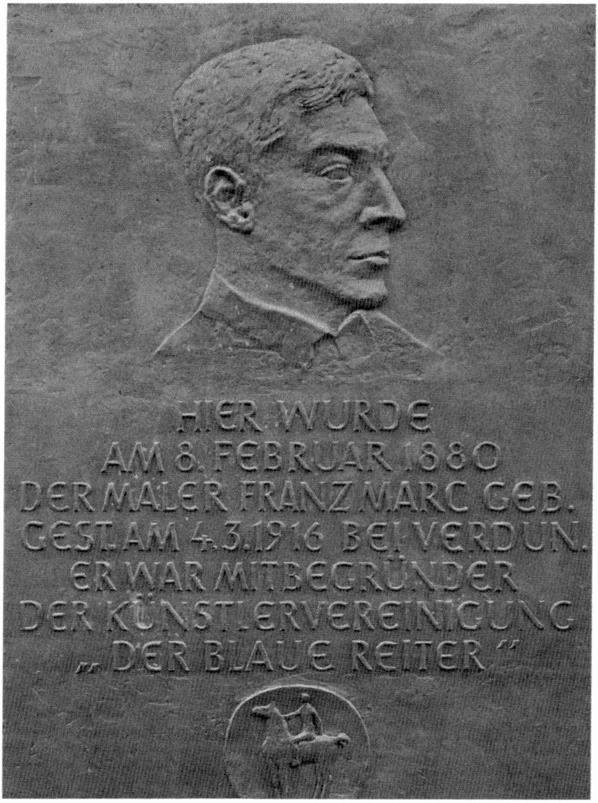

APARTMENT OF PAUL AND LILY KLEE

Ainmillerstrasse 32, from 1906

APARTMENTS OF ALFRED KUBIN

Theresienstrasse 108, 1902–1904
Mandlstrasse 26 (commemorative plaque), 1904–1906

Houses which are not illustrated were destroyed during the Second World War and mostly replaced by new buildings during the 1960s and 1970s.

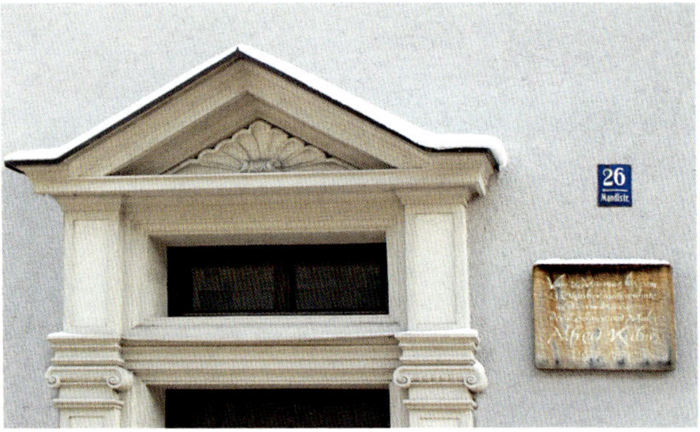

Munich, Mandlstrasse 26:
Apartment of Alfred Kubin
1904–1906

Right page:

Schloss Museum Murnau, exterior

Schloss Museum Murnau, section displaying the Blue Rider collection

MURNAU

SCHLOSSMUSEUM MURNAU

Schlosshof 4–5
82418 Murnau
Tel.: +49 (0) 88 41/476 201

The museum is housed in the former keep of Schloss Murnau, which for over 400 years was inhabited by the "caretakers" from Ettal monastery, who were responsible for the jurisdiction of Murnau.
At the beginning of the twentieth century, Murnau was a popular place among artists and writers. The museum's interesting collection is dedicated above all to the life and works of Gabriele Münter, to the activities of the Blue Rider, and to the writer Ödön von Horvath and his circle. The visitor will also find numerous exhibits and information relating to the countryside around Murnau, especially the Murnauer Moos (moor) with its hiking possibilities, and local crafts including reverse-glass painting, which fascinated both Münter and Kandinsky. Gabriele Münter had learned the technique from the last reverse-glass painter in Murnau, Heinrich Rambold (1872–1953).

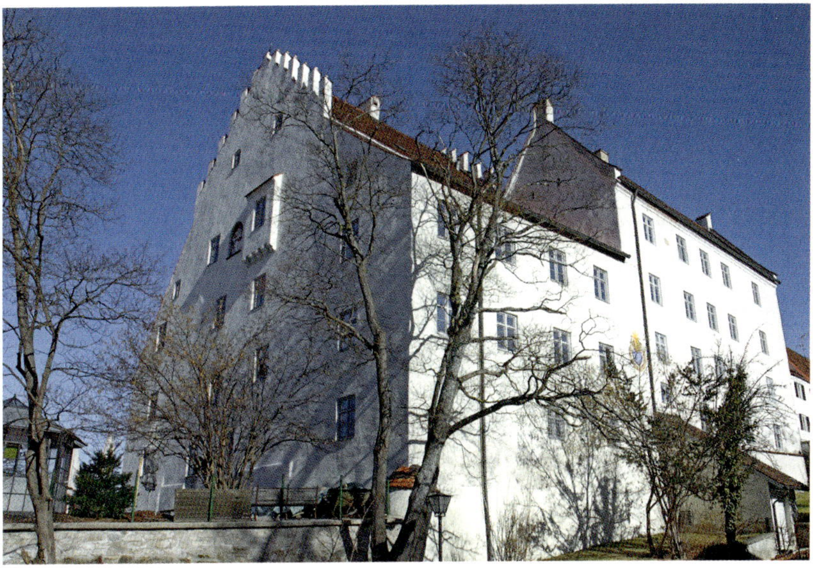

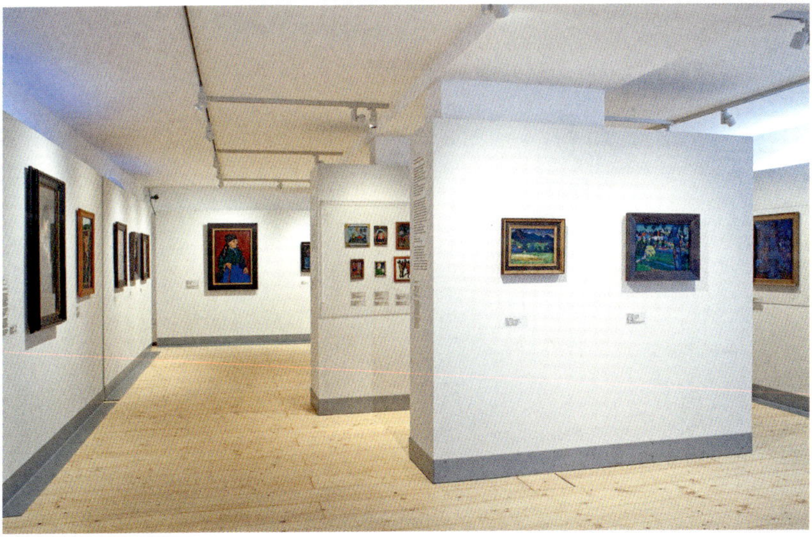

Staircase and banister of the "Russian House" (Münter-Haus) painted by Kandinsky

Right page:

Dining corner in the living-room of the "Russian House," with reverse-glass paintings by Kandinsky

MÜNTER-HAUS

Kottmüllerallee 6
82418 Murnau
Tel.: +49 (0) 88 41/62 88 80

Gabriele Münter purchased the house on the western fringes of the town with its views of Schlosshügel (Castle Hill) in the summer of 1909. Both Kandinsky and Münter painted the view several times. The couple lived here during the summer months from 1909 until 1914. In reference to Kandinsky's origins, the citizens of Murnau also called the house the "Russian House." Kandinsky painted the stair-

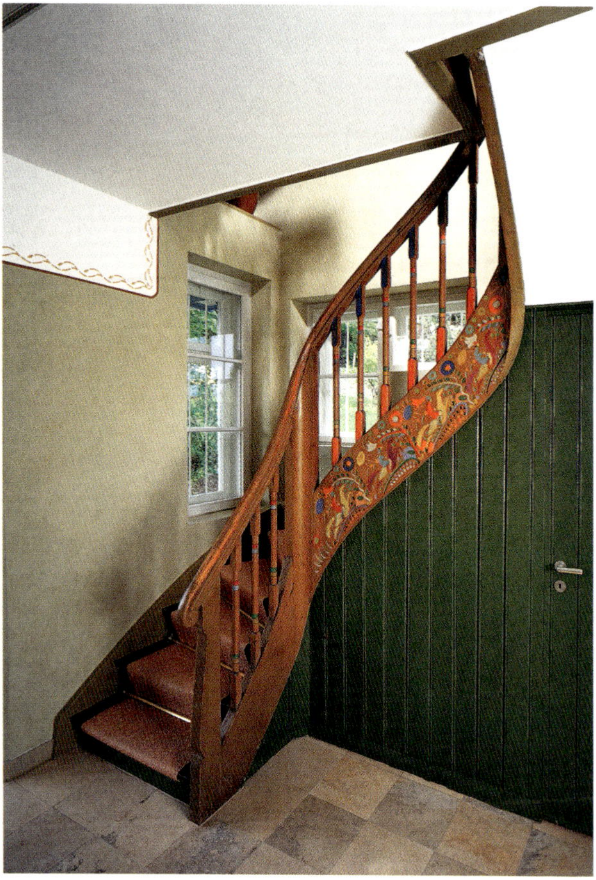

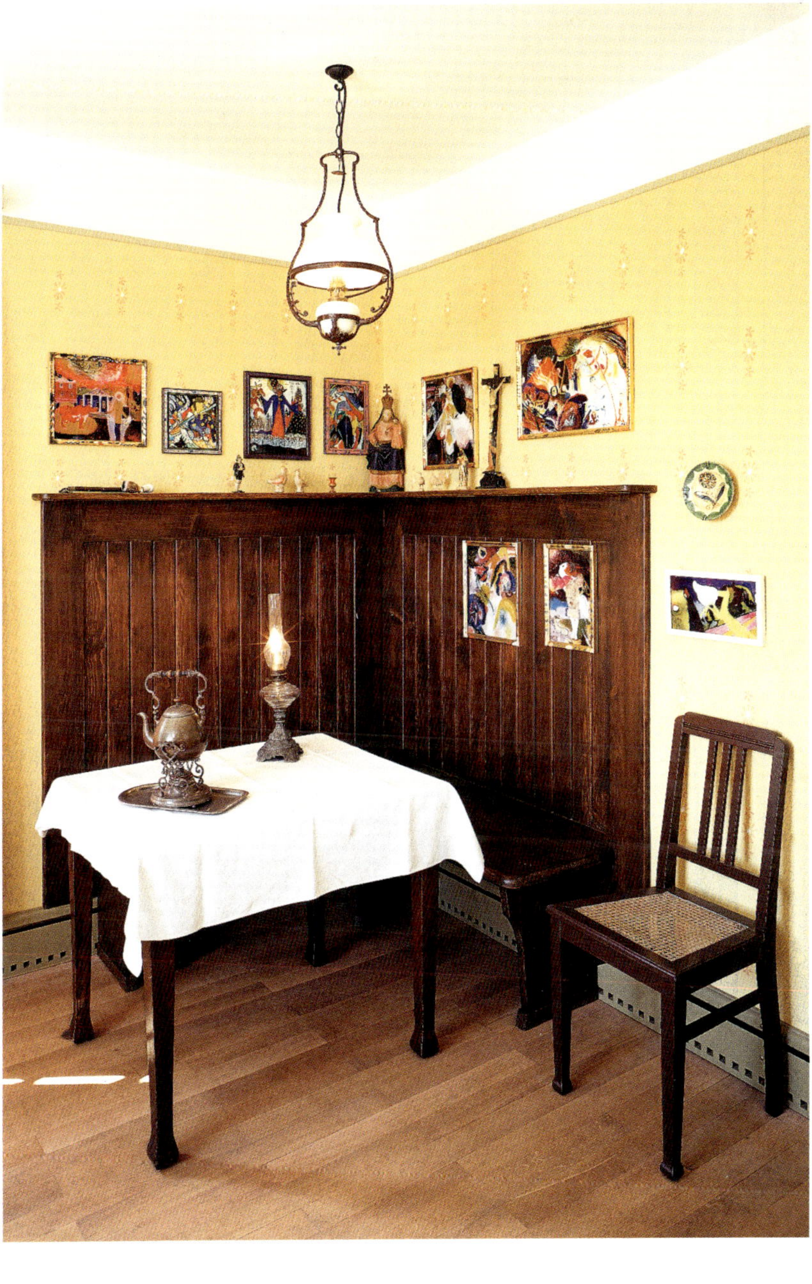

Studio with washstand painted by Kandinsky

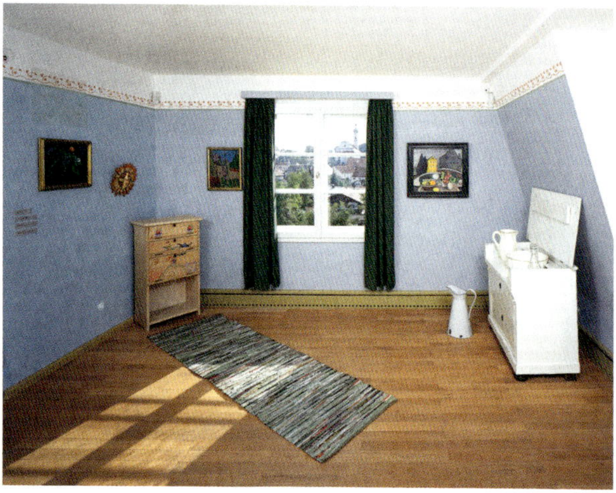

Gabriele Münter
INTERIOR IN THE "RUSSIAN HOUSE,"
1909

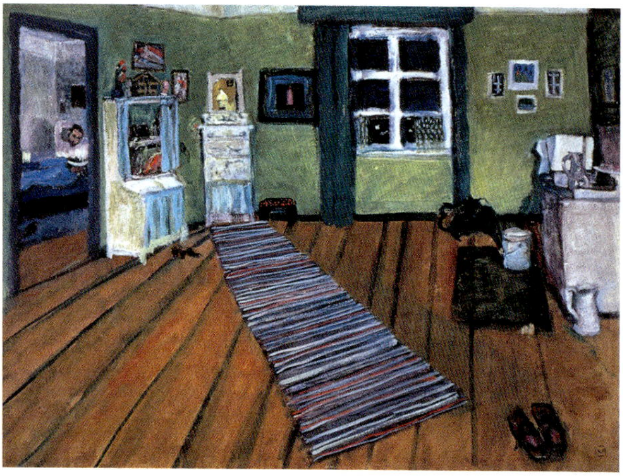

case and furniture and he and Gabriele Münter lovingly furnished it with pictures and objects of Bavarian folk art. Kandinsky looked after the garden, which in recent years has been reconstructed in line with old photographs. The house is also largely still in its original state. Until the outbreak of the First World War, which forced Kandinsky to return to Russia, the couple's artist friends from Munich visited the house, including August and Elisabeth Macke, Franz and Maria Marc, Marianne von Werefkin and Alexej von Jawlensky, and

Arnold Schönberg. Apart from a few interruptions, Gabriele Münter spent most of her life in Murnau. From 1933 until her death in 1962, she lived here with her subsequent partner, the art historian Johannes Eichner.

GASTHOF GRIESBRÄU

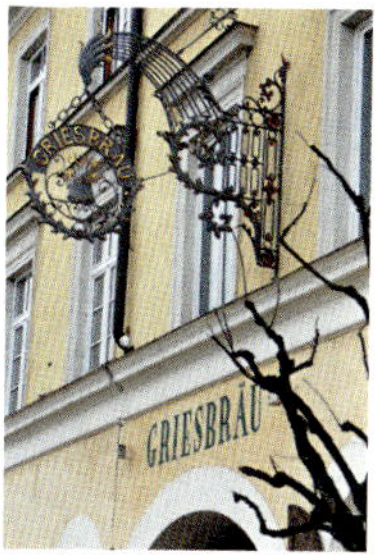

Obermarkt 35

It was in this inn that Wassily Kandinsky and Gabriele Münter, Marianne von Werefkin and Alexej Jawlensky, stayed during the summer of 1908. From his room here Kandinsky painted *View of the Johannisstrasse from the Griesbräu* (below). Today the building complex includes not only the hotel but also an inn, a beer hall with its own brewery, a bar, and a cinema.

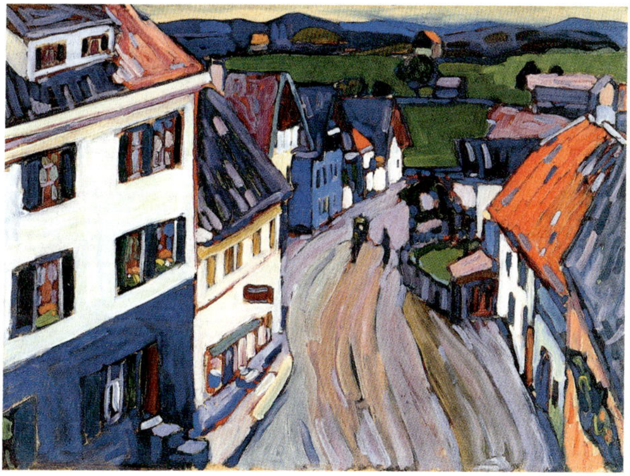

Wassily Kandinsky
JOHANNISSTRASSE MURNAU FROM THE WINDOW OF THE HOTEL GRIESBRÄU, 1908

PARISH CHURCH OF ST. NICHOLAS AND CEMETERY

The large yellow church is perched on Schlosshügel overlooking the town, not far from the museum with its prominent stepped gable. The opulent Baroque building with a large fresco adorning the cupola also contains twenty-three votive pictures; Marc and Kandinsky included several of them in their famous almanac. Gabriele Münter and her long-time partner Johannes Eichner are buried in the cemetery. The simple gravestone was created by the Murnau sculptor

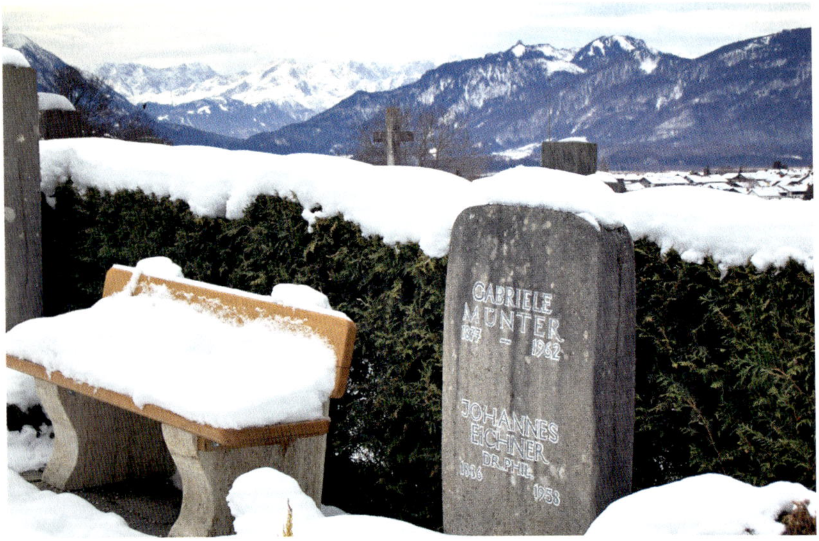

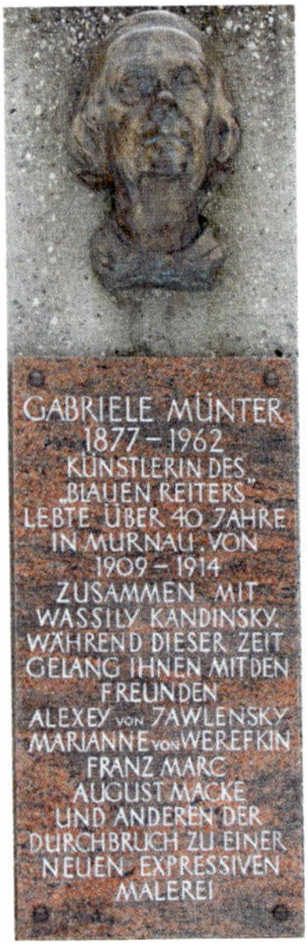

Rudolf Pfefferer, who died in 1986. The grave lies in the southeast behind the church; steps lead up a hill on the right, which also belongs to the cemetery. It is the second grave on the right after the steps. On a clear day there is a magnificent view from here across the marshy landscape of the Murnauer moors to the peaks of the Wettersteingebirge, including the Zugspitze and Alpspitze.

GABRIELE MÜNTER MEMORIAL

Gabriele-Münter-Platz

The fountain by Hans Angerer can be seen as a "sculpture" – it makes playful use of elements of the Münter house in Kottmüllerallee, showing similarities with its layout and the staircase painted by Kandinsky. However, these links will only be obvious to visitors who have previously visited the "Russian House." The bronze cast on the right-hand side with the portrait of Gabriele Münter is the work of the ornamental blacksmith Herbert Elflein from Steingaden as a partial cast of a marble bust by the sculptor Rudolf Pfefferer, which can be seen in the Schloss Museum. The small, casually modeled head looks very realistic.

WALK ACROSS THE MURNAUER MOOS

The footpath, which is clearly signposted, begins beside the little church in Ramsachnext to Gasthof Ähndl (Ramsach 2). It offers a succession of impressive views of the marshland and the mountains. Here you can understand exactly how it was that Kandinsky and Münter captured the character of this unique landscape in their strongly abstracted paintings. The circuit leads for 12.5 km (7.75 miles) across flat countryside, partly on boardwalks through the marshes. You should wear strong shoes and take sufficient water with you on your excursion.

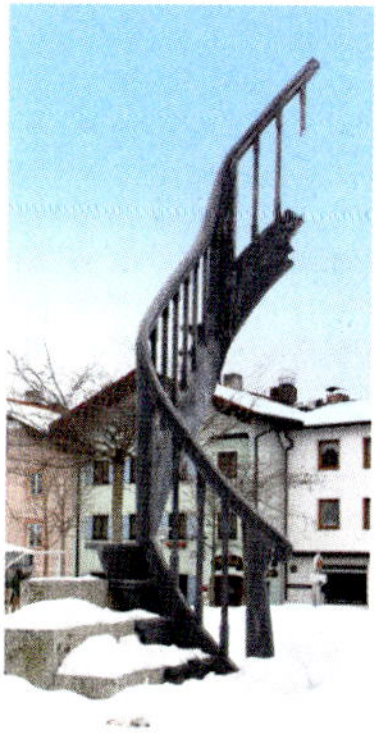

Fountain by Hans Angerer, Gabriele-Münter-Platz in Murnau

KOCHEL

FRANZ MARC MUSEUM

Franz Marc Park 8–10
82431 Kochel am See
Tel.: +49 (0) 88 51/92 488 0

Founded in 1986, the museum lies in an idyllic location on the road between the Kochelsee and the Walchensee. Initially it was housed in a villa dating from the turn of the nineteenth century. The extension was opened in 2008 and provides space for temporary exhibitions which look at Franz Marc's work from a variety of perspectives and establish its relationship with the other artistic movements of the early twentieth century and the present day.
From the café terrace and the vast panorama windows in the new building there are magnificent views of the Kochelsee and the surrounding mountains.

DISCOVERING FRANZ MARC – AN ART WALK

The signposted circuit in the footsteps of Franz Marc through Kochel begins and ends at the rail station and has nine stopping points along the route. It shows in particular the places where some of the artist's famous pictures were created, with signboards pointing out the associations.

Next Page:

Franz Marc Museum in Kochel (Diethelm & Spillmann Architects), 2008

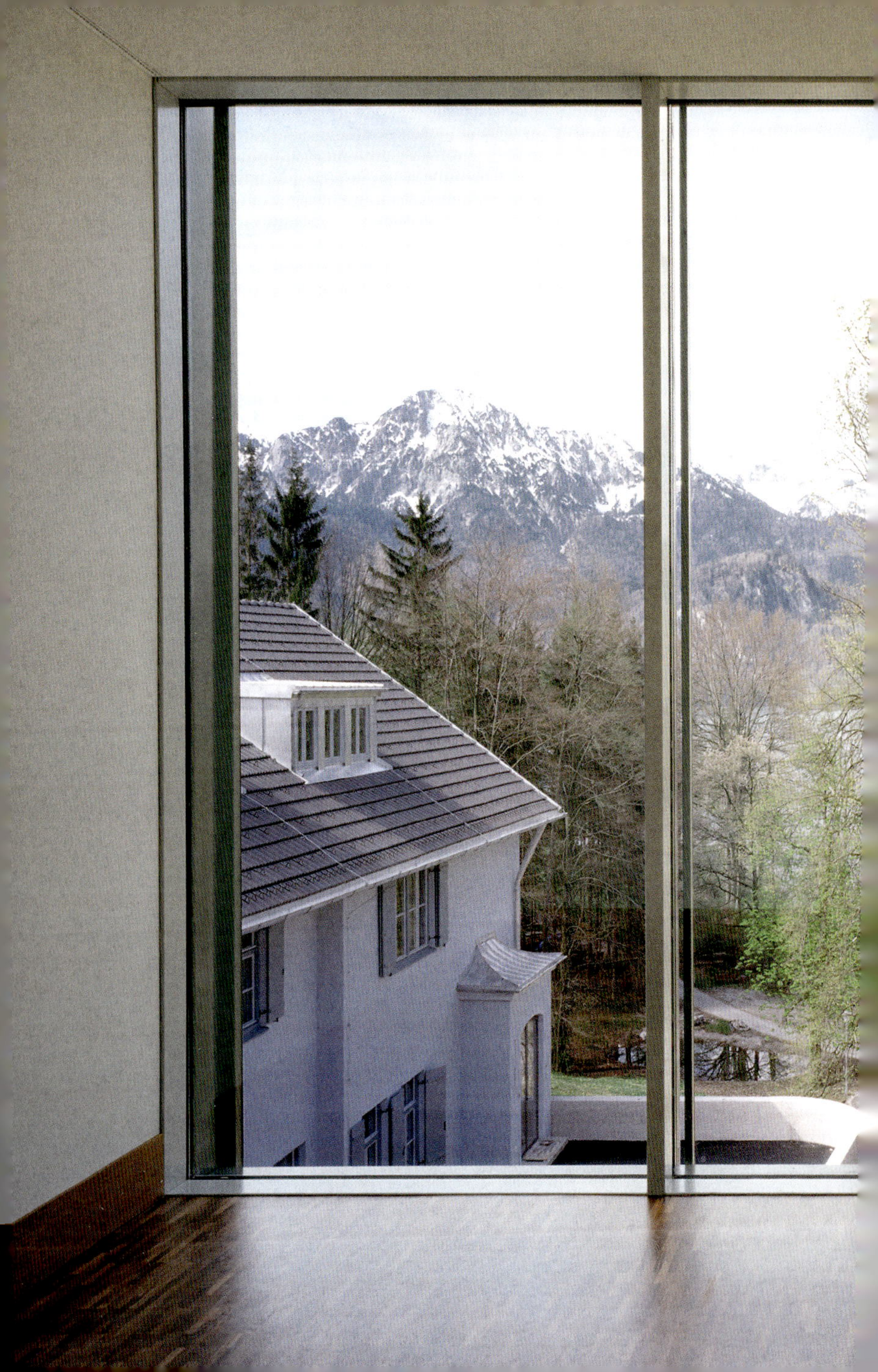

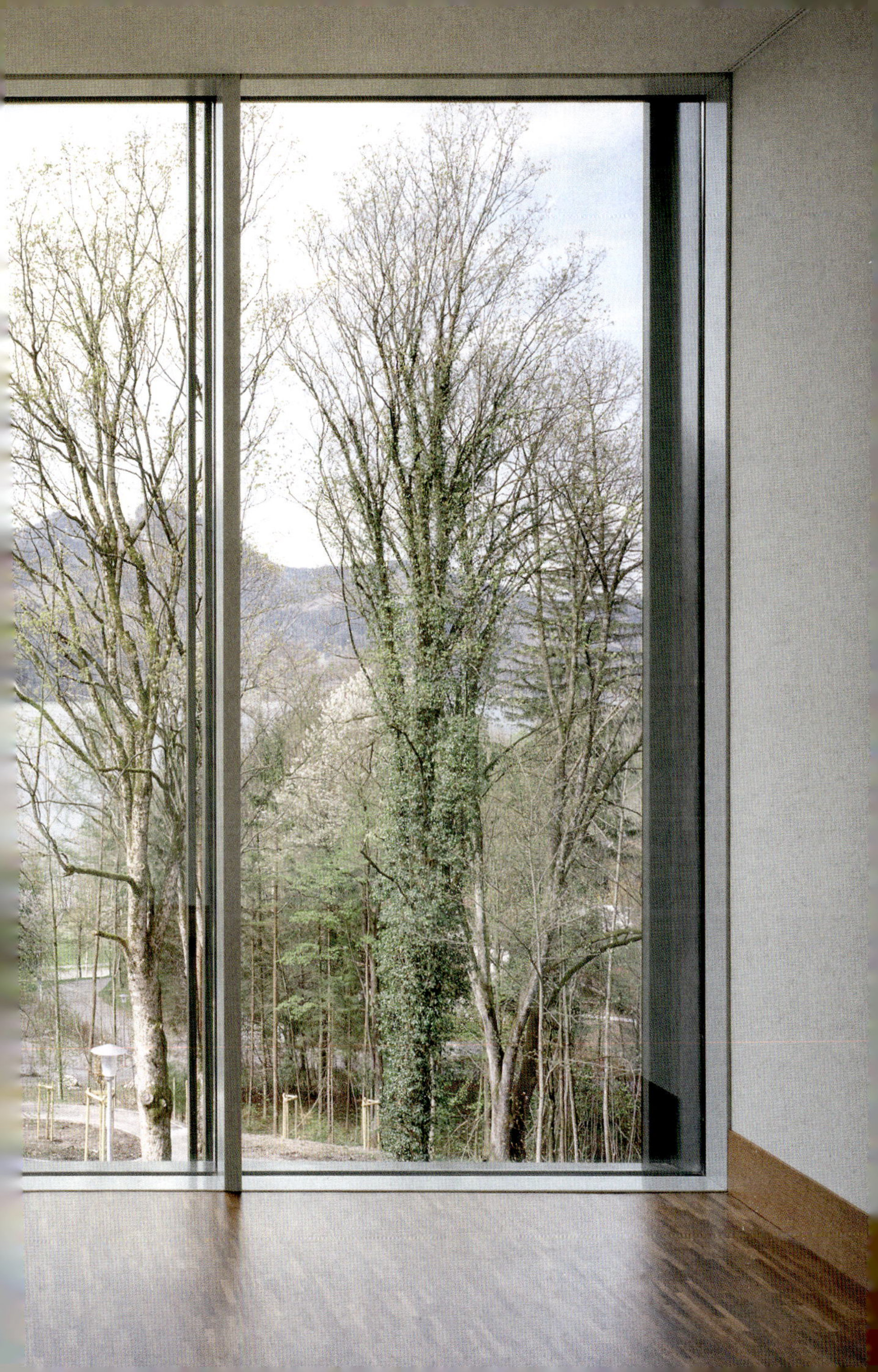

SEEHOTEL GRAUER BÄR

Mittenwalderstrasse 82–86

The Munich architect Oscar Strelin extended the existing inn with the large hotel building and swimming pool in 1899. The hotel was a popular haunt of artists; Wassily Kandinsky and his wife Anja stayed here in 1902.

HOTEL ZUR POST

Schmied-von-Kochel-Platz 6

As was fashionable at the time, the painter Wilhelm Marc and his wife Sophie spent their summer break here with their son Franz almost every year. Franz Marc therefore knew the place and the hotel itself very well. So it is not surprising that during his time as a student he used it as a "love nest" and spent the carnival holiday here with Maria Franck in 1906.

PARISH CHURCH OF ST. MICHAEL AND CEMETERY

Gabriele Münter and Wassily Kandinsky, who were very interested in the folk art of Upper Bavaria, were also fascinated by the wrought-iron grave crosses. During the summer of 1909 in particular they came here frequently in order to draw and to study the forms of the graves and their inscriptions, producing several pictures.

The graves of Franz and Maria Marc are in the cemetery, near the wall and with views of the Jochberg. The remains of Franz Marc, who was killed in 1916 near Verdun, were moved here in 1917; Maria Marc was buried beside him thirty-eight years later.

STAFFELALM BELOW THE RABENKOPF

Visitors who are not deterred by the two-and-a-half-hour ascent from the Sonnental to a height of 1,320 meters (4,330 feet) are recommended to visit one of Franz Marc's favorite places. The artist came on a number of occasions to this alpine summer meadow, established in around 1868. During these visits he painted, among other pictures, two wall pictures, the head of an ox, and a stag and hind (see p. 156). The pictures were later whitewashed over; it was only fairly recently that the farmer Josef Orterer had the wall paintings uncovered again; they have now been restored. During the summer months you can enjoy hearty snacks here while admiring the views of the surrounding mountains.

SINDELSDORF

EHEMALIGES ATELIER VON FRANZ MARC

Franz-Marc-Straße 1

Franz Marc was a close friend of August Macke's, who visited Sindelsdorf on many occasions, sometimes accompanied by his future wife Elisabeth. The latter noted of the Marcs' home: "The village itself is small and straggling, with inhospitable paths which were almost impassable after it had rained. The only largish house was the Gasthof zur Post, in which one could stay and spend the night. […]

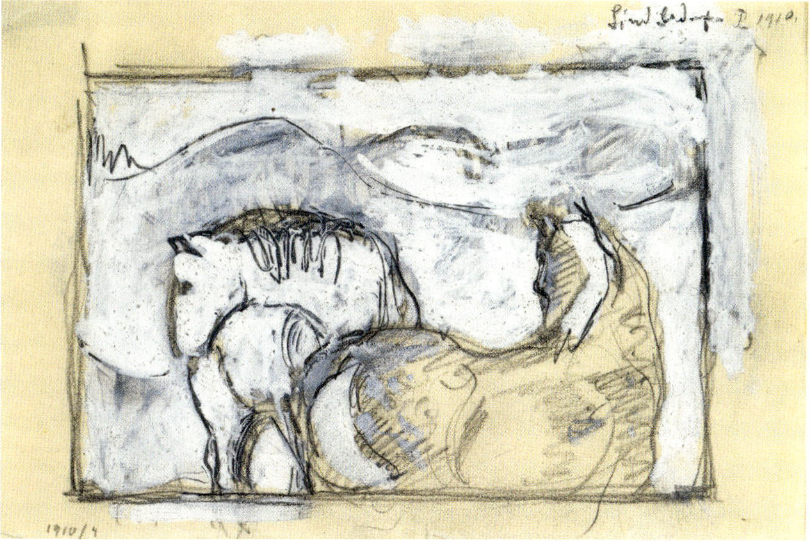

Franz Marc
TWO HORSES, 1910

Marc and Fräulein Franck [his future wife] lived in a little apartment in the house of the master carpenter Josef Niggl in a modern, tasteless farmhouse. […] The rooms which the friends had furnished on the upper floor were all the more comfortable, with fine old furniture and lots of artistic details which lent the whole a very personal note."[76]

The house is now privately owned and is not accessible to the public.

RIED

HOUSE OF FRANZ AND MARIA MARC

(Villa Ried)

Heinrich-Kaminsky-Weg 1

Franz and Maria Marc moved from Sindelsdorf into the spacious villa in April 1914 (see p. 175). They had exchanged the house for the house of Maria's parents in Pasing. Letters and notes indicate that they loved living here. But their happiness was short-lived, since Franz Marc was called up in August of the same year and failed to return from the war. Maria Marc continued to live here until her death in 1955.

The house is privately owned and is not accessible to the public.

LENGGRIES

FORMER PENSION BACHER

Gebhardtgasse 2

During the spring of 1908 Franz Marc took a room in the guest house, which was run by a school friend of his who also owned the Staffelalm (see p. 174).

Maria Franck joined him a few weeks later and a phase of intense artistic activity began. Marc explored the immediate surroundings for his art, drawing and painting in the nearby paddocks and pastures.

TEGERNSEE

APARTMENTS OF AUGUST AND ELISABETH MACKE

Bahnhofsstrasse

The Rhineland artist August Macke and his wife Elisabeth lived in Tegernsee in 1909–1910. In November 1909 they first moved into an apartment in the Villa Brand in Bahnhofsstrasse. The young couple made numerous changes to the rooms. Elisabeth Macke wrote: "Much to the horror of the owners, we mercilessly removed all the kitsch pictures and shelves filled with cheap knick-knacks from the wall and stored them in one of the unused rooms. We completely cleared out one room which served as studio. August was very keen to work and soon the empty canvases were filled with the first pictures."[77]

The landlords were clearly somewhat suspicious of the young artist couple; there was a disagreement and they had to move. They found another place to live, also in Bahnhofsstrasse, in the spacious chalet of a carpenter named Staudacher.

This turned out to be a stroke of luck. The relationship with the landlords developed into a friendship, and Macke began to work in a frenzy of creativity. During a visit to Munich he discovered the works of Franz Marc, which greatly impressed him. He contacted the artist and a very close friendship developed which was characterized by the fact that the two men spoke together very openly and critically about their art, from which both of them ultimately profited. The Mackes' elder son was born in the house of the Staudachers; it was with great reluctance that the young family left the "beloved nest of their home" in November 1910 and returned to Bonn. Macke hoped above all that he would find there better working conditions in the house of his parents-in-law, where a spacious studio awaited him. "I am already dreaming about painting a few things beside you in your studio in Bonn; we would both profit from such an arrangement, I for my part am quite sure of that!" wrote Franz Marc.[78]

GARMISCH-PARTENKIRCHEN

APARTMENT OF ALEXANDER KANOLDT

Am Holzhof 4

Alexander Kanoldt rented the apartment in Partenkirchen for himself and his family. During the years from 1931 he ran a private painting school here and tried to secure the family income by selling prints. In 1933 he was appointed director of the college of art in Berlin.

MARKT SCHWABEN

FRANZ-MARC-GYMNASIUM

Rektor-Haushofer-Strasse

The façade of the school, founded in 1973, is adorned with a vast wall picture of a portrait of Franz Marc, painted by the artist Martina Resch.

The wall was decorated in 2006 following a competition among the pupils majoring in art. The photo-mosaic shows virtually all the pupils of the school. The glass was printed and the color baked on; the technical execution was undertaken by the Mayersche Hofkunstanstalt in Munich.

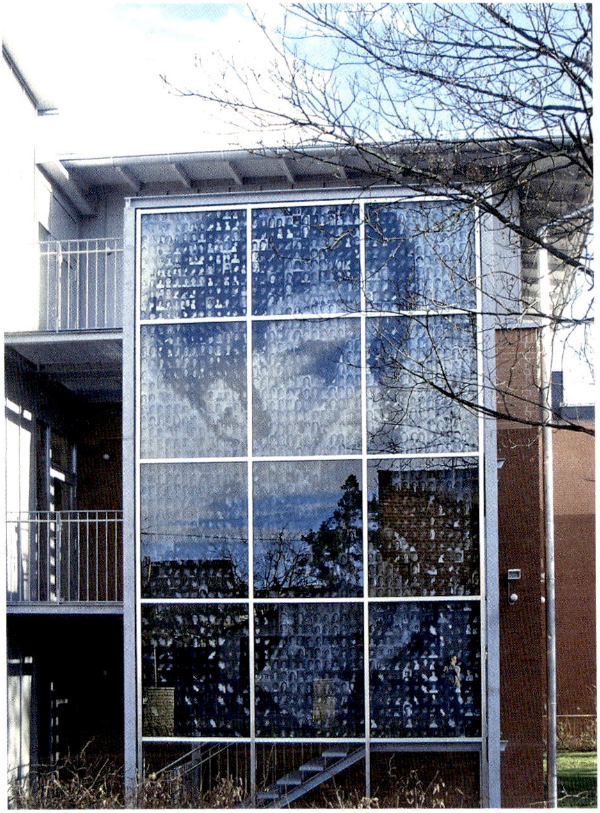

WERNSTEIN AM INN, AUSTRIA

KUBIN-HAUS ZWICKLEDT

A – 4738 Wernstein am Inn
Tel.: +43 (0) 7713 6603

Art-lovers interested in the Blue Rider are strongly recommended to make this excursion to Austria – Wernstein lies directly on the banks of the Inn, which here marks the frontier with Bavaria. Kubin moved here from Munich in 1906 and remained, apart from a few

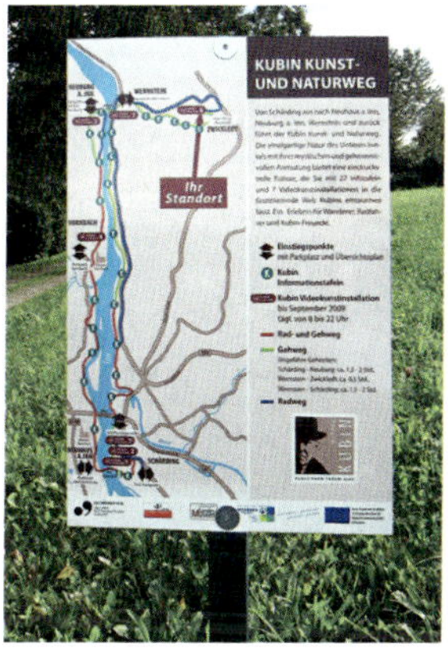

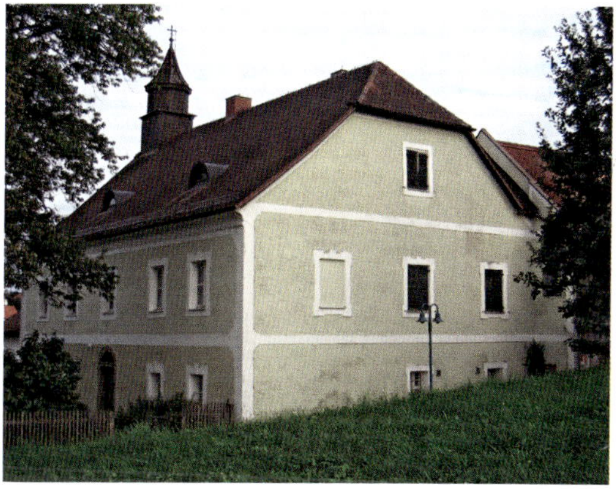

interruptions for extended journeys, until his death in 1959. He lived here with his wife Hedwig. It was here that he produced most of his pictorial work, and it was here that he wrote and illustrated his fantasy novel *Die andere Seite [The Other Side].*

The living accommodation remains completely unchanged; even the pictures and knick-knacks are in their original places (see p. 180). In the study in particular visitors almost feel as if they are intruding into the artist's private quarters, a very special and moving experience. Visitors with sufficient time available can walk along the "Kubin Kunst- und Naturweg" (Kubin Art and Nature Way) to Schärding, a footpath with informative signs. In any case you should follow the half-hour footpath down to Wernstein, which Kubin walked several times a week.

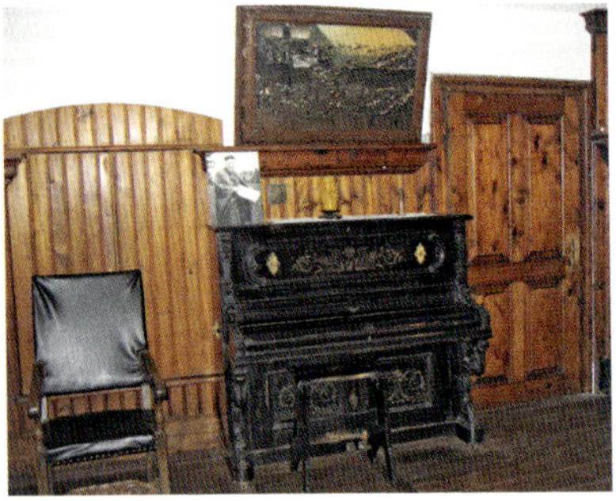

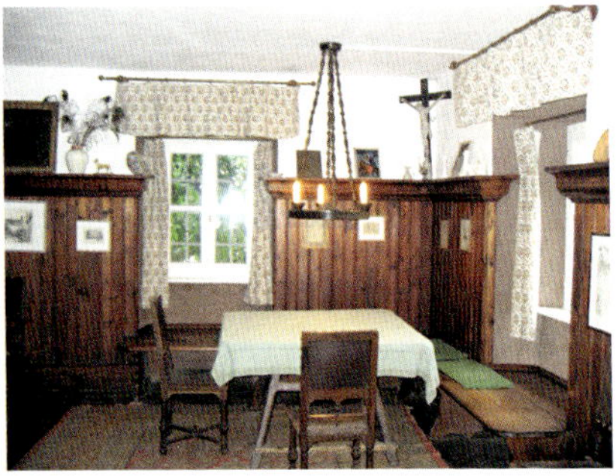

PARISH CHURCH OF ST. GEORGE AND CEMETERY

On the south wall of the church, in the corner between the nave and the extension added in 1966/1967, lies the grave of Alfred and Hedwig Kubin. The gravestone was the work of Karl Prantl, who was also responsible for the partly modern interior decoration of Gothic church. The church windows, designed by Rudolf Kolbitsch, were produced in the glass workshops of the abbey at Schlierbach.

The parish church of St. George is a single-nave Late Gothic building dating from around 1500. The big crucifix also dates from that time. On the exterior, a statue of St. George above the entrance stands watch over the church and the graves. Kubin would certainly have been pleased about that, for St. George served Kandinsky as the inspiration for his figure of the Blue Rider, with whom Kubin felt a close affinity.

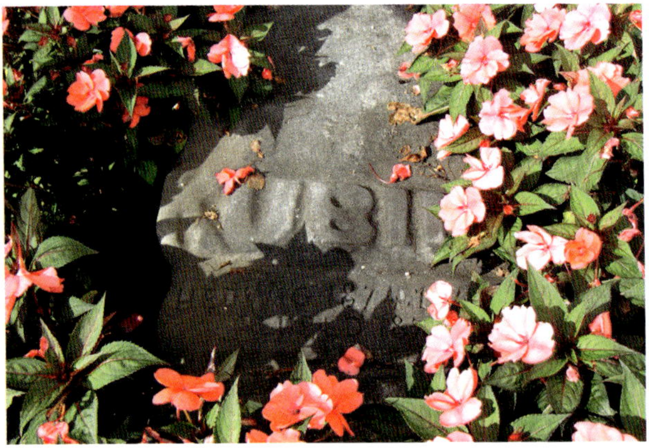

APPENDIX

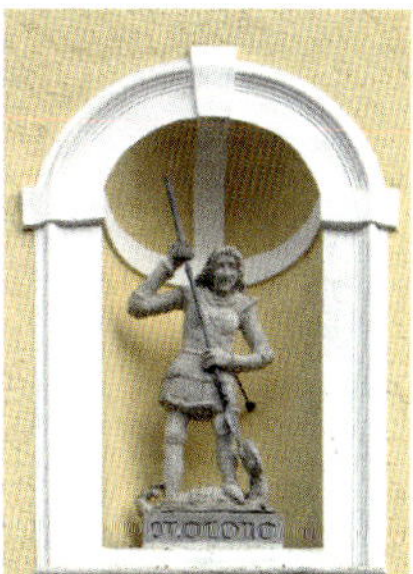

Notes

1 Friedel / Hoberg 2004, p. 20
2 Frèches / Perucchi 1993
3 Hollmann 1996, p. 11
4 Frèches / Perucchi 1993, p. 251
5 Brucher 1999, p. 419
6 Hoberg/Friedel 1999, p. 29
7 Friedel/Hoberg 2004, p. 36
8 Hüneke 1986, p. 257
9 Hüneke 1986, pp. 20 – 21
10 Hüneke 1986, p. 34
11 Hüneke 1986, p. 26
12 Hüneke 1986, p. 29
13 Hüneke 1986, p. 31
14 Friedel/Hoberg 2004, p. 40
15 Friedel/Hoberg 2004, p. 41
16 Friedel/Hoberg 2004, p. 49
17 Hüneke 1986, p. 60
18 Friedel/Hoberg 2004, p. 49
19 Friedel/Hoberg 2004, p. 44
20 Güse 1986, p. 182
21 Almanac 1912
22 Almanac 1912, p. 1
23 Almanac 1912, p. 7
24 Almanac 1912, p. 11
25 Almanac 1912, pp. 24 & 26
26 Almanac 1912, p. 7
27 Almanac 1912, p. 78
28 Hüneke 1986, p. 164
29 Hüneke 1986, p. 170
30 Hüneke 1986, p. 169
31 Roethel 1979, p. 86: "absolute Malerei, entbunden von der Tradition"
32 Kandinsky 2007, p. 30
33 Brucher 1999, p. 419
34 Antonio Pisano, known as Pisanello, Italian artist, b. before 1395 in Pisa, *d.* c. 1455, probably in Verona
35 Meissner 1980, p. 154
36 Meissner 1980, p. 154
37 Hoberg / Friedel 2006, p. 140
38 Hüneke 1986, p. 59
39 Hoberg 2004, p. 3
40 Friedel / Hoberg 2004, p. 40
41 Marks 1977
42 For a detailed description of this relationship in the form of a novel, see: Steinwendter 2009
43 Güse 1986, p. 154
44 Hüneke 1986, p. 93
45 Moeller 1989
46 Güse 1986, p. 178
47 Klee 1957, p. 229
48 Hüneke 1986, p. 283
49 Hüneke 1986, p. 322
50 Hüneke 1986, p. 185
51 Hüneke 1986, p. 189
52 Hüneke 1986, p. 190
53 Schuster 1987
54 Brühl 1983, p. 7
55 Hüneke 1986, p. 182
56 Brühl 1983, p. 36
57 Hüneke 1986, pp. 182 – 183
58 Friedel/Hoberg 2004, p. 70
59 Brühl 1983, p. 50
60 Hüneke 1986, p. 502
61 Hüneke 1986, p. 503
62 Hüneke 1986, p. 519
63 Hüneke 1986, p. 526
64 Jähner 1984, p. 416
65 Jähner 1984, p. 80

66 Hüneke 1986, p. 338

67 Hüneke 1986, p. 355

68 Friedel / Hoberg 2004, picture caption no. 16

69 Maur 1999, p. 30

70 For a brilliant analysis of the picture, see: Brucher 1999, pp. 279 – 280

71 Mommsen 2004, p. 29

72 For a concise, popular introduction to the topic, see: Friedewald 2009

73 For detailed information and exhibition catalogue, see: Schuster, *Nationalsozialismus*, 1987

74 The text of the lecture can be found in: Hanfstaengl 1974, pp. 11 – 12

75 Friedel 2000, p. 5

76 Tworek 2004, p. 51

77 Tworek 2004, p. 205

78 Letter from Marc to Macke 1910

Literature

Almanac 1912
Kandinsky, Wassily and Franz Marc (eds.), *Der Blaue Reiter*, Munich 1912 (English edition: *The Blaue Reiter Almanac*, Introduction by Klaus Lankheit, Boston 2005)

Brucher 1999
Brucher, Günter, Kandinsky – *Wege zur Abstraktion*, Munich 1999

Brühl 1983
Georg Brühl, *Herwarth Walden und "Der Sturm,"* Leipzig 1983

Frèches / Perucchi 1993
Frèches-Thory, Claire, and Ursula Perucchi-Petri, *Die Nabis. Propheten der Moderne*, Munich 1993

Friedel 2000
Friedel, Helmut (ed.), *Städtische Galerie im Lenbachhaus München*, 3rd edition, Munich 2000

Friedel / Hoberg 2004
Friedel, Helmut, and Annegret Hoberg, *Der Blaue Reiter im Lenbachhaus München*, Munich 2004

Friedel / Hoberg 2010
Friedel, Helmut, and Annegret Hoberg (eds.), *"Der Blaue Reiter" Aquarelle, Zeichnungen und Druckgraphik aus dem Lenbachhaus. Ein Tanz in Farben*, Munich 2010 (English edition: *The Blue Rider: A Dance in Colours. Watercolours, Drawings and Graphic Arts from the Lenbachhaus Munich*, Munich, 2011)

Friedewald, 2009
Friedewald, Boris, *Bauhaus*, Munich 2009

Güse 1986
Güse, Ernst-Gerhard, *August Macke – Gemälde, Aquarelle, Zeichnungen*, Munich 1986

Hahl-Koch 1993
Hahl-Koch, Jelena, *Kandinsky*, Stuttgart 1993

Hanfstaengl 1974
Hanfstaengl, Erika (ed.), *Wassily Kandinsky. Zeichnungen und Aquarelle*, Munich 1974

Hoberg 2004
Hoberg, Annegret, *Franz und Maria Marc*, Munich 2004

Hoberg / Friedel 1999
Hoberg, Annegret, and Helmut Friedel (eds.), *Der Blaue Reiter und das Neue Bild*, Munich 1999

Hoberg / Friedel 2006
Hoberg, Annegret, and Helmut Friedel, *Franz Marc – Die Retrospektive*, Munich 2006

Hollmann 1996
Hollmann, Eckhard, *Paul Gauguin – Bilder aus der Südsee*, Munich 1996

Hüneke 1986
Hüneke, Andreas, *Der Blaue Reiter – Dokumente einer geistigen Bewegung*, Leipzig 1986

Jähner 1984
Jähner, Horst, *Künstlergruppe Brücke, Geschichte einer Gemeinschaft und das Lebenswerk ihrer Repräsentanten*, Berlin 1984

Kandinsky 2007
Friedel, Helmut (ed.), *Wassily Kandinsky – Gesammelte Schriften 1889 – 1916*, Munich 2007

Klee 1980
Felix Klee (ed.), *Paul Klee – Tagebücher 1898 – 1918*, Leipzig and Weimar 1980 (English edition: *The Diaries of Paul Klee 1898 – 1918*, (ed.) Felix Klee, Berkley 1964)

Marks 1977
Alfred Marks, *Der Illustrator Alfred Kubin. Gesamtkatalog seiner Illustrationen und buchkünstlerischen Arbeiten*, Munich 1977

Maur 1999
Maur, Karin von, *Vom Klang der Bilder*, Munich 1999

Meissner 1980
Meissner, Günther (ed.), *Franz Marc. Briefe-Aufzeichnungen-Aphorismen*, Leipzig und Weimar, 1980

Moeller 1989
Moeller, Magdalena M., *August Macke – Die Tunisreise*, Munich 1989

Mommsen 2004
Hirschfeld, Gerhard et al. (eds.), *Enzyklopädie Erster Weltkrieg*, Paderborn 2004

Perruchot 1991
Henri Perruchot, *Paul Gauguin – Eine Biographie*, Munich 1991

Roethel 1979
Roethel, Hans K., and Jean K. Benjamin, *Kandinsky*, New York 1979

Schuster 1987
Schuster, Peter-Klaus, *"Der Blaue Reiter präsentiert Eurer Hoheit sein Blaues Pferd." Karten und Briefe*, Munich 1987

Schuster, *Nationalsozialismus*, 1987
Schuster, Peter-Klaus (ed.), *Nationalsozialismus und "Entartete Kunst,"* Munich 1987

Steinwendter 2009
Steinwendter, Brita, *Du Engel Du Teufel. Emmy Haesele und Alfred Kubin*, Vienna 2009

Tworek 2004
Tworek, Elisabeth, *Spaziergänge durch das Alpenvorland der Literaten und Künstler*, Zurich/ Hamburg 2004

Blue Rider Picture list

p. 8: View from the Siegestor of Ludwigstrasse with the Ludwigskirche, Munich, photograph, 1906

p. 11: The Lenbachhaus, photograph

p. 12: Franz von Stuck, Poster for the *VII International Art Exhibition*, 1897, Münchner Stadtmuseum

p. 13 left: *Simplicissimus*, vol. 10, no. 1

p. 13 right: Advertisement for the Munich periodical *Jugend*, Ludwig von Zumbusch, 1898

p. 14: Kandinsky with his painting class from the Phalanx art school in Kochel, 1902, photograph, Gabriele Münter- und Johannes Eichner-Stiftung, Munich

p. 15: Wassily Kandinsky, Poster for the first Phalanx exhibition, 1901, color lithograph

p. 16 above: Wassily Kandinsky, *In the Park at Saint Cloud*, 1906, oil on card, 23.6 x 37.7 cm, Städtische Galerie im Lenbachhaus, Munich

p. 16 below: *Avenue in the Park at Saint Cloud*, 1906, oil on canvas, 40.5 x 50.5 cm, Städtische Galerie im Lenbachhaus, Munich

p. 17: Paul Sérusier, *Talisman*, 1888, oil on wood, 27 x 21.5 cm, Musée d'Orsay, Paris

p. 18: Wassily Kandinsky, *All Saints I*, 1911, reverse-glass painting, frame painted by Kandinsky, 34.5 x 40.5 cm, Städtische Galerie im Lenbachhaus, Munich

p. 19: Wassily Kandinsky, *All Saints I*, 1911, reverse-glass painting, frame painted by Kandinsky, 34.5 x 40.5 cm, Städtische Galerie im Lenbachhaus, Munich (detail)

p. 22: Marianne von Werefkin and Alexej von Jawlensky (top) with Alexander Sakharoff, his sister and a friend; in front, Helene Neznakomova, Munich, 1909, photograph, Fondazione Marianne Werefkin Ascona and Fäthke-Archiv

p. 23 above: Marianne von Werefkin, *Crucifix in Landscape*, 1909, tempera on card, 55 x 74 cm, Private collection

p. 23 below: Gabriele Münter, *Jawlensky und Werefkin*, 1909, oil on card, 32.7 x 44.5 cm, Städtische Galerie im Lenbachhaus, Munich

p. 24: Moderne Galerie Heinrich Thannhauser, Munich, skylit gallery, 1909, photograph from the gallery's opening catalogue, Archiv Meissner

p. 25: Wassily Kandinsky, Poster for the first exhibition of the New Artists' Association of Munich, 1909, color lithograph, 94 x 64 cm

pp. 26-27: Franz Marc, *Dog Lying in the Snow*, 1910–1911, oil on canvas, 62.5 x 105 cm, Städelsches Kunstinstitut, Frankfurt

p. 28: Alexej von Jawlensky, *Portrait of the Dancer Alexander Sakharoff*, 1909, oil on card, 69.5 x 66.5 cm, Städtische Galerie im Lenbachhaus, Munich

p. 29: Adolf Erbslöh, *Nude with Garter*, 1909, oil on card, 103 x 75 cm, Bayerische Staatsgemälde-sammlungen, Munich

p. 30: Paul Baum, *Flat Landscape in Autumn with Meadows and Pond*, c. 1907, oil on canvas, 50.5 x 62.5 cm, Städtische Galerie im Lenbachhaus Munich, On permanent loan from the Gabriele Münter- und Johannes Eichner-Stiftung

p. 31: Vladimir Bechteiev, *Porte de France, Tunis*, c. 1906, oil on card, 37 x 51 cm, Städtische Galerie im Lenbachhaus, Munich

p. 32: Gabriele Münter, *Still Life with Armchair*, 1909, oil on card, 72.5 x 49 cm, Gabriele Münter- und Johannes Eichner-Stiftung, Munich

p. 33: Wassily Kandinsky, *Murnau – Landscape with Tower*, 1908–1909, oil on card, 75.5 x 99.5 cm, Musée National d'Art Moderne, Centre Georges Pompidou, Paris

p. 34: Alfred Kubin, *Women with Grounded Ship*, c. 1907/1908, tempera, 50 x 60 cm, Nuremberg, Graf A. W. von Faber-Castell

p. 35: Karl Hofer, *On a Southern Shore*, c. 1909, oil on wood, 55 x 45 cm, Sammlung Hartmut Garnerus, Munich

p. 36: Pierre Girieud, *Judas*, 1908, oil on canvas, 92.3 x 73 cm, Städtische Galerie im Lenbachhaus, Munich, on permanent loan from the Gabriele Münter- und Johannes Eichner-Stiftung

p. 38: Erma Bossi, *At the Opera*, c. 1909/1910, oil on card, 76.7 x 48 cm, Private collection

p. 39: August Macke, *At the Circus*, 1911, reverse-glass painting, frame painted by Kandinsky, 11.8 x 8.9 cm, Städtische Galerie im Lenbachhaus, Munich

p. 40: Alexander Kanoldt, *A Ray of Sunshine*, 1910, oil on canvas, 66 x 54 cm, Von der Heydt-Museum, Wuppertal (detail)

p. 41: Alexander Kanoldt, *A Ray of Sunshine*, 1910, oil on canvas, 66 x 54 cm, Von der Heydt-Museum, Wuppertal

p. 42: Wassily Kandinsky, Title woodcut for the almanac *Der Blaue Reiter*, 1911, in the blue, red, black, and white, 27.9 x 21.1 cm

p. 43 top: August Macke watering the "Tender Plant of Modern Art," on the balcony of Ainmillerstrasse 36, Munich, 1912, photograph, Gabriele Münter- und Johannes Eichner-Stiftung, Munich

p. 43 bottom: Kandinsky with cigarette and book in a meadow near Murnau, c. 1910, photograph, Gabriele Münter- und Johannes Eichner-Stiftung, Munich

p. 45 top left: Poster for a concert of Arnold Schönberg's compositions in Munich on January 2, 1911

p. 45 top right: Wassily Kandinsky, Sketch for *Impression III (Concert)*, January 3, 1911, chalk on colored drawing paper, each 10 x 14.9 cm, Musée National d'Art Moderne, Centre Georges Pompidou, Paris

p. 45 bottom: Wassily Kandinsky, *Impression III (Concert)*, 1911, oil on canvas, 77.5 x 100 cm, Städtische Galerie im Lenbachhaus, Munich

p. 48: *Wassily Kandinsky, The Last Judgement*, 1911, reverse-glass painting, 21.7 x 11.6 cm, Städtische Galerie im Lenbachhaus, Munich

p. 49: Wassily Kandinsky, *Composition V*, 1911, oil on canvas, 190 x 275 cm, signed: KANDINSKY 1911, New York, Private collection (detail)

p. 50: Wassily Kandinsky, Sketch for the cover of the almanac *Der Blaue Reiter*, 1911, pen and Indian ink, watercolor, opaque white, 27.7 x 21.8 cm, Städtische Galerie im Lenbachhaus, Munich

p. 53: Almanac *Der Blaue Reiter*, first page of Franz Marc's essay "Intellectual Property," 1912

pp. 54-55: Almanac *Der Blaue Reiter*, pages 8–9, with the illustration "Lyrical" from the essay "Two Pictures" by Franz Marc, 1912

p. 56: Franz Marc, *Two Horses*, 1911, colored stencil for the almanac *Der Blaue Reiter*

p. 57: Woodcut by Hans Baldung Grien, from the almanac *Der Blaue Reiter*, 1912

p. 58: Wassily Kandinsky, Vignette for the almanac *Der Blaue Reiter*, 1911

p. 59: Wassily Kandinsky, *Archer*, 1908 – 1909, colored woodcut, 16.6 x 15.5 cm (print), supplement to the luxury edition of the almanac *Der Blaue Reiter*

p. 60: First exhibition of the Blue Rider, Galerie Thannhauser, Munich 1911–1912; Room 2 (from l. to r.): Franz Marc, *The Yellow Cow*; Arnold Schönberg, *Self-Portrait* (From Behind); Wassily Kandinsky, *St. George II*; Vladimir Burliuk, *Portrait Study* (top); Gabriele Münter, Country *Road in Winter* (bottom); Marc, *Deer in the Forest I*; (right, partial view) Wassily Kandinsky, *Composition V*, 1911–1912, photograph, Gabriele Münter- und Johannes Eichner-Stiftung, Munich

p. 61: Wassily Kandinsky, Title woodcut for the almanac *Der Blaue Reiter*, 1911

p. 62: Vladimir Burliuk, *Landscape*, 1909, oil on card, 59.8 x 94.8 cm, Museum Ludwig, Cologne

p. 63: Heinrich Campendonk, *Semi-Nude with Cat*, 1912, woodcut, hand-colored on stiff Japanese paper, 32.2 x 43.5 cm, Städtische Galerie im Lenbachhaus, Munchen

pp. 64-65: Eugen von Kahler, *The Bathers*, 1910–1911, opaque colors and Indian ink on card, 18 x 22.2 cm, Städtische Galerie im Lenbachhaus, Munich

p. 66: Albert Bloch, *The Three Pierrots No. 2*, 1911, oil on canvas, 77.2 x 57.8 cm, The Nelson Atkins Museum of Art, Kansas City

p. 67: David Burliuk, *Dniester Rapids*, c. 1910, oil on canvas, 49 x 65.5 cm, Russian State Museum, St. Petersburg

p.68: Wassily Kandinsky, *Improvisation 26 (Rower)*, 1912, oil on canvas, 97 x 107.5 cm, Städtische Galerie im Lenbachhaus, Munich

p.69: Franz Marc, *The Tiger*, 1912, oil on canvas, 111 x 101 cm, Städtische Galerie im Lenbachhaus, Munich

p. 70: Arnold Schönberg, *Nocturnal Landscape*, 1910, oil on canvas, 58 x 73 cm, Arnold Schönberg Center, Vienna

p. 71: Robert Delaunay, *Saint Séverin*, 1909–1910, lithograph, two colors, chine collé, and copperplate printing paper, 56.5 x 42.5 cm, cm, Städtische Galerie im Lenbachhaus, Munich, on permanent loan from the Gabriele Münter- und Johannes Eicher-Stiftung

p. 72-73: August Macke, *Large Zoological Garden (Triptych)*, 1913, oil on canvas, 129.5 x 65 cm, Museum am Ostwall, Dortmund

p. 74: Gabriele Münter, *Still Life with St. George*, 1911, oil on card, 51.1 x 68 cm, Städtische Galerie im Lenbachhaus, Munich

pp. 78-79: Wassily Kandinsky, *Composition No. V*, 1911, oil on canvas, 190 x 275 cm, signed: KANDINSKY 1911, New York, Private collection

p. 81: Franz Marc, *Deer in the Forest I*, 1911, oil on canvas, 130 x 100 cm, Private collection

pp. 82-83: Franz Marc, *The Yellow Cow*, 1911, oil on canvas, 130 x 100 cm, New York, Guggenheim Museum

p. 85: Henri Rousseau, *The Farmyard*, 1896–1898, oil on canvas, 24.6 x 32.9 cm, Paris, Musée National d'Art Moderne, Centre Pompidou

p. 87: Franz Marc, *Portrait of Henri Rousseau*, 1911, reverse-glass painting, 34 x 22 cm, Städtische Galerie im Lenbachhaus, Munich

p. 88: On the balcony of Kandinsky's and Münter's apartment at Ainmillerstrasse 36 (l. to r.: Maria and Franz Marc, Bernard Koehler (senior), Heinrich Campendonk, Thomas von Hartmann; seated: Wassily Kandinsky), c. 1911/1912, photograph, Gabriele Münter- und Johannes Eichner-Stiftung, Munich

p. 89: Wassily Kandinsky, *Motley Life*, 1907, tempera and gouache on canvas, 130 x 162.5 cm, Städtische Galerie im Lenbachhaus, Munich, on permanent loan from the Bayern LB

pp. 90-91: Wassily Kandinsky, *Motley Life*, 1907, tempera and gouache on canvas, 130 x 162.5 cm, Städtische Galerie im Lenbachhaus, Munich, on permanent loan from the Bayern LB (detail)

p. 92 above: Kandinsky playing the 'cello, c. 1886, photograph, Gabriele Münter- und Johannes Eichner-Stiftung, Munich

p. 92 below: Wassily Kandinsky, *St. George I*, 1911, reverse-glass painting, frame painted by Kandinsky, 19 x 19.5 cm, Städtische Galerie im Lenbachhaus, Munich

p. 93: Wassily Kandinsky, *Murnau with Church I*, 1910, oil on card, 64.7 x 50.2 cm, Städtische Galerie im Lenbachhaus, Munich

p.94: Wassily Kandinsky, *Improvisation Klamm*, 1914, oil on canvas, 110 x 110 cm, Städtische Galerie im Lenbachhaus, Munich

p. 96: Gabriele Münter, *Self-Portrait*, c. 1901, charcoal, 44.7 x 30.8 cm, Städtische Galerie im Lenbachhaus, Munich

p. 97: Gabriele Münter, *Garden at Night with Buildings*, 1905, tempera and white chalk on black paper, 17.3 x 25 cm, Städtische Galerie im Lenbachhaus, Munich

pp. 98-99: Gabriele Münter, *Haystacks*, c. 1909, watercolor and oil on gray paper, 21.4 x 28.8 cm, Städtische Galerie im Lenbachhaus, Munich

p. 100: Franz Marc, *Two Cats*, poster for Franc Marc's first solo exhibition in Josef Brakl's Moderne Kunsthandlung, Munich, February 1910, color lithograph, 4 colors, 40.5 x 42.5 cm (poster size 91.9 x 63.3 cm)

p. 101 left: Franz Marc, *Horses in the Sun*, 1908, color lithograph

p. 101 right: Franz Marc, *Tower of the Blue Horses*, 1913, oil on canvas, formerly in the Nationalgalerie Berlin (whereabouts unknown since 1945)

p. 102: Franz Marc, *Girl with Cat*, 1910, tempera and pencil, 40.5 x 29.5 cm, Stiftung Sammlung Ziegler, Mülheim an der Ruhr

p. 103: Else Lasker-Schüler, *The Gathering of the Wild Jews*, 1923, lithograph, colored pencil, 32 x 23.4 cm, Städtische Galerie im Lenbachhaus, Munich

p. 104 above: Franz Marc, *Head of a Girl (Maria Franck)*, 1906, Staatliche Graphische Sammlung, Munich

p. 104 middle: Franz Marc, *Head of a Woman (Annette von Eckardt)*, 1904 – 1905, whereabouts unknown

p. 104 unten: Franz Marc, *Two Women on the Mountain*, sketch, 1906, Franz Marc Museum Kochel (On permanent loan from the Bayerische Staatsgemäldesammlungen, Munich)

p. 105: Alfred Kubin during his first year in Munich, 1898, photograph, Städtische Galerie im Lenbachhaus, Munich, Kubin-Archiv

p. 106: Alfred Kubin, *Pupated World*, 1906, tempera, 37.5 x 40.3 cm, Städtische Galerie am Lenbachhaus, Kubin-Archiv, Munich

p. 107: Alfred Kubin, *The Foreboding*, 1906, tempera, 30.8 x 25.3 cm, Städtische Galerie am Lenbachhaus, Kubin-Archiv, Munich

p. 108: Alfred Kubin, *The Lady on the Horse*, c. 1900/1901, Indian ink, pencil, washed, sprayed, on cadastral paper, 34.9 x 22 cm, Städtische Galerie am Lenbachhaus, Kubin-Archiv, Munich

p. 109: Alfred Kubin, *The Invaders*, c. 1902/1903, Indian ink, brush, watercolors and opaque white, 20.1 x 29 cm, Städtische Galerie am Lenbachhaus, Munich, Kubin-Archiv

p. 110 above: August Macke, *Self-Portrait with Hat*, 1909, oil on wood, 41 x 32.5 cm, Städtisches Kunstmuseum Bonn, On permanent loan from a private collection

p. 110 below: August Macke, *Portrait with Apples*, 1909, oil on canvas, 66 x 59.5 cm, Städtische Galerie im Lenbachhaus, Munich

p. 111: August Macke, *Promenade*, 1913, oil on card, 51 x 57 cm, Städtische Galerie im Lenbachhaus, Munich

p. 112: August Macke, *St. Germain near Tunis*, 1914, watercolor, 26 x 21 cm, Städtische Galerie im Lenbachhaus, Munich

p. 113: August Macke, *Garden Gate*, 1914, watercolor, 31 x 22.5 cm, Städtische Galerie im Lenbachhaus, Munich, on permanent loan from the Gabriele Münter- und Johannes Eichner-Stiftung

p. 114 below: Paul Klee, *Sacred Stones and Images of Gods*, 1913, Indian ink on Ingres paper, 5.4/5.7 x 16.5/16.8 cm, Städtische Galerie im Lenbachhaus, Munich

p. 115: Paul Klee, *Föhn Wind in Franz Marc's Garden*, 1915, watercolor on paper, glued to card, 20 x 15 cm, Städtische Galerie im Lenbachhaus, Munich

pp. 116-117: Paul Klee, *Street Junction*, 1913, charcoal, Indian ink, watercolored, on Ingres paper, 13.4 x 26 cm, Städtische Galerie im Lenbachhaus, Munich

p. 118 above: Paul Klee, *Figures*, postcard to Alfred Kubin in Wernstein/Zwickledt, June 19, 1913, Indian ink on paper, 4 x 4.5 cm, Städtische Galerie im

Lenbachhaus, Munich, on permanent loan from the Gabriele Münter- und Johannes Eichner-Stiftung

p. 118 below: Paul Klee, *Grotesque Female Figure*, postcard to Gabriele Münter in Munich, June 26, 1913, Indian ink on paper, 6.6 x 5.1 cm, Städtische Galerie im Lenbachhaus, Munich

p. 119 above: Paul Klee, *Figures*, postcard to Alfred Kubin in Wernstein/Zwickledt, June 19, 1913, Indian ink on paper, 4 x 4.5 cm, Städtische Galerie im Lenbachhaus, Munich (detail)

p. 120: Gabriele Münter, *Listening (Portrait of Jawlensky)*, 1909, oil on card, 49.7 x 66.2 cm, Städtische Galerie im Lenbachhaus, Munich

p. 121: Gabriele Münter, *Portrait of Marianne von Werefkin*, 1909, oil on card, 81 x 55 cm, Städtische Galerie im Lenbachhaus, Munich

p. 122: Marianne von Werefkin, *Summer Stage*, 1910, tempera on card, 56 x 74 cm, Fondazione Marianne von Werefkin, Ascona

p. 123: Alexej von Jawlensky, *Meditation*, 1918, oil on card, 40 x 31 cm, Städtische Galerie im Lenbachhaus, Munich

p. 124: Alexej von Jawlensky, *Dark Blue Turban*, 1910, oil on card, mounted on wood, 72 x 69 cm, Private collection, Switzerland

p. 126: Heinrich Campendonk, *Forest, Girl, Goat*, 1917, oil on canvas, 94 x 64 cm, Städtische Galerie im Lenbachhaus, Munich

p. 127: Arnold Schönberg, *Self-Portrait (From Behind)*, 1911, oil on canvas, 48 x 45 cm, Arnold Schönberg Center, Vienna

p. 128: Wassily Kandinsky, colored woodcut from *Sounds*, 1912

p. 129: Wassily Kandinsky, Cover of *On the Spiritual in Art*, Piper-Verlag Munich, published in December 1911

p. 130 above: Franz M. Jansen, Invitation to the first exhibition at the Gereons Club, Cologne

p. 130 below: Ernst Ludwig Kirchner, *Three Bathers (Moritzburg)*, 1910, woodcut, 30 x 21 cm

p. 131: Cover of the catalogue of *The Second Exhibition of the Editorial Team the Blue Rider Black White*, 1912

p. 132: Cover page of the exhibition catalogue of 1912

p. 133: Albert Bloch, *Prize Fight, c.* 1912/1913, washed Indian ink and pencil on card, 35.5 x 30.5 cm, Städtische Galerie im Lenbachhaus Munich

p. 134 left: Gabriele Münter, Woodcut for the cover of the periodical *Der Sturm*, no. 162/163, May 1913

p. 134 right: Franz Marc, Woodcut for the cover of the periodical *Der Sturm*, no. 144/145, January 1913

p. 136: August Macke, *Satire on the Blue Rider*, 1913, watercolor, pencil and black chalk, 24.7 x 34.7 cm, Städtische Galerie im Lenbachhaus, Munich

p. 137: Title page of the leaflet *Aufruf gegen Kunstkritiker [Appeal against Art Critics]*

p. 138: August Macke, *Portrait of Bernhard Koehler*, 1910, oil on canvas, 63.5 x 41 cm, Städtische Galerie im Lenbachhaus, Munich

p. 139: Franz Marc, *Reconciliation*, 1912, woodcut on heavy Japanese paper, 20.1 x 25.7 cm

p. 141: Wassily Kandinsky, *Large Resurrection*, late June-July 1911, colored woodcut on Japanese paper, 21.9 x 21.9 cm

p. 142: Wassily Kandinsky, *Lyrical*, 1911, oil on canvas, 94 x 130 cm, Museum Bijmans van Beuningen, Rotterdam

p. 143 above: Wassily Kandinsky, Cover design for *On the Spiritual in Art, c.* 1910, gouache and Indian ink on white paper, mounted on dark brown paper, 17.5 x 13.5 cm (sheet), Städtische Galerie im Lenbachhaus, Munich

p. 143 below: Hermann Max Pechstein, Poster for the exhibition of the artists' association the Brücke in the Galerie Richter, Dresden 1908. With the portraits of Kirchner, Pechstein, Heckel, and Schmidt-Rottluff, black printing plate for colored woodcut, 82 x 58.3 cm

p. 145: Wassily Kandinsky, study for *Composition VII*, 1913, watercolour, Indian ink and pencil on paper, mounted on grey paper, 18,5 x 27,1 cm, Städtische Galerie im Lenbachhaus, Munich

pp. 146-147: Franz Marc, *Fighting Forms (Abstract Forms I)*, 1914, oil on canvas, 91 x 131.5 cm, Bayerische Staatsgemäldesammlungen, Pinakothek der Moderne, Munich (detail)

p. 148: Wassily Kandinsky, *Untitled, (First Abstract Watercolor)*, 1910 (1913), pencil, watercolor and Indian ink on paper, 49.6 x 64.8 cm, Musée National d'Art Moderne, Centre Pompidou, Paris

pp. 150-151: Wassily Kandinsky, *The Yellow Sound*, from the almanac *Der Blaue Reiter*, 1912

p. 152: "Prophetess of 'The Blue Four'," 1925, newspaper cutting from the *San Francisco Examiner*, November 1, 1925

p. 153: Cover of the magazine *Der Kunsttopf*, César Klein, August 1920

p. 154: Cover of the guide to the *Degenerate Art exhibition*, Berlin 1937

p. 155: Städtische Galerie im Lenbachhaus, Munich. View of Room 25 showing a work by Kandinsky, and of Room 24 with works by Jawlenksy and Münter

p. 156: Staffelalm beneath the Rabenkopf with a wall painting by Franz Marc

p. 157: The historical rooms in the Lenbach Villa

p. 158: View from the Kandinsky room (25) and of Room 24

p. 165 top: Schloss Museum Murnau, exterior

p. 165 bottom: Schloss Museum Murnau, section displaying the Blue Rider collection

p. 166: Staircase and banister of the "Russian House" (Münter-Haus) painted by Kandinsky, photograph, Gabriele Münter- und Johannes Eichner-Stiftung, Munich

p. 167: Dining corner in the living-room of the "Russian House," with reverse-glass paintings by Kandinsky, photograph, Gabriele Münter- und Johannes Eichner-Stiftung, Munich

p. 168 above: Studio with washstand painted by Kandinsky, a painting by Gabriele Münter on the wall, photograph, Gabriele Münter- und Johannes Eichner-Stiftung, Munich

p. 168 below: Gabriele Münter, *Interior in the "Russian House,"* 1909, Gabriele Münter- und Johannes Eichner-Stiftung, Munich

p. 169 left: Wassily Kandinsky, *Johannisstrasse Murnau from the Window of the Hotel Griesbräu*, 1908, oil on card, 49.8 x 69.6 cm, Städtische Galerie im Lenbachhaus, Munich

pp. 172-173: Franz Marc Museum in Kochel (Diethelm & Spillmann Architects), 2008, photograph

p. 175: Franz Marc, *Two Horses*, 1910, tempera over pencil, 14.1 x 20.8 cm, Sammlung Stiftung Etta und Otto Stangl

Photo credits

The illustrations in this publication have been kindly provided by the museums, institutions and archives mentioned in the captions, or taken from the Publisher's archives, with the exception of the following:

akg-images: p. 8
Münchner Stadtmuseum: p. 12
Gabriele Münter- und Johannes Eichner-Stiftung: pp. 14, 32, 43, 60, 88, 92 above, 168 below
Gabriele Münter- und Johannes Eichner-Stiftung/ Anton J. Brandl: pp. 166, 167, 168 above
Städtische Galerie im Lenbachhaus, Munich: pp. 16, 18, 19, 23 below, 28, 31, 39, 42, 45 below, 48 50, 64-65, 68, 69, 74, 87, 92 below, 93, 94, 96, 97, 98-99, 103, 105, 106, 107, 108, 109, 110 below, 111, 112, 114 below, 115, 116-117, 118 below, 120, 121, 123, 126, 133, 136, 138, 143 above, 145, 169 left
Musée d'Orsay, Paris: p. 17
Fondazione Marianne Werefkin Ascona and Fäthke-Archiv: p. 22
Archiv Meissner: p. 24
Städelsches Kunstinstitut, Frankfurt am Main: pp. 26-27
Bayerische Staatsgemäldesammlungen, Munich: pp. 29, 114 above, 146-147
Städtische Galerie im Lenbachhaus, Munich, on permanent loan from the Gabriele Münter- und Johannes Eichner-Stiftung, Munich: pp. 30, 36, 71, 113, 118 above
Musée National d'Art Moderne, Centre Georges Pompidou, Paris: pp. 33, 45 above right, 85, 148
Graf A.W. von Faber-Castell, Nuremberg: p. 34
Sammlung Hartmut Garnerus, Munich: p. 35
Von der Heydt-Museum, Wuppertal: p. 40, 41
Museum Ludwig, Cologne: p. 62
The Nelson Atkins Museum of Art, Kansas City: p. 66
Staatliches Russisches Museum, St. Petersburg: p. 67
Arnold Schönberg Center, Vienna: p. 70
Museum am Ostwall, Dortmund: pp. 72-73
Guggenheim Museum, New York: pp. 82-83
Städtische Galerie im Lenbachhaus, Munich, on permanent loan from the Bayern LB: pp. 89, 90-91
Sammlung Ziegler, Mühlheim an der Ruhr: p. 102
Staatliche Graphische Sammlung, unich: p. 104 above
Franz Marc Museum, Kochel, on permanent loan from the Bayerische Staatsgemäldesammlungen, Munich: p. 104 below
Städtisches Kunstmuseum Bonn, on permanent loan from a private collection: p. 110 above
Fondazione Marianne von Werefkin, Ascona: p. 122
Museum Bijmans van Beuningen, Rotterdam: p. 142
Bayerische Staatsgemäldesammlungen, Pinakothek der Moderne, Munich: pp. 146-147
Tourist Information, Kochel am See: p. 156
Bildarchiv Schloss Museum Murnau: p. 165
Roger Frei, Zurich: pp. 172-173
Sammlung Stiftung Etta und Otto Stangl: p.175
Hans Jais, Puchheim: pp. 158, 160, 161, 162, 163, 164, 169 right, 170, 171, 178, 179, 180, 181

Below: Arnold Schönberg, Self-Portrait, from behind, 1911, Detail

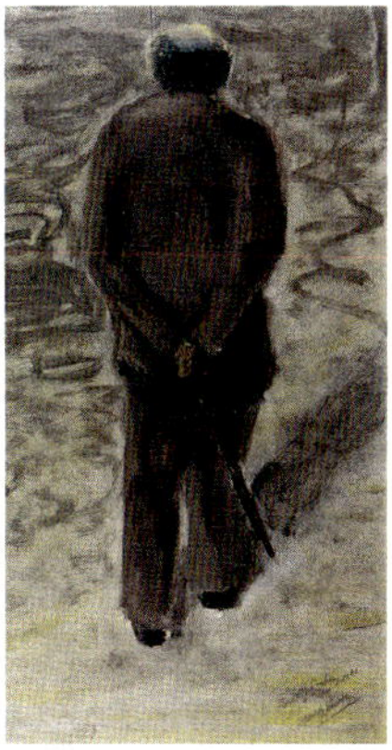

Imprint

Front Cover:
Franz Marc, *Tower of the Blue Horses*, see page 101

Back Cover:
Gabriele Münter, *Portrait of Marianne von Werefkin*, see page 121
Gabriele Münter, *Self-Portrait*, see page 96
On the balcony of Kandinsky's and Münter's apartment at Ainmillerstrasse 36, see page 88
Gabriele Münter, *Listening (Portrait of Jawlensky)*, see page 120
Alfred Kubin during his first year in Munich, see page 105
August Macke, *Portrait Franz Marc*, 1910, oil on cardboard, 50 x 39 cm, Staatliche Museen Preußischer Kulturbesitz, Nationalgalerie Berlin
Franz Marc, *Head of a Girl (Maria Franck)*, see page 104
August Macke, *Self-Portrait with Hat*, see page 110

Prestel Verlag, Munich
A member of Verlagsgruppe Random House GmbH

Prestel Verlag, in der Verlagsgruppe Random House GmbH
Neumarkter Straße 28
81673 München
Tel. +49(0)89 4136 0
Fax +49(0)89 4136 2335

Prestel Publishing Ltd.
4 Bloomsbury Place
London WC1A 2QA
Tel. +44 (0)20 7323-5004
Fax +44 (0)20 7636-8004

Prestel Publishing
900 Broadway, Suite 603
New York, NY 10003
Tel. +1 (212) 995-2720
Fax +1 (212) 995-2733

www.prestel.com

A Library of Congress Control Number is available
British Library Cataloguing-in-Publication Data: a catalogue record for this book is available from the British Library; Deutsche Nationalbibliothek holds a record of this publication in the Deutsche Nationalbibliografie; detailed bibliographical data can be found under: http://dnb.d-nb.de

Prestel books are available worldwide. Please contact your nearest bookseller or one of the above addresses for information concerning your local distributor.

Editorial direction: Claudia Stäuble
Translated from the German by Jane Michael, Munich
Copyedited by Chris Murray
Picture editor: Katharina Knüppel
Art direction: Cilly Klotz
Cover, design and layout: Johannes Hollmann, INDEED – Agentur für Gestaltung, München
Production: Astrid Wedemeyer
Lithography: Reproline mediateam, Munich
Printing and Binding: Tlačiarne BB spol. s r. o., Banská Bystrica

FSC
www.fsc.org
RECYCLED
Made from recycled material
FSC® C022120

Verlagsgruppe Random House FSC-DEU-0100
The FSC-certified paper *Eurobulk* produced
by mill Biberist has been supplied by Papier Union.

Printed in Slovakia

ISBN 978-3-7913-4528-4